THE Painter4 Wow! BOOK

Cher Threinen-Pendarvis

Peachpit Press

**The Painter 4 Wow! Book**

Cher Threinen-Pendarvis

Peachpit Press
2414 Sixth Street
Berkeley, CA 94710
(510) 548-4393
(510) 548-5991 (fax)

Find us on the World Wide Web at: http://www.peachpit.com

Peachpit Press is a division of Addison Wesley Longman

Series Editor: Linnea Dayton
Cover design: TMA Ted Mader + Associates
Cover illustration: Cher Threinen-Pendarvis
Book design: Jill Davis
Art direction and layout: Cher Threinen-Pendarvis
Editing: Linnea Dayton
Copyediting and proofreading: Susan Bugbee
Production and prepress: Jonathan Parker
Service bureau: Adage Graphics

This book was set using the Stone Serif and Stone Sans families. It was written and composed in Adobe Pagemaker 5.0a.

ISBN 0-201-88644-8

0 9 8 7 6 5 4 3 2
Printed and bound in the United States of America.

*To my husband Steven,*
*for his friendship,*
*encouragement and understanding;*
*and to our Creator*
*from whom all inspiration comes. . . .*

*— Cher Threinen-Pendarvis*

Pouring it on with Painter, *illustrated by Corinne Okada*

## ACKNOWLEDGMENTS

*The Painter 4 Wow! Book* would not have been possible without a great deal of help from some extraordinary people and sources.

My special thanks go to Jim Benson, my partner on the first edition of *The Painter Wow! Book*, for his support, encouragement, careful edit and contribution to the organization of the first edition. Thank you, Jim—for helping to launch the book.

My heartfelt thanks go to Linnea Dayton, the *Wow!* Series Editor and a treasured friend and colleague. At times when it was needed most during the first *and* second editions, her inspiration and advice proved invaluable. Thank you, Linnea, for the creative edit of *The Painter 4 Wow! Book*.

Warmest thanks go to my friends at Peachpit Press, especially Ted Nace for his inspiration and guidance, Roslyn Bullas for her sincere encouragement during the development of the book, and the rest of the publishing team for their support. Thank you Peachpit, for giving me the opportunity to do this book.

A big "thank you" goes to the folks at Fractal Design Corporation: Mark Zimmer, Tom Hedges, John Derry and Steve Guttman, for creating such a *Wow!* program and for their inspiration, enthusiasm and openness; to Daryl Wise, Glenna Dailey and Dan DiPaola for helping me locate artists who use Painter; and to Fractal Design's outstanding technical support team for fielding questions about the program: Laurie Hemnes, Bud Daumen, Shawn Grunberger, Leila Kiba and Steve Rathman.

I am grateful to the talented Painter artists who contributed their work and techniques; their names are listed in the Artist Appendix in the back of the book. I would especially like to thank

Pouring it on with Painter, *illustrated by Chelsea Sammel*

Pouring it on with Painter, *illustrated by Mark Jenkins*

Pouring it on with Painter, *illustrated by John Derry*

Sharon Steuer, author of *The Illustrator Wow! Book*, who helped me locate artists who use Painter and became an encouraging friend as our two books developed.

I'd also like to thank the companies who supplied the *Wow!* book team with supporting software during the development of the book—Adobe Systems for supplying me with Photoshop, Illustrator and Adobe Premiere, so I could demonstrate how nicely these programs work with Painter; Macromedia, for contributing Director for the Multimedia chapter; Netscape Communications for providing Netscape for the Web Graphics chapter; MetaTools and Xaos Tools for their filters; Aladdin Systems for Sitcomm; Baseline Publishing for Screenshot; and Insignia for Soft PC.

Thanks to Digital Stock and PhotoDisc for their support during both editions of the book; these two "stock on CD-ROM" companies allowed us to use their photos for demonstration purposes in the book. I am also grateful to the other companies who provided images or video clips for *The Painter 4 Wow! CD-ROM;* their names are listed in Appendix A in the back of the book.

Additionally, the following companies donated, loaned or gave us a good deal on hardware that helped to create the book: Wacom, for their great pressure-sensitive tablets; Epson and Hewlett-Packard for color printers (for testing of printing techniques); and Pinnacle Micro for a Sierra magneto-optical drive.

I'm grateful to Linnea Dayton, Jack Davis, Victor Gavenda, Donal Jolley and Allen Ridgeway for their helpful technical reads. Special thanks also go to Jon Lee and Geoff Hull of Fox Television for sharing their experience of designing for broadcast television; Cindy and Dewey Reid of Reid Creative for sharing their expertise in animation and film; and Lynda Weinman for sharing her knowledge about designing graphics for the Web.

I'd like to thank my co-workers "behind the scenes" on the Wow! book team. Warmest thanks go to Jill Davis for her brilliant book design; Susan Bugbee for her friendship and excellent copyediting and proofreading; Jackie Estrada for her careful indexing; and Pagemaker whiz Jonathan Parker for his production and prepress expertise. His calm assurance during deadlines was much appreciated!

My sincere thanks go to Doug Isaacs and the rest of the team at Adage Graphics in Los Angeles, who did a quick, high-quality job of producing proofs and film for these pages.

Finally, I would like to thank my family, friends and colleagues for their patience and understanding during the development of both editions of this book.

*Mark Zimmer, President of Fractal Design Corporation, and a developer of Painter*

## FOREWORD

"So, Mark . . . this new edition of *The Painter 4 Wow! Book* is pretty cool, don't you think?"

"Yes, John, it's like a fine wine. It just keeps getting better with age!"

"Cher really put Painter 4 (and us!) through our paces!"

"Yeah, but it's definitely worth the effort. This ought to be made into a major motion picture!"

It seems like such a short time ago that the first edition of *The Painter Wow! Book* was released . . . and now, *Wow!,* here's a completely revised edition that includes all the cool new Painter 4 stuff and then some.

Following the format of the first edition, *The Painter 4 Wow! Book* uses real-world examples of artwork created by top-notch artists to walk the reader through the image-making process. Not only do you learn about the inner workings of Painter 4, but you can also pick up a lot of the artistic "inside stuff" that can transform a good image into a great one.

Just what makes Painter tick, anyway? The primary vision behind Painter is that it provides the tools found in a traditional artist's or designer's studio. Many of these tools even *feel* like the traditional studio tools, especially when used with a pressure-sensitive pen and tablet. These tools act as a doorway to personal expression that can provide endless hours of creative exploration.

Other tools are like some of the more interesting graphics gizmos found in the traditional graphic arts studio—flexible French

*John Derry, Vice President of Creative Design, Fractal Design Corporation, and a developer of Painter*

curves, felt-tip markers, Zipatone rub-off textures, and so on. Many have an instant appeal that leaves you wondering how you ever got along without them in the past.

And some of Painter's more outrageous tools—the Image Hose or Shapes, for example—take advantage of the unique properties of the computer and have no traditional counterpart. These tools place you at the trail-blazing digital frontier, where no other pixel has gone before.

All of Painter's tools require a period of experimentation in order to master their unique qualities. Some users delight in this experimentation; others just want to cut to the chase and get productive immediately. This book addresses both groups exceptionally well.

It has been a pleasure to watch Cher enthusiastically take on the task of cataloging Painter's tools and elaborating their subtleties through example. She really understands the experimental stage that occurs when an artist encounters a new expressive tool. *The Painter 4 Wow! Book* provides the reader with valuable insight into this process.

Another contribution of *The Painter 4 Wow! Book* is the novel perspective it provides with regard to Painter's organization. Painter's user manual describes all of the individual tools but can go only so far in detailing the interaction among them. Cher has organized subjects so that not-so-obvious tool combinations are illuminated. This provides Painter users with a new perspective that can expand their expressive range.

"Mark, can we go home now?"

"Not yet, John. You gotta see this cool new feature I just coded!"

As we continue to improve Painter at our typical breakneck speed, we hope that both Cher *and* you will stay along for the ride.


Mark Zimmer
John Derry

June, 1996

# CONTENTS

# WELCOME TO PAINTER 4 WOW!

SOME PEOPLE EMPHASIZE THE DIFFERENCES between traditional and digital art tools—almost as if art and the computer are not compatible. But during the early development of this book, we discovered many working artists who had bought computers specifically because they were thrilled by the promise of Fractal Design Painter. It seemed logical that *The Painter 4 Wow! Book* should become a bridge connecting conventional tools and techniques with their electronic counterparts. Early chapters of the book, in particular, touch on color theory, art history and conventional media, and explain how to translate foundational art theory using Painter's tools.

This book addresses the needs of a wide variety of creative professionals: artists making the transition from traditional to digital media; photographers looking to expand their visual vocabulary; multimedia or print graphic designers hunting for special effects to apply to type; even creative explorers out for some mind-boggling thrills. For those of you with a long history in a traditional art form and a short history with computers, we've done our best to guide you through Painter's complex interface, making it as simple as possible for you to achieve the desired effect. And if you've spent more time with a keyboard and mouse than you have with an artist's palette and paintbrush, you may learn a lot about conventional art terms and techniques as you read the book.

The folks at Fractal Design are famous for their creativity, innovation and dedication to improving and expanding their software tools. Along with new Painter 4 features such as the precision vector-based drawing capabilities of Shapes, the Mosaic brush (which allows you to create resolution-independent tile mosaic images), and tools that make it easy to prepare graphics for use on the World Wide Web, Fractal Design has also made many small

*Painter 4's new features help you get images ready for use on the World Wide Web. For instance, Painter can create some of the coding for interactive buttons and can convert colors to Web-friendly palettes.*

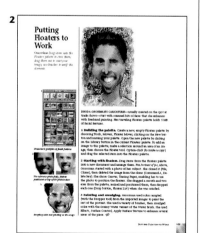

1

2

changes to Painter's interface that make it easier to use. The most noticeable of these are the expanded Toolbox and the new palette menus found on the Art Materials, Brushes, and Objects palettes. The new palette menus help to consolidate your actions to a specific area of the screen, and make procedures such as choosing a brush, customizing a brush variant and building a new library of brushes available within one palette.

To make *The Painter 4 Wow! Book* complete and up-to-date for Painter 4, we've revised every page. And we've expanded the book—adding pages of brand-new real-world tips and techniques that specifically profile features added in version 4.

## DO YOU DO MAC OR WINDOWS?

Because Painter works so similarly on both Macintosh and PC/ Windows platforms, we've taken the path of least resistance by using only one platform's keyboard commands—Macintosh, our native language. (Just to make sure of our techniques, though, we also tested them on a Pentium machine running Windows 95.) If you're a Windows user, use the Control key wherever the Command key is mentioned, and substitute the Alt key when the Option key is used. Additionally, because versions of Windows prior to Windows 95 require shorter file names, PC users looking for texture libraries will need to find them under somewhat different names than their Mac counterparts. For instance, "More Wild Textures" Paper library on the Mac is "morewild.pap" on the PC. The other differences are few, and they're covered in Chapter 1.

## NEWS FOR BEGINNERS AND MORE

If you're new to Painter, welcome! We assume that you're familiar with the basic Mac and Windows mouse functions, that you know how to open and save files, copy items to the clipboard and navigate through the Mac's hierarchical file system or through Windows directories. It's also a good idea, though it isn't essential, to have worked with the *Painter 4 User Guide* and to have completed the tutorial that comes with the program.

Just a few words on some of the "shorthand" naming conventions that we've used to pack more information into the book. Because Painter uses nested palettes that have long names—for instance, the "Art Materials:Paper palette"—we frequently only direct you to the "child" palette. In this case we'd write "Paper palette." Another space-saving measure: In the Brushes palette, we refer to the "Method Subcategory" as the "submethod."

## HOW TO USE THIS BOOK

The information we're presenting generally progresses from simple to complex through each of the ten chapters. We've organized each chapter into four types of information: Basics sections, techniques, practical tips and galleries. In addition, hardware, software and other resources are in one section at the back of the book.

## SAMPLING PAINT

You can temporarily switch to the Dropper tool and sample colors by holding down the Command key while you're using many of Painter's other tools.

**4**

**5**

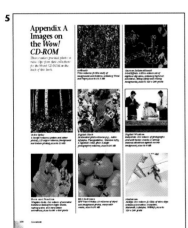

**1** The **Basics** sections teach how Painter's tools and functions work, and give real-world applications for the tools. *The Painter Wow! Book* wasn't designed to be a replacement for the *Painter 4 User Guide*. We've focused on the tools and functions that we think are most useful. In some cases we've explained items covered in the manual, and, where important, we've dug deeper to help you understand how the tools and functions work. In other cases, we've covered undocumented functions and practical applications shared by contributing artists, or that we uncovered in our own research.

**2** Within each **Technique** section, you'll find step-by-step, real-world techniques that give you enough information to re-create the process yourself. In the *Wow!* format, pictures illustrating the stages of the process are positioned alongside the appropriate step in the project. Browse the pictures in the art column within a technique for a quick overview of the development of an image. We've done our best to give you enough information so you won't have to refer to the manual to follow the steps.

**3** The **Tips** are easily identified by their gray title bar. We've placed them in the Basics and Technique sections where we thought they'd be the most useful, but each tip is a self-contained tidbit of useful information, so you can learn a lot very quickly by taking a brisk walk through the book, reading only the tips.

**4** The **Galleries** are there for inspiration, and one appears at the end of every chapter. With each gallery image, you'll find a short description of how the artwork was produced.

**5** No book is an island, so in the **Appendices** in the back of this one, we've included lists of other resources for your use. If you want to contact a vendor, an artist, a fine art service bureau or the name of an art-related book or other publication, you'll find the information you need there.

*The Painter 4 Wow! Book* was created to share useful techniques and tips and to provide creative suggestions for using the program. We hope that you'll use it as inspiration and a point of departure for your own creative exploration. Above all, don't be overwhelmed by Painter's richness. . . Just dig in and enjoy it!

# GETTING
# TO KNOW
# PAINTER

*Steve Guttman's illustration,* Pouring It
On with Painter

SIT RIGHT DOWN AND POWER UP! This chapter explores Painter's basic needs and functions, as well as its unique strengths and idiosyncrasies. If you're new to Painter, you'll benefit the most from this chapter if you've already spent some time with the *User Guide* that ships with the program.

### PAINTER'S REQUIREMENTS FOR MAC AND PC

Here are Painter's *minimum* requirements: If you use a Macintosh you need a 68020 processor (Mac II) or faster and 6.5 MB of application RAM. On a Power Macintosh you'll need at least 8 MB of application RAM. If you have a PC running with Windows 3.1, you'll need at least a 386 processor (although a 486 with FPU is recommended) and 8 MB of application RAM. To run Painter on Windows 95, you'll need 12 MB of application RAM. For both platforms you'll need a hard disk with approximately 20 MB of free space to perform a standard installation.

When you open an image in Painter—for example, a 5 MB image—and begin working with it, Painter needs three to five times that file size in RAM in order to work at optimal speed—in our example, that would be 15–25 MB of RAM. Opening more than one image, adding floaters or shapes, or increasing the number of Undos (under Edit, Preferences,

Here are two ways to make quick copies without going through the clipboard and using valuable RAM. To make a copy of your entire document, use File, Clone. (This is also a quick way to drop all of the Floaters in the document.) To quickly duplicate a floater, choose the Floater Adjuster tool and Option-drag a floater copy.

*On the Mac, Painter runs faster with these settings in the Memory Control Panel: Virtual Memory off (it interferes with Painter's own virtual memory scheme, the Painter Temp file) and Disc Cache Size on a low setting.*

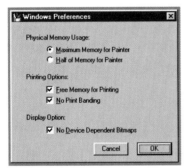

*Setting the Maximum Memory for Painter in Windows 95*

*Setting the Cache Size in the Windows 3.1 Virtual Memory dialog box*

Undos) adds further demands on RAM. When Painter runs out of RAM, it uses the hard disk chosen in Edit, Preferences, General as a RAM substitute. This "scratch disk" holds the Temp file you may have seen. Since hard disks operate much slower than RAM, performance suffers accordingly—even if you have a speedy hard disk or a disk array (two hard disks linked together so they can move data twice as fast).

Ideally, to work with Painter, you would use a computer with a speedy processor; a large, fast hard disk or a disk array; and lots of RAM. In addition, you'll want a large, 24-bit-color monitor—probably no less than 16 inches—and perhaps a second monitor on which to store palettes. Also highly recommended—some might say *essential*—is a drawing tablet with a pressure-sensitive stylus. Not only is it a more natural drawing and painting tool than a mouse, but many of Painter's brushes lose their zip without a pressure-sensitive input device.

**Mac memory allocation.** To allot maximum RAM to Painter on a Mac, first quit all open applications. In the Finder, under the Apple menu, choose About This Macintosh. Write down the number next to Largest Unused Block. This is the total amount of RAM in which you can run applications. Subtract 500 or 1000 K (as a buffer) from this number. Now, in the Painter folder, click once (not twice!) on the Painter application icon and choose File, Get Info. Enter the result of your math in the Preferred Size box. This method won't let you open any other applications of significant size while Painter is running, but it assures you of the use of nearly all available RAM while you're in Painter.

**Windows memory allocation.** To make maximum RAM available for your Windows 95-based PC, choose Edit, Preferences, Windows to access the Windows Preferences dialog box. Under Physical Memory Usage click the "Maximum Memory for Painter" button. Quit all applications and relaunch Painter. Painter will run faster if you let Windows 95 manage the virtual memory scheme. On a PC running Windows 3.1, Painter will run faster if

You can speed up your scratch disk by using hard disk driver software to make a separate partition just for the Painter Temp file. Additionally, use a hard disk utility program like Norton Utilities, Mac Tools or PC Tools (all from Symantec) to regularly defragment the partition. Over time, hard drives become fragmented (space is broken into smaller and smaller blocks)—and thus, slower—as data is slip up in order to be written to them.

Painter reads all open fonts and loaded plug-in filters when it starts up. For faster start-up, consider organizing your fonts with a utility that enables you to turn them on and off (Suitcase or MasterJuggler). And, if you have a large number of third-party filters, create several plug-ins folders. To change to an alternate plug-ins folder choose Edit, Preferences, Other Raster Plug-ins, and navigate to the folder. Restart Painter, and the alternate filter set will appear under the Effects, Other Plug-ins menu.

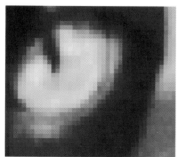

*This scan of a photograph is a pixel-based image. Enlarging it to 1200% reveals the grid of pixels.*

you reduce the size of the Windows Swap File to half of your total system RAM. The swap file takes hard disk space away from Painter's virtual memory scheme and may hurt performance.

## FILE SIZE AND RESOLUTION

If you're new to the computer, here's important background information regarding file sizes: Painter is a *pixel-based* program (also known as a *bitmap*, *painting* or *raster* program), not a *drawing* program (also known as an *object-oriented* or *vector* program). Drawing programs use mathematical expressions to describe the outline and fill attributes of objects in the drawing, while pixel-based programs describe things dot-by-dot. Because its components are mathematically described, art created with drawing programs can be resized or transformed with no loss of quality. Not so with Painter, Photoshop and other pixel-based programs. Increasing the size of an existing image in these programs means that additional pixels must be created to accommodate the larger size by filling in spaces as the existing pixels spread apart. As a result of the interpolated (manufactured) pixels, resized images can lose their crispness.

There are ways of working around this "soft image" dilemma. One solution is to do studies using a small file size (for instance, an 8x10-inch image at 75 pixels per inch), then start over with a large image to do final art at full size (for instance an 8x10-inch file at 300 pixels per inch). You can also block in the basic form and color in a small file, then scale the image up to final size (using Canvas, Resize) to add texture and details (textures seem par-

You can use Painter's Scripts function to record your work at low resolution, then play it back at a higher resolution. This technique gives you a much crisper result than simply resizing the original image to a new resolution. Here's how to do it: Start by opening the Objects:Scripts palette. Choose the Scripts menu, and select Script Options from the pull-down list. In the Script Options dialog box check the Record Initial State box, then click OK. Open a new file and choose Select All (Command-A). Begin painting. When you're finished, choose Scripts, Stop Recording Script. Open a new document two to four times as large as the original (this technique loses its effectiveness if your new file is much bigger than this), press Command-A, then Scripts, Playback Script. Painter will replay the script in the larger image, automatically scaling brushes and papers to perfectly fit the new size. A word of caution—sessions can be quirky: Your higher-resolution image may not match the lower-resolution one if you use imported photos, complex selections, shapes or the Image Hose, for instance.

*Choosing Script Options from the pull-down menu on the Objects, Scripts palette*

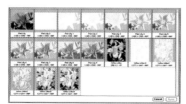

*Expressing width and height in pixels in the New Picture dialog box keeps the file size the same, regardless of how you change the Resolution.*

*Unchecking the Constrain File Size checkbox in the Canvas, Resize dialog box keeps the file size the same, regardless of how you change the Resolution.*

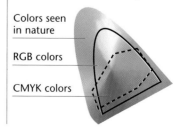

*Click the Browse button in the Open dialog box to preview all of the images in a folder. Some files may not have a preview (for example, some PICT or JPEG files created by other programs), but most of the time you'll see it. The watercolor studies in Mary Envall's "Lilies" folder are shown here.*

ticularly vulnerable to softening). You'll notice that many of the artists whose work is featured in this book use another efficient method: They create the components of a final piece of art in separate documents, then copy and paste the components into a final "master" image. Painter 4 offers yet another solution for working with large file sizes—composing with reference floaters, (a small version of an actual large image that's kept outside the document). Because data for the large image is not kept in the working file, performance improves. The introduction to Chapter 5 contains more information about using reference floaters.

Although it's primarily a pixel-based program, Painter does have some vector capabilities—shapes, paths and outline-based selections. Chapter 4's introduction tells more about them.

**Pixel size and resolution.** There are two commonly used ways of describing file sizes: in terms of their pixel measurements, or in a unit of measure (such as inches) plus a resolution. An image is a fixed number of pixels wide and tall—like 1200 x 1500—or a measurement combined with a resolution—4 x 5 inches at 300 ppi. (Either way, the file is 7 MB.) If you use pixels as a measurement for Width and Height in the New File dialog box, notice that the file size doesn't change, regardless of the numbers you type into the Resolution box. The pixel number does not change unless you resize the image using Canvas, Resize. Uncheck the Constrain File Size check box in the Canvas, Resize dialog box and increase (or decrease) the number of pixels in the width and height fields to add (or reduce) pixel information in the picture.

## OPENING FILES

Images in Painter are 24-bit color, made up of RGB (red, green and blue) components consisting of 8 bits each. Painter will recognize and open grayscale images, not in grayscale mode (since it doesn't have one), but in Painter's own RGB mode. CMYK, CIE LAB, Kodak Photo CD format and other color formats used by other applications will need to be converted to RGB in one of these programs (such as Adobe Photoshop or Equilibrium's Debabelizer) before Painter can read them.

### WORKING WITH CMYK

Here are some hints for working with Painter in a CMYK production environment. If you're starting with scanned images, scan them in RGB instead of CMYK—RGB has a significantly broader color gamut. If possible, avoid importing your image into another program (like Photoshop) to convert it to CMYK until you're ready to print, since you lose colors when you convert from RGB to CMYK. And, it's a good idea to save a copy of the RGB image in case you want to convert it again with different RGB-to-CMYK conversion settings.

Colors seen in nature

RGB colors

CMYK colors

You can preserve floaters in files by saving in either RIFF or Photoshop 3.0 format, but RIFF (even uncompressed) is usually significantly smaller. Rick Kirkman's 663 x 663-pixel image with 150 floaters weighs in at 1.7 MB as a compressed RIFF, 6.1 MB as an uncompressed RIFF, and 7.1 MB when saved in Photoshop 3.0 format.

## SAVING FILES

Painter offers numerous ways to save your image under Edit, Save or Save As. If you've created an image with a mask (Chapter 4 tells how to create masks), some of the formats will allow you to preserve the mask (by checking the Save Mask Layer box in the Save or Save As dialog box), while others won't. Here's a list of the current formats that includes their "mask-friendliness" and other advantages and disadvantages:

**A SAVING GRACE**

Saving multiple versions of your art at various steps along the way makes good sense: It helps you remember how you created your art, and it could be your saving grace if a file gets corrupted.

**RIFF.** Thrifty (files are saved quite small) and robust (allows for multiple layers), RIFF (Raster Image File Format) is Painter's native format. Few other programs recognize RIFF, so if you want to work with a Painter image in another program, save a copy in a different format. If you're using layer or path elements unique to Painter, such as the Wet Layer, floaters, shapes or selections, saving in RIFF format will preserve them. (Shapes and floaters are described in depth in Chapters 4 and 5). If you have *lots* of free hard disk space, check the Uncompressed box in the Save dialog box when you're saving in RIFF: Files will become many times larger, but will open and save much more quickly.

**Photoshop 2.0 and 3.0.** Saving files in Photoshop 3.0 format gives you nearly all the flexibility of RIFF, and is ideal if you frequently move data between Painter and Photoshop. When you use Photoshop to open a file saved in this format, Painter's floaters become Photoshop layers (Chapter 5's introduction contains more information about working with Painter and Photoshop); Painter's background mask (explained in depth in Chapter 4) becomes Photoshop Channel #4; and Painter's Bézier paths translate perfectly to Photoshop's paths and subpaths, appearing in Photoshop's Paths palette. Photoshop 2.0 format saves the image with information from Painter's mask layer (this becomes Channel 4), but without the file's floater or path information.

**TIFF.** Probably the most popular and widely recognized of the bitmap file formats, TIFF allows you to save a mask with your image. Unfortunately, unlike Photoshop, Painter's Save As    dialog box gives you no option to compress the TIFF file—the Uncompressed check box is checked and grayed-out.

**PICT.** PICT is the format of choice for multimedia programs

**QUICK CLOSING KEYS**

To quickly close a file, without having to click the on-screen buttons, use these keyboard shortcuts: press "D" for Don't Save, "C" for Cancel, and "S" for Save.

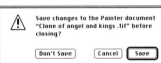

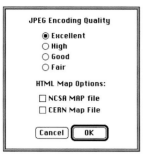

*The JPEG encoding dialog box showing Quality settings and HTML Map Options*

*For a neat "mosaic," tile-like effect on an ordinary image (left), save an image in JPEG format and click the Fair button. Close and open it, then apply Effects, Focus, Sharpen and Effects, Surface Control, Apply Surface Texture with Image Luminance. (This is probably the only practical use for the Fair JPEG setting!)*

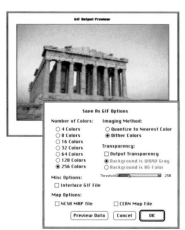

*The GIF file format dialog box has been expanded in Painter 4 to include NCSA and CERN Map Options for HTML.*

and other on-screen display. Painter's PICT format lets you save a mask (but not floaters), and save a Painter movie as a sequence of numbered PICT files to export and animate in another program (described in Chapter 8). Painter also opens PICT files very quickly.

**JPEG.** When you save a file in JPEG format, a dialog box appears with four choices: Excellent, High, Good and Fair. You'll get the best results by choosing Excellent. The advantage of saving a file in JPEG format is that you get superb space savings: a JPEG file is usually 10 times smaller than a TIFF file of the same image if you choose Excellent, and up to 100 times smaller if you choose Fair. The drawbacks: No mask layer, floaters or paths are saved; and the compression is a lossy compression—which means that some data (color detail in the image) is lost in the compression process. While JPEG is a good way to archive images once they're finished (especially images where there are no sharp edges), many artists prefer not to use JPEG because it alters pixels. Don't save in JPEG format if you're continually opening and closing an image—you'll lose more data every time you do so.

JPEG is also useful for preparing 24-bit images with tiny file sizes that are needed for use with World Wide Web site graphics. (See Chapter 10 for more information on JPEG use in projects created for the Web.)

**GIF.** GIF is the graphics format of choice for the World Wide Web on the Internet. Like TIFF, PICT or JPEG, saving in GIF format combines floaters with the background, so remember to Save As in a different file format if you want to be able to access the original image structure again. When you save in GIF, a dialog box appears that gives you a number of options for saving your file. You'll get smoother color transitions if you choose the Dither Colors button. Click the Preview Data button to see how your choices will affect your image.

**EPS.** Saving in this format drops floating elements into the background and ignores the mask layer, so it's best to choose Save As in another format if you'll want to make changes to your document at a later time. Saving in EPS format also converts the file into a five-part DCS file: four separate files for the four process printing colors, and a fifth file as a preview of the composite image. Check Painter's *User Guide* for a complete explanation of the EPS Options dialog box.

**PC formats.** BMP, PCX and Targa are formats exclusive to the PC. BMP (short for "bitmap") is a Windows-based graphics file format, and PCX is the PC Paintbrush native format. Neither of these two formats supports floaters or masks. Targa is a popular format used on the PC for creating sophisticated 24-bit graphics; it

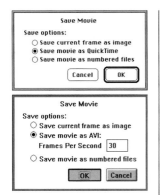

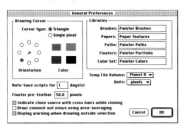

Choosing Save As with an open Painter Movie gives you these three options for Mac (top) or Windows (bottom).

The Place dialog box gives you options for transforming the image, retaining a mask, and creating a Pyramid data structure.

The General Preferences dialog box lets you specify libraries, cursor type and orientation, Temp File Volume (location of scratch disk), and units, among other defaults.

Making a stroke in the Brush Tracking dialog box

was originally developed by TrueVision Company as a proprietary format for use with its video capture boards. The Targa format is often used (in place of PICT) when preparing numbered files for import into Windows animation applications.

**Movie formats.** Movies in Painter (described in Chapter 8), are saved as Frame Stacks, but you can choose Save As to export the current frame of your movie, the entire Frame Stack as a Quicktime or AVI/VFW (on the PC) movie, or the entire Frame Stack as numbered PICT files. See Chapter 8's introduction for more information about multimedia formats.

**Pyramid files.** The Pyramid file structure is useful for composing high-resolution documents. A file with Pyramid data structure is capable of containing multi-resolution information. When an image is placed into a document (File, Place), it comes in as a reference floater (a low-resolution *reference* to the original placed image). The introduction to Chapter 5 contains more information about working with reference floaters and Pyramid files.

## SETTING PREFERENCES

Painter's Preferences (under the Edit menu) go a long way in helping you create an efficient workspace. A few pointers:

**Brush Tracking.** Before every work session, it's a good idea to first choose Edit, Preferences, Brush Tracking. Make a brushstroke with your stylus using a typical amount of pressure. Painter adjusts to give you the maximum amount of range and pressure-sensitivity based on your sample stroke. Unfortunately, Painter doesn't remember your custom setting after you quit the program; hence the need to re-establish your typical brushstroke every time you launch the program.

**Multiple Undos.** Painter lets you set the number of Undos you want under Edit, Preferences, Undos. It's important to note that this option applies cumulatively across all open documents within Painter—if you have the number of Undos set to 5 (the default) with two documents open, and you use two Undos on the first docu-

**CUSTOM INTERFACE SCREENS**

Change the look of Painter's interface with Edit, Preferences, Interface. Load an interface set from the Painter 4 CD-ROM, or choose any paper texture or pattern and apply it in the current color as an interface background. Shown on the left is the Standard Colors palette with the Sky interface from the Painter 4 CD-ROM, and on the right, the same palette with Wheat String texture (from the More Wild Textures library) and a plum color.

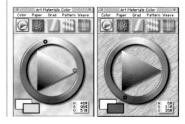

ment, you'll be able to perform only three Undos on the second document. And, since a high number of Undos will burden your RAM and scratch disk, unless you have a good reason (such as working on a small sketch where you'll need to make many changes), it's best to leave the Undo setting at 5—enough for even finicky artists.

## PAINTER BASICS

Here's a guide to some of Painter's basic operating procedures. As you work with the program, it may help to think of Painter's interface as a lovable but slightly eccentric relative: friendly and fun to be with, but occasionally exhibiting quirky behavior.

**Dragging off palettes.** Painter lets you tear off inactive "child" palettes from the "parent" palette to customize your workspace. For example, in the Art Materials palette, click on the Colors icon to make the Colors palette active, then click and drag the Papers icon to another location on your monitor. An outline of the palette appears as you drag, and when you release, the Papers palette appears. Although adding palettes in this manner can quickly fill your screen, if you frequently use palettes that are on the same parent palette (such as Colors and Papers), creating child palettes will save you many a mouse-click. To return a child palette to its parent, click the close box in the child palette's upper-left corner.

**Opening drawers.** Many of Painter's palettes display a pushbar with a green arrowhead that you can click on to open or close a drawer. An open drawer gives you access to a wide choice of brushes, gradients, papers and so on from whatever library is active at the time. A closed drawer (you see only the "front" of the drawer) shows your five most recent choices (as in the case of Brushes and Papers) or gives you additional controls (as in the case of Grads or Weaves). Clicking the "grow" or the "zoom-out" box in

As a shortcut for Window, Zoom To Fit Screen (fitting your entire image in the window), double-click on the Grabber tool in the Tools palette.

the upper-right of the palette will show more controls—brush methods and submethods, for instance.

**Screen management shortcuts.** Like other programs, Painter offers lots of shortcuts designed to cut down on your trips to the menus, palettes or scroll bars. To *scroll* around the page, press the spacebar (a grabber hand appears), then click and drag on your image. To *zoom in* on an area of your image at the next level of magnification, hold down Command-spacebar (a magnifier tool appears) and click in your image. Add the Option key to *zoom out*. (You can also use Command-plus to *zoom in* one magnification level and Command-minus to *zoom out*.) These are the same scrolling shortcuts used in Photoshop and Adobe Illustrator.

To *rotate the page* to better suit your drawing style, press Option-spacebar (the Rotate Page icon appears) and click and drag in your image until the dotted outline preview shows you the angle you want. (The Rotate Page command only rotates the view of the image, not the actual pixels.) Restore your rotated image to its original position by holding down Option-spacebar and clicking once on your image.

Two other frequently used screen management shortcuts include Command-M (Window, Screen Mode Toggle), which replaces a window's scroll and title bars with a frame of gray (or toggles back to normal view), and Command-H (Window, Hide Palettes), which hides (or restores) all palettes.

**Helpful icon buttons.** At the top right on the Painter Window scroll bar are three very helpful icon buttons: the Tracing Paper icon (allowing you to toggle Tracing Paper on and off), the Grid overlay icon (which turns the Grid View on and off) and the Color/Mask Edit Mode icon, (to toggle between the full-color view and Mask Edit Mode, a black-and-white view of the current background mask).

**Measuring and positioning elements.** The Ruler, Guides and Grid overlay can help you measure and position shapes and floaters. All three of these features reside under the Canvas menu. They are especially helpful for aligning type shapes and selections (see Chapter 4 for more about working with type in Painter).

To set up a guide using precision measurements or to change the default guide color, double-click on the Ruler to access the

If you're getting frustrated because you choose a new color in the Colors palette (or sample a new color from your image with the Dropper), but your brush still paints with the old color, you've probably chosen the back color rectangle in the Colors palette when setting the new color. Click on the front color rectangle, then choose the desired color and begin painting.

Back color rectangle
Front color rectangle

*The Tracing Paper, Grid overlay and Color View icon (Color toggles to a black circle in Mask Edit Mode) reside at the top of Painter's vertical scroll bar.*

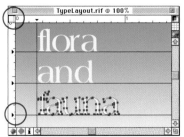

*Positioning the baseline of active letterform shapes with the help of the Ruler and horizontal Guides pulled from the ruler. The circled items show the Ruler Origin field (top), and a triangular marker (bottom).*

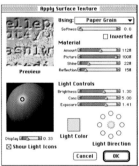

*Using the Grid overlay to help when positioning text selections*

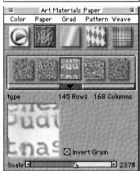

*The Surface Texture dialog box preview window (here shown Using Paper Texture) updates when a new choice is made in the Paper palette.*

Guide Options. Double-click on a triangle marker on the Ruler to access options for an individual guide. Delete guides by dragging them off the document window, or by pressing the Delete All Guides button in Guide Options.

To easily measure the exact *width* of an item, try moving the Ruler Origin. Press and drag it from the upper left corner of the Ruler, where the horizontal and vertical measurements meet, to the left end of the item you want to measure. Then see where the right end falls on the ruler.

The Grid overlay is useful for aligning items. Choose Canvas, View Grid, or click on the checkered Grid icon on the upper right of the scroll bar. To change the grid's appearance (for example, to create a grid of only horizontal lines), choose Canvas, Grid Options and adjust the settings.

## ALIGNING SHAPES AND FLOATERS AUTOMATICALLY

The Align dialog box (Effects, Objects, Align) is helpful for lining up several shapes or floaters (or a combination of the two). To align a series items, select the Floater Adjuster tool, press the Shift key and click on each item. When all the items are selected, go to the Effects menu and choose Objects, Align, and choose your settings. The dialog box preview will update to show you how your horizontal and vertical choices will affect alignment of the objects, and you can click OK to accept, or Cancel. Items will be aligned based on their bounding boxes. The shapes (below, center,) are aligned using Horizontal: Center, and Vertical: None. The floaters (below, right), were aligned using the tops of their bounding boxes. The settings were Horizontal: None, and Vertical: Top.

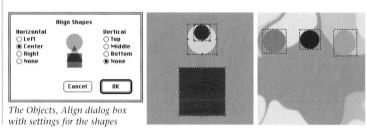

*The Objects, Align dialog box with settings for the shapes*

**Interactive dialog boxes.** In most programs, clicking to make choices outside of a dialog box will reward you with an error beep, but Painter's interactive dialog box design encourages such radical behavior. As an example, if you open a piece of artwork or a photo, and then choose Effects, Surface Control, Surface Texture and click and drag in the Preview window until you see a part of the image that you like, if you then choose Paper Grain in the pop-up menu you can go outside the dialog box to choose a different paper (even a paper in another library) in the Papers palette. You can even move the Scale slider in the Papers palette, and watch as the Preview image in the Surface Texture dialog box updates to reflect your choice. When you've arrived at a result that you like, you can click OK in the Surface Texture dialog box. The

Effects, Surface Control, Color Overlay dialog box behaves in a similar way, allowing you to choose Uniform Color in the pop-up menu and test different colors from the Colors palette before you click OK. The Edit, Fill dialog box (Command-F) is also interactive, giving you the ability to preview your image before it's filled with a Current Color, a Gradation or a Weaving.

## LIBRARIES AND MOVERS

Painter uses *libraries* and *movers* to help you manage the huge volume of custom textures, brushes and other items that the program can generate. Libraries are the "storage bins" for those items, and movers let you customize those bins by transferring items in or out of them.

The Wow! Texture 08 library, available on the CD-ROM that accompanies this book

**How libraries work.** On the inside of almost any of the palette drawers you'll find a Library button. Click the button to display the standard Mac or Windows Open dialog box and dig through folders on any hard disk or CD-ROM (like the *Painter 4* CD or the *Wow!* CD) until you find the library you want and double-click to open it. Fortunately, Painter is smart enough to show only libraries that can be opened in the palette of origin. For instance, if you clicked on the Library button in the Papers palette, you'll see Papers libraries only, not the Grad or Brushes libraries.

**Using movers to customize your libraries.** If you find that you're continually clicking on the Library button—for example, in the Papers palette—it's probably time to use a mover to compile your favorite textures into a single library. Here's how:

From the Paper pull-down menu on the Art Materials palette,

*Choosing Paper Mover from the pull-down menu on the Art Materials:Paper palette*

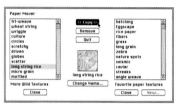

*Copying an item into the Favorite paper textures library*

*The open Papers drawer showing the newly created Favorite paper texture library*

choose Paper Mover. Create a new, empty Paper library by clicking on the New button on the right side of the mover, then name your Paper Texture file and save it. To move a texture from the left side of the mover (your currently active library) into the new library, click on a texture's name on the left side of the mover: A preview of the texture will appear in the center of the mover window; click the Copy button to move the texture.

Continue adding textures to the new library in this fashion. To add textures from different libraries to your new library, click on the left-hand Close button, then click again when it changes to an Open button and open the next library that you want to draw from. (Don't forget the libraries on the *Wow!* and *Painter 4* CDs!) When you've finished, click Quit. Now open your new library by clicking on the Library button in the Papers palette. If it contains over 25 papers, a scroll bar will appear so you can scroll to items at the bottom of the drawer. If you want your new library to open every time you launch Painter, choose Edit, Preferences, General and type its exact name in the Paper Textures box.

All movers work in the same way, so you can follow the above procedure to, say, create a new Brushes library that contains the only five brushes that you ever use. (See "Expressive Custom Brushes" on page 42 for an example of using the Brush mover.) 🖐

## LIBRARIES OF SPECIAL EFFECTS

To save libraries of "effects scripts" separate from the Painter Script Data file, you can make new script libraries to store automated effects. First, open the Objects palette and choose the Scripts palette, then select Script Mover from the pull-down menu. When you've finished copying, delete the items from the Settings file to keep file size trim. (For more information about effect scripts, see Chapter 8.)

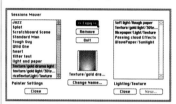

*Using the Script Mover to import scripts saved in the Painter Script Data file (left side) into a custom library of special effects scripts (right side)*

*The new Script library containing special effects "macros" that can be applied to images*

# THE POWER OF COLOR

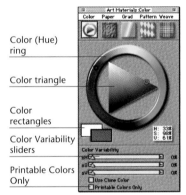

Color (Hue) ring

Color triangle

Color rectangles

Color Variability sliders

Printable Colors Only

*The Standard Colors palette (with the Hue ring), expanded to show the Color Variability (± H, ± S, ± V) sliders*

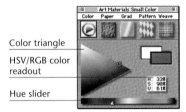

Color triangle

HSV/RGB color readout

Hue slider

*Change to the Small Colors palette by selecting Compact Colors from the Color pull-down menu list.*

*Change to the RGB Colors palette by choosing RGB Colors from the Color list.*

"COLOR, THE FRUIT OF LIGHT, is the foundation of the painter's means of painting—and its language." Abstract painter Robert Delaunay's observation mirrors our own appreciation of color as an expressive and essential element of the visual arts. Getting the most out of Painter's powerful color tools is an important first step for those of us who work with "the fruit of light."

## HUE, SATURATION AND VALUE

Painter's interface for choosing color is built around a model that uses *hue*, *saturation* and *value* (HSV) as the three basic properties of color. The program is designed so that you'll typically first choose a hue, then alter it by changing its saturation or value. Painter's Standard Colors palette and Small Colors palette are designed to work with these properties, but the program also includes an RGB (red, green, blue) palette for those who prefer working in that color space. Click the Color button in the Art Materials palette to open the Color palette. Switch palette views by choosing from the Color menu on the Color palette.

**Hue.** The term *hue* refers to a predominant spectral color, such as red or blue-green. Hue indicates a color's position on the color wheel or spectrum, and also tells us the color's temperature. A red-orange hue is the warmest color; a blue-green hue is the coolest. (Keep in mind, though, that temperatures are relative. Blue-violet is a cool color, but it warms up when it's placed next to blue-green.)

In the traditional pigment-based color system, red, yellow

**QUICK SWITCH TO RGB**

Click once on the HSV color readout on either the Color or Small Color palette to display the current color in RGB mode. Click again to switch back to HSV.

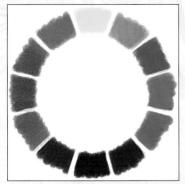

A pigment-based color wheel

A study created in a fiery, analogous palette dominated by orange

Saturating a color

Desaturating a color

Creating a shade of a color

Creating a tint of a color

An example of atmospheric perspective. The illusion of distance is enhanced in this piece because distant hills are painted with reduced saturation and less value contrast.

and blue are *primary* hues—colors that cannot be obtained by mixing. *Secondary* hues—green, orange and violet—are those colors located midway between two primary colors on the color wheel. Yellow-green, blue-violet and red-orange are examples of *tertiary* hues, found between a primary and a secondary color.

*Analogous hues* are adjacent to each other on the color wheel and have in common a shared component—for instance, blue-green, blue and blue-violet. *Complementary hues* sit opposite one another on the color wheel. Red and green are complements, as are blue and orange. (Painter's Hue ring is based on the RGB components of the computer screen, so it doesn't exactly match a traditional pigment-based color wheel.)

To change hues in Painter's Color palette, drag the slider on the Hue ring or click anywhere on the ring. Dragging and clicking also work with the Hue slider in the Small Colors palette.

**Saturation.** Also known as *intensity* or *chroma*, *saturation* indicates the color's purity or strength. The most common way of changing a color's saturation is by adjusting the amount of its gray component. In the Color triangle, move the Color ring to the left to desaturate a color, or to the right to saturate it. Fully or very saturated colors—those at or near the tip of the Color triangle—won't print the way they look on the screen. To see their printed (CMYK) equivalent colors while you paint, select the Printable Colors Only button in the expanded Color palette.

**Value.** A color's lightness or darkness is its *luminance* or *value*. A color's most pure value is that taken from the spectral hue. To create a *tint* of a color (lightening it, or increasing its value), move the Color ring higher in the Color triangle. To create a *shade* of a color (darkening it, or decreasing its value), move the Color ring lower in the Color triangle.

## PUTTING HSV TO WORK

Here are several practical suggestions and creative solutions for solving artistic problems using hue, saturation and value.

**Reduce saturation and value to indicate distance.** Artists have been creating *atmospheric* (or *aerial*) *perspective* in their work for thousands of years. The wall paintings of Pompeii in the first century B.C. show this technique. Hills we see in the distance have less intensity than nearer hills, and they also have less variation in value. This effect increases in hazy or foggy conditions. To depict this in your art, you can reduce the color saturation and value range as the landscape recedes from the foreground.

**Use saturation to indicate time of day.** At dawn or dusk, colors appear to be less saturated, and it becomes more difficult to distinguish colors. At noon, on a bright sunny day, colors seem saturated and distinct. (See Richard Noble's solutions on page 25.)

*A study in value contrast, based on a drawing by Michelangelo*

*Detail from Dennis Orlando's* Bend in the Epte, *showing shadows modulated with complementary color*

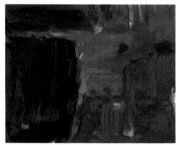

*The colors in this study (based on Hans Hofmann's* Twilight) *were blended using the Just Add Water and the Total Oil Brush variants.*

*Simultaneous contrast at work. Notice how the gold looks brighter next to the dark blue than it does next to pink.*

**Use color temperature to indicate distance.** The eye puts warm colors in front of cool colors. For example, orange flowers in the foreground of a hedge appear closer than blue ones.

**Create drama with light-to-dark value contrast.** Baroque and Romantic period artists as diverse as Caravaggio, Zurbarán, Géricault and Rembrandt are known for their use of extreme light-to-dark contrast. They accomplished this by limiting their palette to only a few hues, which they either tinted with white or shaded by adding black. A close look at the shadows and highlights that these artists created reveals complex, modulated tone. Digital artists can use Painter's Apply Lighting feature to add a dramatic splash of contrast to an image and also to unify a painting's color scheme, although achieving genuine tonal complexity requires additional painting.

**Use complementary colors to create shadows.** The Impressionists Monet, Renoir and Degas frequently avoided the use of black in the shadow areas of their paintings. They embraced a more subjective view of reality by layering complementary colors to create luminous shadows.

**Neutralize with a complement or gray.** One way to tone down a hue is to paint on top of it with a translucent value of its complement. El Greco painted his backgrounds in this manner to draw attention to more saturated foreground subjects. Try painting with a bright green hue, then glaze over it with a reduced opacity of red. The result will be an earthy olive. You can also neutralize a hue using shades of gray, as did the French artist Ingres. Although he often limited his palette to red, blue, gold and flesh tones, he created an illusion of a larger palette by adding varying proportions of gray and white.

**Blending, pulling and thinning colors.** Subtle changes in hue and saturation take place when colors are blended in a painting. Use the Just Add Water or Grainy Water variants of the Water brush to blend, for instance, two primary colors (red and blue) to get a secondary color (purple). For a more dramatic blending, you can pull one color into another by using the Total Oil Brush variant of the Liquid brush. Artists using traditional tools often thin paint by mixing it with an extender. In Painter, you get a similar effect by reducing a brush's opacity in the Controls palette.

**Draw attention with simultaneous contrast.** If two complementary colors are placed next to one another, they intensify each other: Blue looks more blue next to orange, and white looks more white next to black. In the 1950s, Op artists used the principle of simultaneous contrast to baffle the eye. Advertising art directors understand the power of simultaneous contrast and use it to gain attention for their ads.

*The flowers were painted in reds and red-oranges to unify the composition.*

*A landscape with figures, based on Mahana no atua (The Day of the God) by Paul Gauguin*

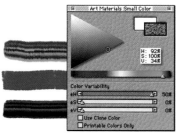

*These brushstrokes were painted with the Loaded Oils variant of the Brush and varying amounts of Color Variability: top, Hue slider only set to 50%; middle, Saturation slider only set to 50%; bottom, Value slider only set to 50%.*

**Use a family of colors to evoke an emotional response.** Create a calm, restful mood by using an analogous color theme of blues and blue-greens. Develop another family of hues using reds and red-oranges to express passion and intensity. You can also use a color family to unite a composition.

**Create your own color world.** Post-Impressionist Paul Gauguin (among others) created a powerful, personal color language by combining several of the above techniques. He used warm, bright colors to bring a subject forward in his composition, and used cool, dark colors to convey distance and mystery. He also made the bright foreground colors seem brighter by surrounding them with darker, more subdued colors.

## PAINTING WITH MULTIPLE COLORS

Painter has several brushes that paint with several colors at once; for instance, nearly all of the Artists brushes do so. Here are some customizing tips:

**Randomize colors with Color Variability.** Choose a multiple-bristle brush such as the Big Loaded Oils variant of the Brush. (If you keep the Brush Controls:Spacing palette open as you choose various brushes, you'll see their Stroke Types appear. Both Multi and Rake are multiple-bristle brushes.) Now zoom-out the Color palette to display the Color Variability sliders. Choose a color and paint with the brush, then experiment by adjusting the Hue (± H), Saturation (± S) or Value (± V) slider and painting again. You can see the effects of the sliders more easily if you make a series of short strokes rather than one long one.

**Change colors with stylus pressure.** Use your pressure-sensitive stylus to paint in two colors. Start by choosing the Graduated Brush variant of the Brush. In the Standard Colors or Small Colors palette, click on the front Color rectangle and choose a bright blue color. Choose the back Color rectangle and select a rose color. If you paint with a light touch, you'll be painting in rose. If you press heavily, the stroke turns blue. (If the balance between the two colors seems uneven, choose Edit, Preferences, Brush Tracking. Make a typical brushstroke in the Scratch Pad area, click OK, and try the Graduated Brush again.)

## COLOR ADJUSTMENTS ON EXISTING IMAGES

Painter offers several ways to modify color in your art *after* it's been created. To see the results of your choices in many of these dialog boxes, you'll need to click and drag in the Preview window.

**Correct Colors.** Do you see an unnatural color cast in your image? The Correct Colors, Curves feature can help you correct this problem. This feature is especially useful when working with scanned photos, for instance.

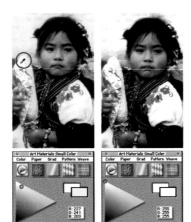

Before and after: Sampling in the image with the Dropper to determine the color cast on a bright highlight on the aluminum foil reveals these values: Red: 227, Green: 241, and Blue 203: (left); and the corrected image (right) with pure white highlights shows Red, Green and Blue values of 255.

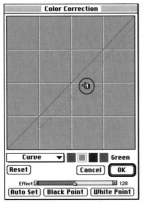

Pulling the Green color curve in the Correct Colors dialog box to lessen the green cast in the image above

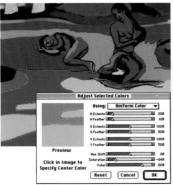

Using Adjust Selected Colors to neutralize a bright blue

To adjust an image, begin by determining the color cast. Use the Dropper tool to sample a bright highlight in your image. (The brightest highlights should be pure white.) In the Color palette, click on the HSV values box to toggle the palette to RGB view. Check the RGB values in the Color palette. In our example, the color and numbers show that the unwanted color cast is green. A bright white should have R, G and B values of 255 in the Color palette. Choose Effects, Tonal Control, Correct Colors, and choose Curve from the pop-up menu. Curve will allow you to adjust the individual RGB values. Click on the color that you want to adjust. (We clicked on the Green icon—to constrain the adjustment to *only* the green values in the image.) Then, position the crosshair cursor over the diagonal curve, and when you see the hand cursor appear, pull down and to the right. Pulling down (as shown), will decrease the selected color in the image. Click the Reset button to try out another adjustment without leaving the dialog box.

**Adjust Colors.** To change the hue, saturation or value of all of the colors in an image, choose Effects, Tonal Control, Adjust Colors. Experiment with the sliders and view the changes in the Preview window. Adjust Colors is also useful for quickly desaturating a full-color image—converting it to black and white. To desaturate an image, move the Saturation slider all the way to the left.

**Adjust Selected Colors.** You may want to make color adjustments in particular areas of your image. Painter's Adjust Selected Colors feature lets you make dramatic changes (turning a blue sky yellow) or more subtle ones (removing the red cast from a subject's face). Choose Effects, Tonal Control, Adjust Selected Colors. In the dialog box, click in your image (*not* in the Preview window) on the color you want to change. Adjust the Hue Shift, Saturation and Value sliders at the bottom of the dialog box. When the basic effect is in place, use the Extents sliders to fine-tune the color range. Use the Feather sliders to adjust transitions between colors: 100% gives a soft transition, 0% gives an abrupt one.

**Color Overlay and Dye Concentration.** Found under Effects, Surface Control, these two dialog boxes don't allow the radical color replacement options you get with the Adjust Colors feature, but they have their strengths. Color Overlay lets you tint an image with a color using either a dye concentration model (which makes the paper appear to absorb the color) or a hiding power model (which covers the image with the color). Dye Concentration adds or removes pigment. Both of these dialog boxes allow you to add texture by selecting Paper Grain in the pop-up menu.

**Negative.** Creating a negative of all or part of an image can have dramatic, artistic purposes or more practical ones—such as converting a scanned negative to a positive. Select Effects, Tonal Control, Negative to convert your image.

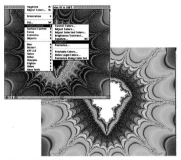

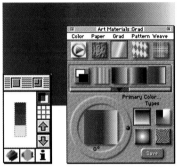

*Using Tonal Control, Negative on a brightly colored image*

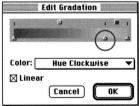

*You can create your own custom gradation based on selected colored pixels using Art Materials, Grad, Capture Gradation. Create a new document (ours was 144 x 144 pixels) and zoom-in to 1200%. Choose the Single Pixel variant of the Pens brush. Paint a single row of pixels (similar to one above). Now marquee the pixels with the Rectangular Selection tool and choose Grad, Capture Gradation from the pull-down menu on the palette. When the Save Color Ramp dialog box appears, give the grad a descriptive name. Click OK and the new grad will appear in the Grad palette.*

### Edit Gradation

Color: **Hue Clockwise**

☒ Linear

[ Cancel ] [ OK ]

*Moving a Color control point in the gradation editor; the Hue Clockwise Color option is chosen.*

### SAMPLING PAINT

You can temporarily switch to the Dropper tool and sample colors by holding down the Command key while you're using many of Painter's other tools.

**Printable and Video Colors.** Your monitor is capable of displaying more colors than can be reproduced in the four-color printing process, and if you are creating images for video, some highly saturated colors will not make the transition to video tape. It's a good idea to convert your out-of-gamut colors while you're in Painter so there won't be any surprises. Choose Effects, Tonal Control and either Printable Colors or Video Legal Colors, depending on whether your image is destined for paper or tape.

## MORE COLOR TOOLS

**Adding color with Gradations.** Painter's powerful Grad palette lets you fill selected areas with preset gradations or ones that you've created. Turn to "Adding Color and Gradations to Line Art" on page 22 to see Linda Davick's technique. You can also colorize an image with a gradation using Grad, Express in Image.

The gradation editor is a powerful tool for creating custom color ramps. You can't use this tool to alter all of Painter's existing gradations, however—it's used primarily for creating new ones. On the Art Materials palette, click on Grad, and choose Edit Gradation from the pop-up menu to bring up the gradation editor. Select one of the triangular color control points and choose a color from the Color palette. The color ramp will update to reflect your choice. Add new color control points by clicking directly in the color bar; the sliders can be positioned anywhere along the ramp. To delete a control point, select it, and press the Delete key; Option-click on the color bar to add a new control point in the current color. Clicking on the squares above the ramp brings up the Color pop-up menu; experiment with the options available there to get quick rainbow effects, or to change to RGB color view.

**Filling images.** You can fill images using either Effects, Fill (Command-F) or the Paint Bucket tool. The Fill command lets you fill your image or a selected portion of it with a color, a gradient, a clone source or a weave. The Paint Bucket gives you the same fill options, and gives you additional choices of what to fill: the image, the image's mask or a cartoon cell. (All of the Paint Bucket options appear on the Controls palette when you select the Paint Bucket tool.) Cartoonists and others who fill line art with color will want to explore the Lock Out Color feature (to preserve black line art, for example) by double-clicking on the Paint Bucket tool icon in the Tool palette.

**Keep colors in Color Sets.** Like an artist's palette, Painter can store your most frequently used colors in the Color Sets palette, found under the Art Materials:Color, Adjust Color Set pull-down menu. Painter Colors is the default set. You'll find more Color Sets (including a full set of Pantone colors) on the Painter 4 CD in the Goodies folder. Switch Color Sets by clicking on the Library button in the Color Sets palette. 🐾

# Filling with Gradations

***Overview*** *Fill the background image with a custom gradation; add texture using Dye Concentration and Color Overlay; bring in paths from the Paths palette; resize, reposition and fill them.*

**1**

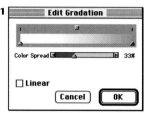

*Adding more white to the gradation using the gradation editor*

**2a**

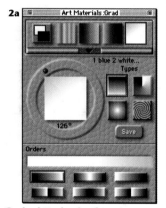

*The Grad palette showing the custom gradation, ready to fill the background*

**2b**

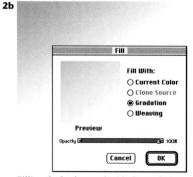

*Filling the background with the gradation*

PAINTER'S TWO-POINT GRADATION is a great way to create an equal blend of two colors, but if you want to see a larger percentage of one of the colors, you'll need to create a custom gradation. For this interface design for a flying service's interactive CD-ROM, we initially tried a two-point, blue-to-white gradation on the background, but later chose to make a custom gradation to reduce the amount of blue.

**1 Modifying a color ramp with the gradation editor.** To create a custom two-color gradation that emphasizes one color more than another, you could select colored pixels in an image and choose Art Materials, Grad, Capture Gradation, but Painter's gradation editor gives you greater precision and flexibility. Begin by choosing the two colors you want to blend (we chose white and a sky blue). Select the Two-Point gradation in the Art Materials:Grad palette, then close the drawer so you can see the gradation with the surrounding direction ring. Choose the Linear Type (the top left of the four icons to the right of the ring). Open the gradation editor by choosing Art Materials, Grad, Edit Gradation. Click on the triangular slider under the color that you want to de-emphasize (blue, in our example), and uncheck the Linear box so the Color Spread slider bar appears. Drag the Color Spread slider to the left (we set the slider to 33%). The color ramps in the gradation editor and in the Grad palette will update as you move the slider. Click OK. Back in the Grad palette, click the Save button if you want to keep your new gradation for later use.

**2 Filling the background image.** Choose File, New and create a 640 x 480-pixel document, a standard size for an interface screen. In the Grad palette, drag the red ball on the direction ring so that the darker color (in our example, the blue) starts at the upper left. To fill with the gradation, choose Effects, Fill (Command-F) with Gradation at 100% Opacity and click OK.

**3**

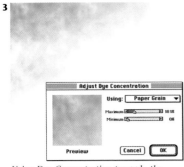

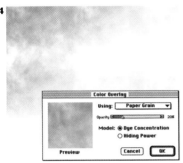

*Using Dye Concentration to apply the Clouds paper texture to the background*

**4**

*Using Color Overlay to add more clouds and a blue tint*

**5**

*Resizing the square path with the Path Adjuster tool*

**6**

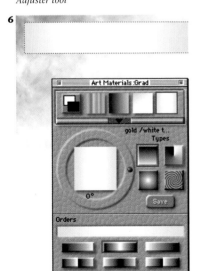

*Applying the gradation to the title bar*

**3 Applying a paper grain to the gradation.** To add "atmosphere" to the image, we added a paper texture using Dye Concentration, since that method adds grain based on an image's luminance (darker areas receive more texture). Start by choosing a texture in the Paper palette (we chose the Clouds paper texture from the Nature paper library), then choose Effects, Surface Control, Dye Concentration. Choose Paper Grain from the pop-up menu and experiment with the Maximum and Minimum sliders until you're pleased with the result in the Preview window (we set Maximum to 181% and Minimum to 0%). Click OK.

**4 Finishing the background.** To complete the background, we added a hint of clouds to the entire image using Color Overlay, keeping the same paper texture and color. Choose Effects, Surface Control, Color Overlay. Choose Paper Grain from the pop-up menu, and experiment with the settings. We set Opacity to 20% and selected the Dye Concentration button. Click OK.

**5 Preparing the title bar.** The easiest way to create a long, editable rectangular selection is to resize an existing path from the Paths palette. In the Objects palette, click on the P. List icon, and choose Paths, to open the Paths drawer. Click on the square path icon and drag it into your document. Choose the Selection Adjuster tool and turn the square into a rectangle by clicking and dragging on one of the corner or side handles. You can reposition the path by clicking inside of it and dragging it to a new location.

**6 Creating and applying a gold gradation.** We wanted a gold color on both ends of the title bar and a large area of white in the center. Our tests with the two-point gradation did not accomplish this, so we created a custom gold-and-white gradation using the same gradation-editing process as in step 1.

To apply the gradation, first make sure the title bar selection is active. In the Grad palette, set the angle to 0 and choose the Linear (top left) Type. To create a gradation with gold at the ends, zoom-out the palette to display the Orders options; click the top center or bottom center option. Apply the gradation by choosing Effects, Fill (Command-F). Click on Gradation and click OK.

**Adding other elements.** We repeated the above process to add gradations and solid colors to the remaining elements of the design. We created the drop shadows behind several of the buttons by floating the selections (Option-clicking with the Floater Adjuster tool) and using Effects, Objects, Create Drop Shadow. Finally, we added text using the Text tool, kerning the type with the arrow keys and filling with blue. (To kern the type, choose the Floater Adjuster tool, click outside the newly set type to deselect it, then click individual letters with the Floater Adjuster tool and move them using either the left or right arrow key.)

# Capturing a Color Set

**Overview** *Capture color from a reference using the Dropper; build and customize a Color Set; use the Color Set to paint a new image.*

**1a**

*The reference photograph*

**1b**

H: 38%
S: 90%
U: 68%

*Using the Dropper to sample color from the image*

 **2**

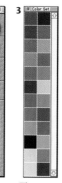 **3**

*The Color Set palette*

*The Autumn Colors Set*

**4**

*Applying watercolor washes using the Autumn Colors Set*

TRADITIONAL ARTISTS USE PALETTES to hold paint; digital artists can turn to Painter's Color Sets. Use this technique of sampling color from a photo or painting to quickly build a full palette of colors. If you're planning a series of illustrations based on the same color theme, you'll find Color Sets invaluable.

**1 Sampling the color.** Open an image that contains the color range you want. To sample the color, choose the Dropper tool and click it on a colored pixel in the image. The Colors palette will display the color. If the displayed color isn't the one you want, you can click and drag the Dropper around your image. The Color palette will update to show the new color as you drag.

**2 Creating a Color Set.** In the Art Materials palette, choose Color, Adjust Color Set from the pull-down menu to open the Color Set palette, and click on the New Set button. A Color Set palette title bar will appear. Click on the Add Color button to add the selected color to the Color Set. Continue to sample and add more colors in this way. To save your colors, click on the Library button in the Color Sets palette, then click Save, name the set and click OK. We named ours "Autumn Colors."

**3 Arranging the Color Set display.** You can arrange your colors in the Color Set to fit your drawing environment. To change the shape of the individual color squares, click on the Color Square Size arrow buttons, and click on Color Set Size arrow buttons to change the shape of the layout. We built our Color Set of 32-pixel-wide squares with 2 columns and 12 rows.

**4 Using your new colors.** To paint with the new Color Set, click on a color in the set, choose a brush and begin painting. We drew a sketch using a dark blue-gray from our set with the 2B Pencil variant, and added washes in other colors using the Simple Water variant of the Water Color brush.

### NAMING COLORS

To name your colors, click on the Display Text button at the bottom of the Color Sets palette, double-click on the color in the Color Set, type a name and click OK.

# Colorizing Scratchboard

***Overview*** *Create black-and-white art; float it and apply the Gel Composite Method; paint on the background in color.*

CHET PHILLIPS

*Phillips' black-and-white scratchboard art*

*Choosing the Gel Composite Method*

*Adding color with the Thin Stroke Airbrush variant*

ADDING COLOR TO BLACK-AND-WHITE ARTWORK without covering the black areas requires forethought. One option is using Painter's Wet Layer, but brushwork there can become slow and laborious. Artist Chet Phillips discovered his own "wet layer" technique—shown here on his whimsical *Ant Farm*—using a floater and the Gel Composite Method.

**1 Creating black-and-white art.** Start a new document with a white background. Choose black, then Effects, Fill (Command-F) using Current Color. Click OK. Use white and the Scratchboard Tool variant of the Pens brush to "etch" into the black fill.

**2 Floating the image.** Select All (Command-A), choose the Floater Adjuster tool and click once on the image to float it. The black-and-white image is now floating over a white background. In the Controls palette, choose Gel from the Composite Method pop-up menu. This method makes the white areas of the floater transparent, allowing any color on the background to completely show through without affecting the black in the floater.

**3 Painting on the background.** In the Floater List palette, click in the blank area below the floater's name to deselect it. This makes sure that you'll be painting on the background. Choose a brush and a color and begin painting. Phillips used the Thin Stroke Airbrush variant in varying sizes and colors, switching occasionally to the Dodge and Burn brushes to add highlights or darken areas. If you need to edit the black areas, click on the floater's name in the Floater List before painting. ▞

# Adding Color and Gradations to Line Art

**Overview** *Use the Pens brush to create line art; fill areas with flat color and gradations; add highlights with the Airbrush.*

LINDA DAVICK

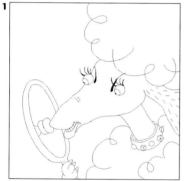

*Line art created with the Single Pixel variant of the Pens brush*

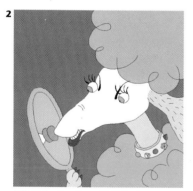

*Filling the drawing with flat color*

FILLING LINE ART WITH COLOR AND GRADATIONS is slick and efficient in Painter, using what children's book illustrator Linda Davick calls "the coloring-book technique." Davick employed the Paint Bucket tool to create the vain, arrogant Zuba, the protagonist in Debbie Smith's *Beauty Blow-Up.*

**1 Creating a black-and-white line drawing.** Choose the Pens brush, Single Pixel variant, and choose the Flat Cover submethod. Flat Cover lets you draw a solid-color line, a necessity for this technique that fills all neighboring pixels of the same color. Choose black (in the Color palette) and draw your line art, making sure all your shapes are completely enclosed with black lines. If you need to correct your work, switch the color to pure white in the Color palette and erase.

**2 Filling with flat color.** To test color choices and tonal values, fill areas of your illustration with flat color. Choose the Paint Bucket tool, and in the Controls palette, choose Image under What To Fill and Current Color under Fill With. Choose a color, then click in the area of your drawing you want to fill. Since the Paint Bucket fills all neighboring pixels of the same color, you can refill by choosing another color and clicking again. If you're filling small areas, it's important to know that the Paint Bucket's "hot spot" (where it fills from) is the tip of the red paint in the icon. Davick filled all areas except Zuba's face using this method.

**3 Adding color ramps.** To fill the background with a gradation, open the drawer of the Art Materials:Grad palette and choose Two-Point from the pop-up menu. Close the drawer, choose the upper left Types button and set an angle for your fill by rotating the red ball around the direction ring. In the Color

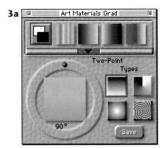

**3a**

*A Two-Point linear gradation*

**3b**

*Filling the background with the gradation*

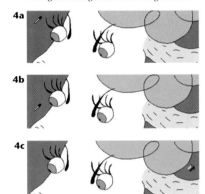

**4a**

**4b**

**4c**

*Sampling the gradation across from the top of the area to be filled (a); sampling across from the bottom of the area to be filled (b); filling the area with the gradation (c). Repeat this process for each flat color (negative) area to be filled.*

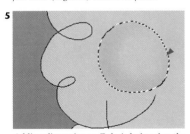

**5**

*Adding dimension to Zuba's hair using the Fat Stroke Airbrush inside a selected area*

palette, choose colors for both the front and back Color rectangles. In the Controls palette, choose Fill with Gradation. Finally, to apply the gradation, click in the area that you want to fill. Davick filled the largest background area and the mirror with linear gradations.

**4 Duplicating color ramps.** To duplicate the large background gradation in each of the smaller background shapes—under Zuba's chin and below and above her ear—Davick created a new gradation using color sampled from areas in the background gradation. She then filled the smaller background shapes with the new gradation. If you need to do this on the "negative" shapes in your image, first check the Color palette to make sure that the Color rectangle that contains the starting color of your original gradation is selected. Choose the Dropper tool and position it over the existing gradation at approximately the same height as the top of the negative area that you want to fill. Click in the gradation to sample the color. To sample the bottom portion of the gradation, select the opposite Color rectangle, then position and click the Dropper at about the same height as the bottom of the area to be filled. Click in the negative area with the Paint Bucket to fill with the new sampled gradation.

**5 Adding airbrush details.** Davick finished the piece using the Fat Stroke variant of the Airbrush within circular selections to add dimension to Zuba's hair and fur. (You can make roughly circular selections using the Lasso tool.) She used the same Airbrush with unrestricted strokes on Zuba's face and ear.

*Davick used her "coloring-book technique" for this editorial illustration for* Aspire *magazine. The related article offered suggestions on how to keep kids entertained during the summer.*

■ Judicious use of saturated color, loose, illustrative strokes, and an eclectic mix of brushes and paper textures let **Susan LeVan**, of LeVan/Barbee Studio, create a strong emotional quality in her work.

To create the impression of a cloudy day in *A Boy and His Dog* (above), LeVan used a palette composed primarily of low-saturation colors, including a lot of gray and brown. She began the image with a brown paper color, and applied and mixed strokes using the Simple Water variant of the Water Color brush. She used the Artist Pastel Chalk variant and Rough Water Color paper texture to apply strokes on the grass and the sweater. LeVan painted with a soft touch, allowing the underpainted areas and brown paper color to show through.

In *The Dinner Hour* (right), she combined dark, somber colors with a few highly saturated ones to help create an unspoken tension between parent and child. She roughed in the image with the Fine Tip Felt Pens variant of the Felt Pens, then added and blended transparent color with the Simple Water variant of the Water Color brush. She used the Pens, Water, Airbrush and Chalk brushes for the details, switching between Basic, Cotton, Rougher, and Wriggle paper textures.

■ Artist **Richard Noble** has successfully recreated the look of traditional acrylic using Painter. He generally begins a piece by importing a reference photograph into Painter to use as a template. He roughs in the colored areas of the composition with the Sharp Chalk and Large Chalk variants of the Chalk brush; he blends colors with the Just Add Water variant; he uses the Distorto variant of the Liquid brush to pull one color into another; he adds highlights with the Airbrush. Noble outputs his pieces onto canvas, then stretches and finishes them with a clear glaze and touches of acrylic paint. The pieces shown here reveal his sensitivity to color at varying times during the day.

In *Marina by Moonlight* (above), he used a limited palette and soft brush work to create an atmosphere of low light. Highlights and shadows are subdued and painted with reduced detail.

For *Harley* (left), he switched to a more vivid palette of saturated colors. The motorcycle and figures are rendered crisply in the midday sun, and details in the highlights and shadows are clearly visible.

■ **Dennis Orlando's** sensitive use of light combined with layered, luminous shadow areas in his paintings has given him the moniker "The Modern Impressionist." Orlando typically starts with a sketch using the Thick & Thin Pencils variant. He lays color down using the Artist Pastel Chalk, and he increases the Color Variability settings in the Colors palette to create activity, or "noise" in the color. He then blends colors with the Grainy Water variant of the Water brush.

Orlando's friend Jack Twelves commissioned him to paint *Dock with Colorful Boats* (right), based on a photograph Twelves took 20 years ago in New England. To create linear strokes in the dock and boats, Orlando used the Straight Lines Draw Style (chosen in the Controls palette) with the Artist Pastel Chalk variant. To retain the color activity in the boats, he reduced the Opacity setting for the Grainy Water variant before blending his pastel brush strokes. This technique let him develop rich, subtle color detail in the highlights and shadows.

Orlando painted *The Bend in the Epte* (below)—inspired by Monet's technique of light and shadows—with soft, warm, light on the backlit trees and blue and purple hues in the shadows. He used Grainy Water and the Total Oil Brush variant of the Liquid brush to pull and blend colors into each other.

■ **Richard Biever's** brushy, spontaneous style translates nicely to the digital realm. Value contrast plays a primary role in his compositions. He typically begins with a gestural sketch on paper, which he then traces on his digital tablet. He uses a custom variant of the Chalk brush to block in areas of color, then moves the color around in a painterly fashion with a modified Water Rake variant of the Water brush.

In *Grounder* (left), Biever painted dark, low-saturation blue and gray strokes behind the ball player to make the background recede and bring the player forward. He added type with the Text tool, filling the letters with a bright red, and then desaturating them by softly stroking over them with a low-opacity white Chalk brush. He blended the colors in the type using his custom Water Rake.

*The King's Musketeer* (below) was inspired by the light-to-dark value contrast used by the masters Rembrandt and John Singer Sargent. Biever began the image with a light background, then decided a dark background would create a more dynamic balance in his composition. He painted the left side of the background slightly lighter than the right to play against the dark and light sides of the figure. This technique adds to the depth of the composition.

# PAINTING WITH BRUSHES

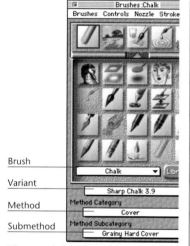

Brush

Variant

Method

Submethod

*The expanded Brushes palette*

*Although it's fun to assign whimsical names (such as Monster Airbrush), informative names are more useful. Try listing brush size, color variability, percentage of opacity, and any change in method or submethod in your variants.*

PAINTER'S BRUSHES ARE THE PROGRAM'S HEART: without them, Painter would be a lot like other image editors. What sets Painter apart is the way it puts pen to paper and paint to canvas—the way its brushes interact with the surface below them. Here's a primer on getting the most from Painter's brushes.

**Brush variants.** Variants are the options that appear in the pop-up menu under the five brushes on the front of the Brushes palette drawer (not zoomed-out). Every brush has its own variants, so every time you choose a different brush, the list of variants changes. While many artists will be content to use only a few of the many brush variants that come standard with the program, others will enthusiastically create dozens of their own. Even if you're an intuitive artist, you'll probably find yourself wanting, for instance, "that scrubby-edged oil paint brush." Since you lose your custom settings when you switch brushes or brush variants, you'll want to save a variant of that special paintbrush so you're not continually adjusting your settings. (For in-depth information on creating your own brushes, turn to page 34, "Building Brushes.")

To make a variant, check that all your settings are the way you want them and the brush under which you want to save the variant is selected in the Brushes palette. Then from the Brushes pop-up menu choose Variants, Save Variant, name it and click OK. Your

(For in-depth information on creating your own brushes, turn to page 34, "Building Brushes.")

## YOUR FAVORITE BRUSHES

Choosing a brush from the inside of the Brushes palette's drawer moves it to the front of the drawer, replacing a less recently used one. You can keep a favorite brush on the front of the drawer by clicking and holding on it for 1 second. A tiny green light will appear below the brush, signaling that it's locked in place. To unlock the brush, click and hold again until the green light goes out.

To change the settings of a variant temporarily, first modify the settings of the current variant, then (on the Brushes palette) from Brushes pull-down menu choose Variants, Save Built Variant. To recover the brush, choose Brushes, Variants, Restore Default Variant. This works with Painter's standard brushes as well as with brushes that you have built and saved.

*Switch methods to make dramatic changes in brush characteristics. Here we've applied the Crayons brush over a gradient using the default Buildup method (top), Cover method (center), and Eraser method (bottom).*

*The Gritty Charcoal variant of the Charcoal brush was applied using various submethods: the semi-anti-aliased default Grainy Hard Cover (top); the aliased Grainy Edge Flat Cover (middle); and the anti-aliased Soft Cover (bottom).*

*Sketch created with the 2B Pencil variant*

new variant will appear at the top of the variant list for that brush and will stay there, even after you leave the program, until you remove it by selecting Brushes, Variants, Delete Variant.

**Methods.** Methods are the backbone of the brushes. To see the methods pop-up menu, click the zoom-out box in the Brushes palette. Methods describe how the paint will interact with the background and with other paint. For instance, the Pencil brush uses the Buildup method, meaning that overlapping strokes will darken. The Chalk brush uses the Cover method, which means that strokes—even light-colored ones—will cover other strokes. You can, however, switch methods at any time. For example, you can save a Cover method variant of the Pencil brush.

**Submethods.** While each method gives a radically different effect to a brush, the submethods make more subtle changes, affecting the edges of brush strokes. Submethods that include the word *flat* produce hard-edged, aliased strokes. Those that include the word *hard* give medium-soft, semi-anti-aliased strokes. Strokes made using *soft* submethods appear with feathered, anti-aliased edges. And strokes with the word *grainy* in their submethods will be affected by the active paper texture.

**Paper textures.** "Grainy" brush methods will reveal the paper texture you've selected in the Art Materials:Paper palette. You can use Painter's standard papers or create your own (see page 38, "Applying Scanned Paper Textures"). Adjust the Grain slider on the Controls palette to vary the intensity of the grain on your brush strokes. A lower grain setting means that less of the color will penetrate the grain, so your strokes will actually look grainier: They are hitting only the "peaks" of the paper surface.

## EMULATING TRADITIONAL TECHNIQUES
Here's a brief description of a several traditional art techniques and how to re-create them in Painter. There are a number of ways to obtain similar results, so only one or two techniques for each medium are outlined as a starting point for your own experimentation. If you are working with large, high-resolution files, consider increasing your brush size and scaling up paper textures: Choose the Brush Controls:Size palette (from the Controls pull-down menu on the Brushes palette), and adjust the Size slider. To scale up a paper texture, use the Scale slider on the Paper drawer; if you don't see this slider, click on the pushbar on the Paper drawer to reveal it.

**Pencil.** Pencil sketches using traditional materials are typically created on location. Tools include soft-leaded graphite pencils (HB to 6B), various erasers and white paper with a smooth to medium grain. To create a pencil sketch in Painter, select a relatively

*Still life study painted with Sharp Chalk, Artist Pastel Chalk and Square Chalk*

smooth paper (such as Regular Fine) and choose the Pencils brush, 2B Pencil variant. Select a black or dark gray and begin sketching. To erase or add white highlights, choose a white color and switch the method from Buildup to Cover.

**Colored pencil.** Conventional colored pencils are highly sensitive to the surface used: Layering strokes with light pressure on a smooth board will create a shiny look, while switching to a rougher surface creates more of a "broken color" effect (color that doesn't completely cover the existing art). To closely match the grainy, opaque strokes of a soft Prismacolor pencil on cold-pressed illustration board with Painter, select a finer medium-grained paper (such as Cotton Paper). Choose the Pencils brush, Colored Pencils variant. Switch the method from Buildup to Cover and change the submethod to Grainy Edge Flat Cover. See "Drawing with Colored Pencils" on page 46 for a full description of this technique.

*Detail from* Coastal Meadow. *The Artist Pastel Chalk and Large Chalk variants were used on Big Canvas texture to paint this pastel image.*

**Pastel.** Pastels encourage a bold, direct style: Edgar Degas preferred pastels for his striking compositions because they simultaneously yield tone, line and color. A great variety of hard and soft pastels are used on soft or rough-grain papers. Pastel artists often use a colored paper stock to unify a composition.

Use Painter's Chalk brush variants to mimic traditional hard or soft pastels, and if you want to use a colored paper, click on the Paper Color box in a new document and choose a color. The Chalk brushes are among Painter's most popular; turn to page 47, "Blending and Feathering with Pastels," or page 40, "Spontaneous Pastels," for two different techniques using them.

**Conté crayon.** Popular in Europe since 1600 and used today for life drawing and landscapes, Conté crayons have a higher oil content than conventional chalk or pastel; as a result, they work successfully on a greater variety of surfaces.

To get a realistic Conté crayon look in Painter, start with the Chalk brush, Sharp Chalk variant. Reveal more paper grain in the brushwork by moving the Grain slider in the Controls palette to 14%. On the Brushes palette, choose Controls, Spacing to open the Spacing palette. Drag the Spacing/Size slider to 25%. Now open the Size palette (Controls, Size) and choose the upper left brush tip. Move the ± Size slider to 1.45, increasing the brush's effective diameter by 45%. Click the Build button and begin drawing. To see another Conté variant, turn to "Spontaneous Pastels" on page 40.

*Inspired by a Michelangelo drawing, this charcoal study was drawn with Gritty Charcoal and blended with Grainy Water.*

**Charcoal.** One of the oldest drawing tools, charcoal is ideal for life drawing and portraiture in *chiaroscuro* (high value contrast) style. Renaissance masters frequently chose charcoal because images created with it could be transferred from paper (where

*A study created with the Scratchboard Tool variant of the Pens brush*

*To create a wet-into-wet look, the sky and water in this study were painted with the Diffuse Water and Broad Water variants on Rough Watercolor paper.*

*Using a glazing technique for a watercolor portrait study of Sabina Gaross*

corrections could be made easily) to canvas or walls in preparation for painting.

To create a charcoal drawing in Painter, select a rough paper and the Soft Charcoal variant of the Charcoal brush. Create a gestural drawing, then blend the strokes—as you would traditionally with a tortillion, a tissue or your fingers—with the Water brush, Grainy Water variant, changing the submethod to Grainy Soft Cover. Finish with more strokes using the Charcoal brush, this time using the Gritty Charcoal variant.

**Scratchboard illustration.** Scratching white illustrations out of a dark (usually black) background surface became popular in the late 1800s. Illustrations created in this manner often contained subtle, detailed tone effects, making them a useful alternative to photographic halftones in the publications of that era. Modern scratchboard artists use knives and gougers on a variety of surfaces, including white board painted with India ink. To duplicate this look in Painter, start with the Pen tool, Flat Color variant and increase its size in the Size palette. Choose black from the Color palette and rough out the basic shape for your illustration. To "scratch" the image out of the shape with hatch marks, switch to white and change to the Scratchboard Tool variant. Use the Scratchboard Rake to add texture. Turn to Chapter 5's gallery to see Chet Phillip's Painter-generated scratchboard work, or check out John Fretz's blending of traditional and digital scratchboard in Chapter 4's gallery.

**Calligraphy.** With the exception of "rolling the nib" and a few other maneuvers, you can imitate nearly all conventional calligraphic strokes in Painter. Choose the Calligraphy variant of the Pens brush and begin your brushwork. To make guides for your calligraphy, select Canvas, Rulers and drag guides out from the ruler, or you can use Painter's Grid overlay (Canvas, Grid). If you want a rougher edge to your strokes, try switching submethods to Flat Cover or Grainy Edge Flat Cover. To fine-tune the "nib," choose Size from the Controls pull-down menu and zoom-out the palette. Create a narrower nib by setting a smaller value on the Squeeze slider; if you want to adjust the angle of the brush, drag the Angle slider until you like what you see in the preview.

**Watercolor.** Landscape artists like Turner and Constable helped popularize watercolors in the nineteenth century, and the medium's portability lends itself nicely to painting on location. Traditional watercolor uses transparent pigment for color, and the paper is often moistened and stretched prior to painting.

Painter lets you achieve many traditional watercolor effects—without paper-stretching! Choose the Simple Water variant of the Water Color brush, a rough paper (such as Big Grain Rough from More Paper Textures) and a color, and begin painting. When you choose a Water Color brush, you automatically paint on Painter's

*A pen and wash of the king of beasts. Washes were added with the Simple Water and Broad Water variants.*

*Detail from John Dismukes' airbrushed Ktema logo*

*Marker comp created with the Felt Marker variant, Cover method*

Wet Layer, which stays "wet" until you choose Canvas, Dry to drop it to the background. For more details about repeatedly drying the Wet Layer for a *glazing* (translucent layering) effect, read about Mary Envall's watercolor technique on page 48. If you want your strokes to appear to *diffuse* into the paper, switch to the Diffuse Water variant. (If the color created with this variant is too intense, reduce the opacity in the Controls palette.) You can also diffuse all existing strokes in the Wet Layer using the Post-diffuse command: Shift-D. Repeat the keystroke to increase the effect.

**Pen and wash.** Tinted, translucent washes over pen work has been the medium of choice of Asian painting masters for many centuries. Painter's Wet Layer lets you add a wash to any drawn (or scanned) image without smearing or hiding it. Choose the Simple Water or Broad Water Brush variant of the Water Color brush, pick a color and a medium-textured paper and begin painting on top of line work.

**Airbrush.** The trademark of most traditional airbrush work is a slick, super-realistic look; photo retouching is a more subtle use of the tool. A traditional airbrush is a miniature spray gun with a hollow nozzle and a tapered needle. Pigments include finely ground gouache, acrylic, watercolor and colored dyes, and a typical support surface is a smooth illustration board. Airbrush artists protect areas of their work from overspraying with pieces of masking film, or flexible friskets cut from plastic.

In Painter, choose one of the Airbrush variants and begin sketching or retouching. To get the most from the tool, use Painter's paths just as you would traditional airbrush friskets. Turn to "Selections and Airbrush" in Chapter 4 to see John Dismukes' masterful airbrush work using paths and selections.

**Marker rendering.** To create traditional comprehensive sketches ("comps"), art directors use pointed and wedge-tipped felt markers on marker paper. In Painter, start by opening a photograph or photomontage. Clone the image (File, Clone), delete the clone (Edit, Select All, then press Delete) and turn on Tracing Paper (Canvas, Tracing Paper). The original image will appear "screened back," ready to be traced with a marker. To emulate a wedge-tipped marker, choose the Felt Marker variant of the Felt Pens brush, choose a color and begin sketching. To apply light strokes over dark you may want to switch to Cover method. Turn off Tracing Paper occasionally to check your progress. If you want to add type, use the Type tool to set text shapes. Resize and reposition the text shapes using the Floater Adjuster tool, then convert the shapes to selections (Shapes, Convert to Selection). Stroke with the Felt Marker inside of the selections. You can also import type or other elements from a drawing program by choosing File, Acquire, Adobe Illustrator format. The Acquire command will

*Detail of Nancy Stahl's* Tennis Woman, *showing her gouache technique*

*Richard Noble blends color with a Liquid brush variant to get the look of conventional acrylic.*

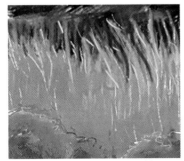

*Creating texture in grass by scratching out with the Scratchboard Tool variant and white paint*

create a new file. Copy and paste the shapes from the new file into your illustration. Reposition the shapes and convert them to selections, then paint within the selections using the Felt Marker.

**Gouache.** Roualt, Vlaminck, Klee and Miro were a few of the modern artists who experimented with this opaque watercolor, used most frequently in paintings that called for areas of large, flat color. Gouache contains a blend of the same type of pigment used in transparent watercolor, a chalk that makes the pigment opaque, and an extender that allows it to flow more easily.

Artist Nancy Stahl has created several complex brushes in Painter that emulate traditional gouache applied to cold-pressed illustration board. To learn her secrets, turn to page 51.

**Oil paint and acrylic.** These opaque media are "standards" for easel painting. Both can be applied in a thick impasto with a palette knife or stiff brush, and both can be *extended* (thinned) with a solvent or gel and applied as transparent glazes. They are typically applied to canvas that has been primed with paint or gesso.

To get the look of oil or acrylic in Painter, choose a very rough paper (Big Grain Rough, Big Canvas or Small Canvas, all from More Paper Textures) and one of the Brush variants (Penetration Brush, Small Loaded Oils, Hairy Brush or Oil Paint) and begin painting. Blend colors using short strokes with a Liquid brush. To get textured brushstrokes (the "3D paint" look), when you're finished, choose Effects, Surface Control, Apply Surface Texture. Choose Image Luminance from the pop-up menu, and an Amount setting of 20–30%. If you want to mimic the look of acrylic paint extended with a glossy gel medium, drag the Shine slider to 100%. To get a semi-matte finish, move the Shine slider to between 40% and 50%. For a variation on this technique, see Dennis Orlando's version of a traditional oil look on page 54.

**Mixed media.** You can create media combinations in Painter that would be impossible (or at least very messy!) in traditional media. Try adding strokes with a Water Color or Pencil brush atop oils, or use a Pens brush on a base of chalk and gouache. See how artist Phil Howe mixes media on page 50.

**Erasing techniques.** Painter provides several ways to emulate traditional erasing techniques. Use the Pure Water Brush variant of the Water Color brush to pull up pigment from a "wet" watercolor (similar to *sponging up* a traditional watercolor). Use the Scratchboard Tool variant of the Pens brush and a white or light color to *scratch out* pigment from a pastel or oil painting; to create strokes with a hint of texture, switch to the Grainy Hard Cover submethod. *Pull paint out* of an image but leave some pigment in the "valleys" of the paper grain by using one of the Bleach variants of the Eraser brush, lowering the Opacity slider (in the Controls palette) to 10%. 🖌

# Building Brushes

***Overview*** *Creating these custom brushes will give you insight into the workings of the palettes that control them.*

## OPEN THE PALETTES

To save time, open as many of the palettes that affect brush behavior as screen real estate will allow. At the very least, keep the Brush Size and Sliders palettes and the Controls palette open as you work.

## VIEWING THE DAB

Click on the brush footprint in the Size palette's Preview window to switch between "hard" (showing the maximum and minimum sizes) and "soft" (showing bristles) views.

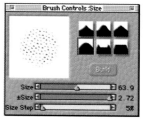

*The Brush Controls: Size palette showing a "soft" view of the bristled dab used to create the Colorful Texture Brush*

IF YOU'RE CONTENT WITH THE HUGE VARIETY of brushes that ship with Painter, you can skip this section. If you like trying new brushes but don't want to build them, check out the Brush librar- ies on the Wow! CD-ROM in the back of this book—you'll find the brushes shown on these pages and more. But if you're one of those folks who doesn't rest until you get exactly the brushstroke you want, you've come to the right place. *Lighthouse Wall*, above (based on a photo by Melinda Holden), was created with six of the custom brushes described here.

### DAB TYPES

It's important to distinguish between the terms *dab* and *stroke*. Think of a *dab* as the footprint of the brush—a cross-section of its shape. Open the Brush Controls:Size palette by choosing Brushes, Controls, Size. You can switch Dab Types at the bottom of the zoomed-out Size palette. Painter has four Dab Types:

**Circular.** Most of Painter's brushes use this Dab Type. Don't be fooled by the term "Circular"; you can change a brush's Squeeze setting so that its footprint looks elliptical, but it's still considered a Circular Dab Type.

**1-Pixel.** Just like it sounds, this is a 1-pixel-wide brush.

**Bristle.** Since Bristle brushes are made up of several "hairs," they have a richer potential than Circular brushes. You can make ad- justments in Bristle Thickness, Clumpiness and other settings in the Spacing and Bristle palettes (found under the Controls menu).

**Captured.** You can capture any area of a document to act as a footprint for a Captured brush. Use the Rectangular Selection tool and draw a marquee (press the Shift key to constrain the selection to a perfect square) around a mark or group of markings. Go to

the Brushes palette and choose Brushes, Capture Brush; the brush footprint will appear in the Brush Controls:Size palette.

## STROKE TYPES

The *stroke* is a dab applied over a distance. You can switch Stroke Types in the Brush Controls:Spacing palette.

**Single.** Just as it sounds, Single Stroke Type brushes have only one stroke path. Because of this, they're fast. If you use a Bristle or Captured Dab Type, you can create a fast Single Stroke Type brush with a lot of complexity.

**Multi.** Painter's computation-intensive Multi Stroke brushes are the slowest (and therefore least spontaneous) of Painter's brushes. For example, try drawing a line with the Hairy Brush variant of the Brush. Instead of a stroke, you'll see a dotted "preview" line that shows its path; the stroke appears a moment later. Multi brushes are built from several randomly distributed dabs that may or may not overlap. Lovely, variable strokes can be made using a Multi Stroke brush, however you can create much faster, "real-time" brushes using a Rake Stroke, or a Single Stroke brush with a Bristle Dab Type.

**Rake.** The Rake Stroke Type is like a garden rake; each of the evenly-spaced tines is a bristle of the brush. Painter gives you a lot of control over the bristles, for instance, you can make them overlap, letting you create wonderfully complex, functional brushes. You can change the number of Rake Bristles in the Spacing palette (keeping in mind that fewer bristles make faster brushes), and adjust the way the bristles interact in the Bristle palette and also the Advanced Controls:Rake palette. To try out an existing Rake brush, paint with the Big Wet Oils variant of the Brush.

## BUILDING CUSTOM BRUSHES

For the custom brushes that follow, we start with an existing Painter brush and radically modify its appearance by making adjustments in the palettes that affect brush behavior. After you've created the brush (and perhaps after having made further modifications on your own), you may want to choose Brushes, Variant, Save Variant to save it into your current Brush palette.

Try these settings on images of 1000 pixels square or less. If you work with larger files, you'll want to proportionally increase the Size slider settings that we list here. Also, don't worry if your slider numbers don't exactly match ours—just get them as close as you can. And don't think your computer has crashed if you hit the Build button (or Command-B) and nothing happens for a while: Painter is working away, building a very complex brush.

To make room for more brushes, we've shortened descriptions. For instance, "*Well:* Resaturation, 80" means, "In the Advanced

*Blocking in window panes with the Fast Flat Oil brush*

*Marks made with Opaque Oil paint*

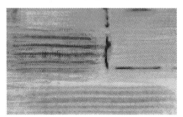

*Adding horizontal strokes to masonry with the Feathering brush*

*Using the Blender brush to add graduated tones to masonry*

*Footprint of the Random Leaves brush and strokes made in a lighter color. To cover an area with fallen leaves, try recording a stroke and playing it back automatically. Choose Brushes, Stroke, Record Stroke and paint a stroke with the Random Leaves brush, then choose Brushes, Stroke, Auto Playback, and watch the leaves fall!*

Controls:Well palette, set Resaturation to 80 and leave all other sliders where they are." "*Color Variability*" stands for the Color Variability settings in the zoomed-out Color palette. For a full description of the functions of the controls in each of the palettes, you can refer to Painter's *User Guide*, although painting with the brush after you make each adjustment will teach you a lot, too.

**Fast Flat Oil brush.** A Circular Dab Type and a Single Stroke Type make this a fast-painting brush, great for painting short dabs of color with a hint of transparency at the end of the stroke.

Start with the Fine Brush variant of the Brush. *Submethod:* Grainy Hard Cover. *Controls:* Opacity, 100; Grain, 18. *Size:* Size, 25.3; ± Size, 1.00; Size Step, 5; Squeeze, 25; Angle 0; Dab Type, Circular. *Sliders:* Opacity/Pressure; all others/None.

**Opaque Oil paint.** Use this springy, speedy, Single Stroke, Bristle brush to paint teardrop-shaped dabs with rough edges.

Start with the Big Wet Oils variant of the Brush. *Submethod:* Grainy Hard Cover. *Controls:* Opacity, 100; Grain, 75. *Size:* Size, 14.5; ± Size, 1.80; Size Step, 5. *Spacing:* Spacing/Size, 5; Min Spacing, 1.0; Single Stroke Type. *Bristle:* Thickness, 60; Clumpiness, 53; Hair Scale, 351; Scale/Size, 0. *Color Variability:* ± H, 1; ± V, 2. *Well:* All sliders to maximum. *Sliders:* Size/Pressure; Grain/Velocity; all others/None.

**Feathering brush.** Created for feathering over existing color to add interest and texture, this Single Stroke, Bristle brush paints tapered strokes quickly, thanks to optimized Spacing settings.

Start with the Loaded Oils variant of the Brush. *Submethod:* Soft Cover. *Controls:* Opacity, 9; Grain, 100. *Size:* Size, 21.0; ± Size, 1.41; Size Step, 5. *Spacing:* Spacing/Size, 8; Min Spacing, 0.1; Single Stroke Type. *Bristle:* Thickness, 40; Clumpiness, 0 (for smooth strokes), Hair Scale, 495; Scale/Size, 0. *Color Variability:* ±H, 1; ± V, 5. *Well:* Resaturation and Dryout, maximum; Bleed, 0.

**Blender brush.** The *Well* palette settings for this Single Stroke, Bristle brush lets you pick up existing color and blend with it.

Start with the Fine Brush variant of the Brush. *Controls:* Opacity, 100; Grain, 20. *Size:* Size, 20; ± Size, 1.44; Size Step, 5; Bristle Dab Type. *Spacing:* Spacing/Size, 1; Min Spacing, 2.0. *Bristle:* Thickness, 71; Clumpiness, 100; Hair Scale, 221; Scale/Size, 0. *Well:* Resaturation, 74; Bleed, 51; Dryout, 4.95. *Sliders:* Size/Pressure; Grain/Velocity; all others/None.

**Random Leaves brush.** This Single Stroke, Captured Dab Type brush with variable color, random size and direction is useful for texturizing—adding a natural look of random fallen leaves to a painting. It looks richest when used over a rough paper texture.

To create the brush dab, use the Smooth Ink Pen variant of the Pens brush to make a few simple leaf shapes—similar to the

To speed up Rake Stroke brushes that use a Bristle Dab Type, try switching them to Single Stroke. Increase Size in the Size palette to compensate for the narrower stroke and adjust the Spacing/Size slider in the Spacing palette.

Footprint of the Soft Captured Oil brush with strokes

Footprint and lettering made with the Bamboo Pen brush

Soft horizontal strokes of color made with the Soft Oil brush

Grainy strokes made with the Colorful Texture brush

footprint shown—and capture the dab (see Captured, on page 34). *Submethod:* Grainy Soft Cover. *Controls:* Opacity, 83; Grain, 9; *Size:* Size, 25.3; ± Size, 2.72; Size Step, 16; Squeeze, 98; Angle Range, 180; Angle Step, 5. *Color Variabilty:* ± H, 20; ± V, 7; *Sliders:* Size/Random; Angle/Random; all others/None.

**Soft Captured Oil brush.** The captured gray dots and a medium Dryout setting give this Single Stroke brush a soft feel.

Start with the Loaded Oils variant of the Brush. To create the dab, draw several tiny black and gray dots in a circular pattern, then capture the dab. *Submethod:* Soft Cover. *Controls:* Opacity and Grain, 100. *Size:* Size: 26.6; ± Size, 1.34; Size Step, 10. *Spacing:* Spacing/Size, 10; Min Spacing, 1.0; Single Stroke Type. *Well:* Resaturation, 100; Bleed, 75; Dryout, 90.4.

**Bamboo Pen brush.** This Captured, Single Stroke brush's irregular edges, color variability and changing stroke thickness make it an expressive calligraphy brush. The bleed and resaturation settings make brushstrokes appear to soak into the image surface and pick up color when the brush is dragged over existing strokes.

Use the Sharp Chalk variant of the Chalk brush to draw a rough-edged oval footprint, with "splinters" on the leading and ending edges. Switch to the Dirty Marker variant of the Felt Pens brush and capture the dab. *Controls:* Opacity, 16; Grain, 79. *Size:* Size, 25.3; ± Size, 1.91; Size Step, 10; Squeeze, 60, Angle Range, 180; Angle Step, 5. *Spacing:* Spacing/Size, 10; Min. Spacing 0.6; *Well:* Resaturation 42%, Bleed 43%; *Sliders:* Size/Direction; Angle/Direction; all others/None.

**Soft Oil brush.** This Rake Stroke Type, Bristle brush was created to feel like a traditional soft, flat brush with long bristles.

Start with the Big Wet Oils variant of the Brush. *Submethod:* Soft Cover. *Controls:* Opacity, 50; Grain, 100. *Size:* Size, 22.1. *Spacing:* Bristles, 7. *Bristle:* Thickness, 50; Clumpiness, 70; Hair Scale, 323; Scale/Size, 0. *Color Variability:* ± H, 1; ± V, 3. *Well:* Resaturation, 70; Bleed, 40; Dryout, maximum. *Sliders:* Opacity/Pressure; Grain/Pressure; all others/None. *Rake:* Contact Angle, 1.04; Brush Scale, 0; Turn Amount, 20; check Soften Bristle Edge; uncheck Spread Bristles.

**Colorful Texture brush.** This Bristle Dab Type, Rake Stroke Airbrush is great for painting grainy textures. Decrease the Hue (± H) Color Variability setting for more monochromatic strokes.

Start with the Spatter Airbrush variant of the Airbrush. *Submethod:* Grainy Hard Cover. *Controls:* Opacity, 68; Grain, 44. *Size:* Size, 63.9; ± Size, 2.72; Size Step, 5; Squeeze, 75; Dab Type, Bristle. *Spacing:* Rake Stroke Type. *Color Variability:* ± H, 40. *Rake:* Turn Amount, 136; *Random:* Placement 4.00, *Sliders:* Size/Pressure; Grain/Velocity; Opacity/Pressure; all others/None.

# Applying Scanned Paper Textures

***Overview** Scan a textured paper; open the file in Painter and capture the texture; use a grainy brush and Painter's special effects to apply the texture to your image.*

CORRINE OKADA

*The scanned paper textures: rice paper (left) and maple leaf (right)*

**1b**

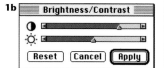

*Increasing the contrast of the paper scan*

**2a**

*Capturing a selected area of the paper scan*

**2b**

*Saving and naming the new paper texture*

WHILE PAINTER OFFERS A SEEMINGLY ENDLESS assortment of paper grains, many artists still choose to create their own surfaces. They draw from many sources: video grabs, scanned photos, texture collections on CD-ROM, scans of natural objects (leaves or richly grained wood), scans of papers or patterns and images drawn in Painter. They also generate their own seamless textures with Fractal's Make Paper Texture and Make Fractal Pattern features.

When Corrine Okada first began using Painter, she began scanning her extensive paper collection, capturing the images in Painter and saving them into her own texture libraries. Her skill in applying these custom textures is evident in *Crane Maiden*, a CD-ROM cover commissioned by Silicon Graphics.

**1 Scanning the papers.** Okada scans her papers on a flatbed scanner in grayscale mode. She scans an 8 x 10-inch area at 300 ppi. If you're scanning a thin, light-colored sheet—like the piece of lacy rice paper that Okada scanned for this job—you may want to place a sheet of black paper behind it to create more contrast. Okada also scanned a sheet of Japanese maple leaf paper.

You'll have more flexibility when you apply the texture if the scan you apply has good contrast and a broad tonal range. Open your scanned texture and choose Effects, Tonal Control, Brightness/Contrast. Drag the top slider to the right to increase contrast. If necessary, adjust the lower slider (Brightness) and then click Apply.

**2 Capturing the texture.** Use the Rectangular Selection tool to isolate an area of your image. Start by selecting an area of about

**3a**

*Detail of the Rice Paper texture brushed behind the head*

**3b**

*Detail of the Rice Paper texture brushed onto the kimono*

**4a**

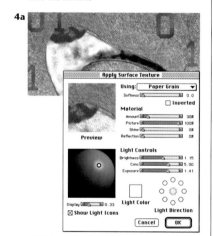

*Applying a Surface Texture using Painter's Rice Paper texture*

**4b**

*The Maple Leaf texture on the brushstroke (created with special effects) and the computer monitor (applied with the Soft Charcoal variant)*

200 x 200 pixels (read the Width and Height dimensions in the Controls palette). The repetition of your pattern may be too obvious if your image is much smaller. On the Art Materials: Paper palette, choose Paper, Capture Texture. Name your paper and click OK to accept (you'll get the smoothest results if you leave the Crossfade setting at 16), and a picture of the texture will appear in your current Paper library.

**3 Applying grain with brushes.** Painter lets you apply textures in two ways: with a brush or as a special effect. Okada used both of these methods (within selections and on floaters), in this piece. To brush the Rice Paper texture behind the woman's head, she first inverted the texture by checking the Invert Grain box on the front of the closed Paper drawer. She selected the area behind the head, then brushed the texture into the selected area using the Soft Charcoal variant of the Charcoal brush and a white color. Okada selected a purple color to brush the same texture (without inverting the grain) onto the woman's kimono. Near the end of the project, she used the same brush to apply the Maple Leaf texture onto the computer screen in blue, yellow and white.

**4 Special effects with grain.** To create a subtle woven look across the entire image, Okada selected Painter's Rice Paper texture from the Wild Textures library. She selected Effects, Surface Control, Apply Surface Texture. In the pop-up menu she selected Paper Grain and dragged the Amount slider to 30%. She set the Shine slider to 0 and clicked OK.

To add color, value and texture to the brushstroke that sweeps across the lower half of the image, Okada applied multiple special effects using the Maple Leaf texture. She selected, then floated the brushstroke, and used Color Overlay, Apply Lighting, and Apply Surface Texture (all under Effects, Surface Control) a few times each with various settings to get the effect she wanted. 🐾

# Spontaneous Pastels

***Overview*** *Add texture to a new document; use variants of the Chalk brush to create a sketch; block in color; add detail.*

CHELSEA SAMMEL

**1a**

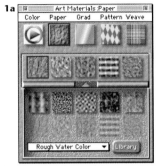

*Selecting the Rough Water Color paper*

**1b**

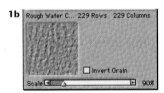

*The front of the Paper palette drawer*

**1c**

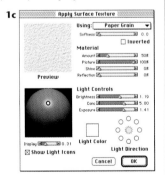

*Sammel's Apply Surface Texture settings*

**2a**

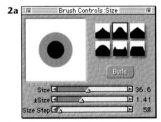

*Adjusting the settings for Tapered Chalk*

THE CHALK BRUSH VARIANTS ARE AMONG PAINTER'S most responsive brushes, making them a natural match for artist Chelsea Sammel's spontaneous style. The Chalk family is also grain-sensitive—another good match for Sammel, who worked for many years with traditional pastels on rough paper. She began *Poppies* at a Macworld demonstration and finished it in her studio.

**1 Preparing the drawing surface.** Sammel created a rough, textured surface across her entire canvas. To do this, create a new document with a tan paper color. Choose a rough paper texture in the Art Materials:Paper palette. Click on the Paper drawer's push bar to reveal the Scale slider, and drag it to the left to make a finer grain. Sammel chose Rough Water Color from the Grains library and scaled it to 90%. To apply the texture, choose Effects, Surface Control, Apply Surface Texture. Choose Paper Grain from the pop-up menu and experiment with the settings. Click OK when you're done. Sammel set Amount to 50%, Picture to 100%, and Shine to 0%.

**2 Building brush variants.** Sammel likes Painter's default Chalk brushes and makes only minor adjustments to their settings. She works quickly and spontaneously, creating a few variants on the fly and switching frequently among them. To create her Tapered Chalk, choose the Artist Pastel Chalk variant of the Chalk brush. In the Brush Controls:Size palette (Brushes palette, under the Controls pull-down menu), set Size to 36.6 and ± Size to 1.41. Open the Advanced Controls:Sliders palette (also found under the Controls pull-down menu) and set Size to

## THE VANISHING SURFACE

Applying Surface Texture to an empty canvas is a good way to give an entire surface a texture, but it will be covered as you paint if the brush you're using doesn't show grain (doesn't have the word "grainy" in its submethod). Some artists apply Surface Texture before *and* after they paint.

**2b**

*The Tapered Chalk variant as it appears in the Brushes palette*

**3a**

*Drawing the poppy with the Conté variant over the ochre background*

**3b**

*The original finished poppy image, before the image was extended to incorporate the second poppy*

**4**

*Duplicating the poppy to balance the composition*

Pressure. This setting, combined with a moderate ± Size setting, creates more taper at the end of each stroke. Click the Build button (or press Command-B) to build the brush. To save the variant, choose Brushes, Variants, Save Variant, then name your brush and click OK. To create Sammel's Conté Crayon, start with the Sharp Chalk variant. In the Size palette, change Size to 9.4 and ± Size to 1.41. In the Sliders palette, set Size to Pressure. Click the Build button. For a grainier stroke, drag the Grain slider in the Controls palette to 13%. Save the variant.

**3 Sketching the first poppy.** Sammel brushed a warm ochre onto the background using the Tapered Chalk, adding a few strokes of complementary blues and greens. She switched to the Conté variant, chose black, and sketched loose, dynamic shapes. She switched back to Tapered Chalk and began to block in areas of color, starting with the large poppy. She wanted an active, random look to the color, so she placed varying colors next to each other. Once she had blocked in the major areas, she chose the Frosty Water variant of the Water brush and smudged her strokes into the background. She switched to the Grainy Water variant in areas where she wanted to preserve the textured look.

**4 Adding the second poppy.** To balance the composition, Sammel decided to add another poppy, so she needed to enlarge her image. If you need to make more room in an existing image, choose Canvas, Canvas Size, and enter the number of pixels you want to add to each edge of your image.

Sammel created a duplicate poppy by floating a copy of the original. To do this, she carefully selected the large poppy with the Lasso tool, switched to the Floater Adjuster tool, held down the Option key (to copy) and clicked on the selected area. While the copy was floating, she scaled it smaller, flipped it horizontally, and rotated it slightly to distinguish it from the original (all of these effects are found under Effects, Orientation). When she was satisfied with floater's position in the composition, she dropped it by clicking on the Drop button in the Objects:Floater List palette.

**Finalizing the image.** Sammel extended the petals of the small poppy with the Tapered Chalk, blending and adding fresh color where needed. To further define the shapes, she added dark green line work with the Conté Crayon set to Buildup method, Grainy Hard Buildup submethod. (The Buildup method lets the color darken to black as strokes overlay each other.) She switched back to Cover method, Grainy Hard Cover submethod to finish the image by adding lighter complementary hues over the dark ones.

# Expressive Custom Brushes

***Overview*** *Build custom brushes before sketching; create a line drawing; brush in soft fills; colorize with a Water Color brush; add a tinted texture.*

AYSE ULAY

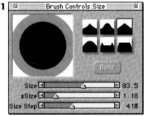

*Settings for Ulay's Large Light Fill variant in the Size palette*

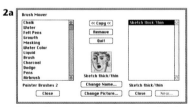

*Using the mover to create a custom brush*

*Ulay's Brush icon after being moved back into Painter Brushes*

AYSE ULAY'S FLUID DRAWING STYLE APPEARS to be a quick, spontaneous expression, but what's not visible is the careful foundation she laid before she began her pieces. Ulay prefers to not interrupt the creative process by building variants as she works, so she prepares them in advance. Her *Musician*, painted from her imagination, was featured in a promotion for a new screenplay.

**Open a new file.** Create a new document with a white background color. Ulay created a 4 x 4-inch image at 300 ppi.

**1 Creating variants.** Ulay created seven custom variants of the Charcoal brush. Three of them, intended for line work, were slight modifications (Size) of the Gritty Charcoal variant. She created four other versions of the Soft Charcoal variant and used these to brush in soft, graduated fills. To build Ulay's Large Light Fill, start with the Soft Charcoal variant. In the Brush Controls:Size palette (found under the Controls pull-down menu on the Brushes palette) increase the Size to 83.5. Drag the ± Size slider to 1.18. In the Controls palette, adjust both the Opacity and Grain to 15%. Save the variant by choosing Brushes, Variants, Save Variant. Name it and click OK. Repeat the process, modifying existing variants to create new ones.

**2 Storing variants in a custom brush.** Once you've created a number of variants, you can create a brush container just for them. This is handy if you use certain brushes for specific jobs (as Ulay did here). Since Painter doesn't have a variant mover that would allow you to swap variants between brushes, the process is a bit involved. You'll create an icon for your brush in the process,

**4a**

*Choosing Big Canvas in the Papers palette*

**4b**

*Detail of Ulay's expressive line work*

**4c**

*Adding dimension with the Fill brushes*

**5**

*Adding color with the Simple Water brush. Notice how the color "pools" along the stroke edges.*

**6**

*Adding a tint and a grain simultaneously with Color Overlay*

so begin by using the Rectangular Selection tool to select a square area of an image that you want to represent your brush. On the Brushes palette choose Brushes, Brush Mover. Click New and name a new Brush palette when the dialog box appears, saving it into the Painter 4 Folder (Ulay named hers Sketch Thick/Thin). Then select the brush on the left side of the mover that contains your new variants and click Copy to place it into your new Brush palette on the right side of the mover. Select the brush on the right, click on Change Picture, and click OK to change from the original icon to the new one (your selected image). Click on Change Name, rename the brush and click OK. Click Quit to exit the mover. Now, back in the Brushes palette, click on the Library button and open the palette you just created. Select your brush and delete the variants that you don't want by selecting them one at a time and choosing Brushes, Variants, Delete Variant. Click Yes when the dialog box appears. If you want to add your new brush to either Painter's default Brushes palette or one of your own, you'll need to use the Brush Mover again.

**4 Sketching in black.** Ulay started with a line sketch. She chose black from the Color palette and the Big Canvas paper texture from the Grains paper library, then began drawing the figure. She switched among her three custom line brushes throughout the sketching process. After completing the line work, she used her Fill brushes to add dimension and contrast to the background, hat, face, and other areas of the image.

**5 Adding color in the Wet Layer.** When she had finished all black brushwork, Ulay colorized her image with varying sizes of the Simple Water variant of the Water Color brush. Using a Water Color brush (or any brush set to the Wet method) automatically turns on Painter's Wet Layer, allowing color to be applied without disturbing the drawing on the background. After colorizing the image, Ulay "dried" it (dropped it onto the background) by selecting Canvas, Dry.

**6 Using Color Overlay.** Ulay wanted to add warmth to her completed brushwork with a sepia tint. She chose a brown color, and with Big Canvas still selected in the Paper palette, she chose Effects, Surface Control, Color Overlay. She chose Paper Grain from the pop-up menu, set Amount to 75%, checked the Dye Concentration button and clicked OK.

**BRUSHES FROM SCRATCH**

If you want to create custom brushes from scratch instead of basing them on pre-existing brushes, first select a square area of your image with the rectangular selection tool. Choose Brushes, Variants, Save Brush. Name your brush category and click OK. You'll see your selection appear in the Brush palette with no variants below it. You've just created an empty "variant holder," ready to be filled with custom variants.

# Painting with Pastels

***Overview*** *Rough out a composition in gray; add color with a custom Chalk variant and fills; blend colors with a Water brush; use "scrumbling" for texture to finish.*

*An original "sketchbook" pencil sketch*

*Sketching in gray with the Chalk brush*

*The custom Pastel variant*

INSPIRED BY THE SOFT, WARM LIGHT of a sunrise in Baja California, *Punta San Antonio* was painted primarily from memory with Painter's Chalk brushes, although we occasionally referred to pencil sketches made on location. To achieve the soft atmosphere, we blended colors with a Water brush, and added a few accents of broken color to finish the piece.

**1 Selecting a reference and opening a new file.** Choose a photo or a sketch to use as a reference and open a new file. We started with an 11.5 x 7.5-inch file at 144 ppi and later doubled the image's resolution (using Canvas, Resize) midway through the painting process so it could be printed larger.

**2 Choosing a gray color, a texture and a brush.** It's often easier to work out the artwork's light and dark values in a neutral gray. Choose a gray tint from the Colors palette and a textured paper from the Paper palette (we chose Rougher). Select the Chalk brush, choose one of the variants and begin sketching. We used Artist Pastel Chalk to create the thick, flowing lines of the landscape. To keep the freshness and energy of a sketch while you draw, don't get bogged down with details.

**3 Building a custom Pastel variant.** When you're done sketching and you're ready to add color, create a midsized, soft Pastel brush. First choose the Large Chalk variant and change the submethod to Grainy Soft Cover. In the Brush Controls:Size palette (chosen from the Controls submenu on the Brushes palette), set the Size slider to 12.0. In the Controls:Brush palette, lower the Opacity slider to 30% (a lower opacity will allow you to build up color slowly with more sensitivity). To save this custom brush as a variant, choose Brushes, Variants, Save Variant, name your variant and click OK. The new name will appear in the Brushes palette. Choose a color and begin painting. We adjusted our new variant's

**4**

*Blending with the Just Add Water variant of the Water brush*

**5a**

*Using the Lasso tool to select the sky*

**5b**

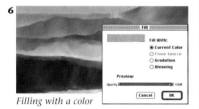

*Feathering the selection in the Controls: Adjuster palette*

**6**

*Filling with a color*

**7a**

*Scrumbling on the white water*

**7b**

*Adding texture to the foreground foliage*

size and opacity as we worked, switching to a 50% opacity, for instance, while creating the gold lighting effect on the water.

**4 Blending colors.** To achieve a smooth look with traditional pastels, you rub them with precise blending tools like a tortillion or a blending stump. Use the Just Add Water or Grainy Water variants of the Water brush to mimic these traditional tools. In the Size palette, choose the top left brush tip profile (the profiles are located above the Build button). Begin blending, and experiment with various brush sizes while you work.

**5 Making selections for the underpainting.** To quickly visualize color choices for the underpainting in the sky and the ocean, we made loose freehand selections of those areas using the Lasso tool. Select the Lasso and on your image, click and drag around the area you want to select. Click the Close button on the Controls:Lasso palette to complete the selection. Now, switch to the Selection Adjuster tool, and in the Controls:Adjuster palette, set the Feather to 2.1 (to slightly soften your selection). If you want to edit the selection, convert it to a shape by opening the Objects palette and choosing P.List, Shapes, Convert to Shape. Chapter 4 contains more information about selections and shapes.

**6 Underpainting with fills and brushwork.** Choose a color to fill the selection. If you want to use a color from your artwork, select the Dropper tool and click on your painting to sample color. To fill the selection, select Effects, Fill (Command-F), choose Current Color and click OK. To avoid a static, flat look, you'll want to lightly brush over the filled areas to create movement and variation in tone. Choose a color that blends well with the fill color, then select the Chalk variant you created in step 3 and apply strokes over the fill. We switched to a very rough paper texture (Big Canvas, Grains paper library), then added darker orange strokes to the center of the sky, and darker and lighter blues to the water. We covered most of the filled areas with brushstrokes.

**7 Finishing with scrumbling.** Artists using traditional media will often finish a pastel drawing by brushing the side of the pastel lightly along the peaks of the rough art paper. This technique, called *scrumbling*, causes colors to blend optically and adds texture. To scrumble electronically, select the Large Chalk variant and adjust Opacity to 25% (Controls palette). Choose a very rough paper. In the Brush Controls:Size palette, move the ± Size slider all the way to the right (for maximum pressure sensitivity), and select the lower left brush tip profile. Build the brush (Command-B) and apply strokes lightly using a color sampled from your image with the Dropper. We used scrumbling to add density to the shadows on the hills and to show wind activity on the water. To add a semi-transparent texture to the plant life in the foreground, we switched to the Grainy Soft Cover submethod. 🖌

# Drawing with Colored Pencils

***Overview*** *Create a sketch with the Colored Pencils variant; customize the brush to further develop the drawing; adjust Color Variability settings for a more active color effect.*

1

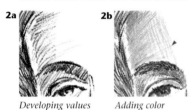

*The line sketch drawn with Colored Pencil*

2a 2b

*Developing values*          *Adding color*

3

*Building dimension using increased Color Variability settings and strokes that follow the form*

YOU CAN MODIFY THE COLORED PENCILS variant and get a broken color effect (where the color only partially covers the background or underdrawing) by brushing lightly across a textured surface.

**1 Starting with a sketch.** Open a new, 4 x 2.5-inch, 225 ppi document with a white background, then choose the Cotton Paper texture. Choose a dark brown color, select the Colored Pencils variant of the Pencils brush and sketch the portrait.

**2 Developing value and adding color.** Change the Colored Pencil's method to Cover and the submethod to Grainy Edge Flat Cover. In the Size palette, set Size to 3.4 and ± Size to 1.54. Use this brush and a lighter brown to develop values throughout the sketch. Choose a skin color (we chose a tan for this portrait of Steve Pendarvis) and apply strokes with a light touch to partially cover some of the brown sketch. Follow the form with your strokes, switching colors and brush sizes as you draw.

**3 Building dimension.** To give a shimmery look to the color as it's applied, drag the Hue (± H) and Value (± V) sliders in the zoomed-out Color Palette to 3%. Use this new pencil to apply a fresh layer of strokes in the areas of strongest color (in our drawing, the forehead and nose shadows and the hair). Remember to use a light touch to allow the underpainting to show through. 🖌

## COLORED PENCIL WASHES

If you're using Colored Pencils on grainy paper, you can create a wash effect. Choose the Grainy Water variant of the Water brush, reducing Opacity and Grain penetration in the Control palette to 40% or less. Stroke over your pencil work to blend colors while maintaining texture on the "peaks" of the paper grain.

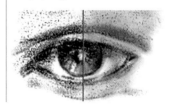

# Blending and Feathering with Pastels

***Overview*** *Create and soften a sketch; build color and form; blend the painting; add feathered strokes to finish.*

*Creating a loose sketch with Sharp Chalk*

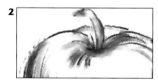

*Smudging with the Grainy Water variant*

*Roughing in color and value with Chalk*

*Blending the underpainting with Water*

*Finishing with feathered Chalk strokes*

FEATHERING—THIN, PARALLEL STROKES over a blended underpainting—is a traditional pastel technique that yields texture and freshness. Because the feathered finishing strokes remain unblended on the painting's surface, the viewer's eye must work to blend the colors. Here is an example of optical color blending.

**1 Starting with a sketch.** Open a new file with a white background—our file was 3 x 3.3 inches and 225 ppi. Select a rough paper texture from the Papers palette (we used Rougher texture), choose a neutral color (we chose a red-brown), and select the Sharp Chalk variant of the Chalk brush. To get a more sensitive response, we moved the ± Size slider in the Size palette to 1.54, and in the Advanced Controls:Sliders palette, we set Size to Velocity. Use this brush to create a sketch.

**2 Softening the sketch.** Select the Grainy Water variant of the Water brush and blend your sketch, allowing your strokes to follow the direction of the form.

**3 Building the underpainting.** Use the Artist Pastel Chalk variant of the Chalk brush and add color and value to your sketch. To blend your strokes, switch to the Grainy Water variant of the Water brush; we lowered our variant's Opacity setting (Controls palette) to 40%. Add layers to the underpainting with these two tools until you're pleased with the form.

**4 Adding feathered strokes.** To create thin, textured strokes on top of the blended form, decrease the Size of the Artist Pastel Chalk variant to 4.2, increase the ± Size to 1.54, and in Advanced Controls:Sliders, set Size to Pressure. Stroke with this brush in the direction of the form. In our example, feathering is most noticeable in the upper portion of the apple. Finish the piece by using Grainy Water to soften the feathering in the shadow areas.

# Glazing with Watercolor

***Overview*** *Make a pencil sketch; apply layers of color to the sketch with Water Color brushes, drying the image between applications of color; add final highlight detail to the dried image with an Eraser brush.*

MARY ENVALL

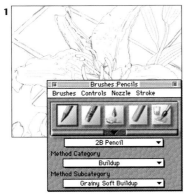

The line sketch made with the 2B Pencil

**2a**

Adding very light tinted washes to the pencil sketch with the Simple Water brush

**2b**

Adding slightly darker washes after drying

TWO COMMON TRADITIONAL WATERCOLOR techniques that are easily emulated with Painter are *wet-into-wet* and *glazing*. Wet-into-wet creates a softer-edged look—the painting surface is kept wet as new color is applied, so new paint blends easily with old. Glazing involves applying transparent washes of watercolor, drying the painting between successive washes; colors are usually built up in layers from light to dark. Drying an image after applying each new layer of color allows crisper rendering than is possible with the wet-into-wet technique.

Mary Envall frequently paints a close-up view of her subject to emphasize subtle details. Before beginning *Stargazer Lily*, one of a series of watercolor flower studies, Envall shot photos to use for reference. She began this image with a tight pencil sketch in Painter and used transparent glazes to build layers of color and value, progressing from light to dark.

**1 Starting with a sketch.** Open a new file with a white background (Envall's file was 1593 pixels wide); then choose a texture from the Papers palette. Envall used Cotton Paper because she felt its natural-looking fine grain would complement her watercolor rendering. Choose a neutral gray color, select the 2B Pencil variant and draw your line sketch.

**2 Adding the first washes.** Using highlight colors for the first glaze layer, Envall added washes to her pencil sketch. Choose light colors and block in the large areas with the Large Simple Water and Simple Water

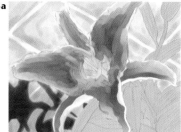

3a

*Applying long strokes of color from the center of the flower toward the petals*

3b

*Adding midtone detail with the Diffuse Water and Simple Water brushes*

4

*Painting the foliage and adding final detail with the Simple Water brush*

Brittany in Sailor Hat *was painted using the Simple Water variant and a freer wet-into-wet style (the painting was kept wet—saved in RIFF format—throughout the painting process). Paying careful attention to her light source, Envall applied washes of highlight colors and the lightest skin tones, then added detail overall, varying color in the shadows.*

variants of the Water Color brush. (Selecting a Water Color brush automatically activates Painter's Wet Layer.) With conventional watercolor, you can't paint on areas that you want to keep white, but Painter lets you lighten or remove color: Use the Wet Eraser variant of the Water Color brush.

If you want to erase linework on the background, do so with a "dry" Eraser variant before you dry the Wet Layer, since drying the Wet Layer drops it permanently to the background. Envall kept the pencil lines she needed for emphasis and erased others with the Ultrafine Eraser.

To complete the first glaze, choose Canvas, Dry to dry the Wet Layer, then start the next glaze by choosing a Water Color brush and continuing to paint. Select the Simple Water variant, for example, and add a slightly darker series of washes with more detail, as Envall did before developing the midtones in the next step.

**3 Building form and midtone values.** Choose medium-value colors and develop your midtones, applying lighter colors first, then darker ones to create form. Keep your light source in mind and let your strokes follow the direction of the forms.

Envall dried her image again, then added the larger intermediate-value shapes and some of the shadows. She applied a darker red to the interior of the lily (to help make it appear to recede), and used the Diffuse Water variant of the Water Color brush to paint long, soft strokes from the interior of the lily toward the tips of the petals. She also used the Diffuse Water variant to paint bright red spots on the interior of the lily. She defined the petal edges and added shadows with a small Simple Water brush. Changing brush sizes intuitively as she worked, Envall painted and dried her image many times, developing subtle layers of color and contrast.

**4 Adding final details.** Using the Simple Water variant, Envall painted the foliage more loosely than she did the flower. She also sharpened areas in the image that needed definition with a tiny Simple Water variant. After drying the image a last time, she defined highlights along the edges of the petals with the Ultrafine Eraser variant. Finally, she sprayed soft spots onto the cement background with the Spatter Water variant.

**COMBINING WET AND DRY**

You can easily switch between working in the Wet Layer and painting on the "dry" background: Switch to a "non-wet" brush to add linework or erase lines on the background, then return to the Water Color brushes to continue your work in the Wet Layer.

**USING POST-DIFFUSE**

To soften the edges of brushstrokes in the Wet Layer, press Shift-D—Painter's Post-Diffuse command. Repeat the key combination to increase the effect.

# Mixing Media

***Overview*** *Create a sketch with the Pencil and the Pens brushes; add color with the Chalk and the Airbrush brushes; finish the piece with Chalk, Charcoal, Liquid and other brushes.*

PHILIP HOWE

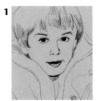

*Sketching with the Sharp pencil (left); then adding value with the Loaded Oils*

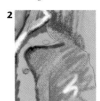

*Laying in loose color with Chalk (left); then airbrushing with color on the face*

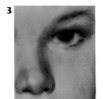

*Adding detail with pencil and charcoal (left); then blending an area with Just Add Water and the Distorto variant*

## FAST TEXTURE ACCESS

To make it easier to switch textures on-the-fly, you can use the Paper Mover to combine your favorite papers from several libraries into a single large Paper palette.

TO CREATE *PORTRAIT OF SEAFTH,* Philip Howe combined no fewer than seven digital brushes—many of which would not mix well in conventional media—yet his finished piece retains the freshness of a sketch. You may want to loosely follow Howe's steps and experiment with your own "media mixing."

**1 Sketching and adding value.** Howe selected Surface 2 from the More Paper Textures library and used the Sharp Pencil to create the sketch. He switched to the Fine Grain texture from the Grains paper library and added detail to the eyes with the Fine Point variant of the Pens brush. To establish values, Howe chose the Loaded Oils variant of the Brush and painted loose, gray strokes on the hair, face and jacket.

**2 Laying in color.** To stroke color onto the jacket and background, Howe chose Eggscape from the Paper Textures library and the Large Chalk variant of the Chalk brush. He used a low-opacity Fat Stroke Airbrush to sculpt the boy's face with soft color.

**3 A veritable brush frenzy.** Using the Just Add Water brush, Howe softly blended selected areas of the image. He added more color to the face with the Large Chalk, blended it with Just Add Water, then darkened detail in the eyes and nose with Gritty Charcoal. Howe chose the Brushy variant of the Brush and painted loose strokes onto the background, hair and jacket. Using tiny strokes with the Thick & Thin Pencils brush, he redefined and enhanced the boy's facial features. He used the Distorto variant of the Liquid brush to smear areas of the hair and to create a soft, irregular edge on the background and jacket to make the boy appear to emerge from the paper's surface. 🖌

# Gouache and Opaque Watermedia

**Overview** *Create a finely grained surface; create custom variants of the Camel Hair Brush, Cover Brush and Huge Rough Out; begin with a line sketch on a dark background; sculpt highlights and details using the custom variants; blend colors with a Liquid brush.*

NANCY STAHL

*Scaling the Micro Grain texture to 25%*

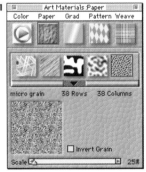

*Sketching with the Cover Brush variant*

ARTIST NANCY STAHL HAS WORKED WITH TRADITIONAL gouache on illustration board since 1976. Her clients would accept her digital art only if the quality matched her conventional style, so after much experimentation with Painter's brushes and surfaces, she has been able to fully re-create the effect of traditional gouache. Her self-promotional pieces *Woman with Braid* (above) and *Tennis Woman* (at the bottom of page 53) were two of her electronic pieces juried into the *Communication Arts Illustration Annual*.

**Beginning the illustration.** Create a new file. Stahl created a 5.7 x 8-inch file at 300 ppi with a white background color.

**1 Emulating a traditional gouache surface.** Stahl's favorite traditional gouache support is a Strathmore kid finish illustration board. The kid finish is soft and allows for a smooth application

**3**

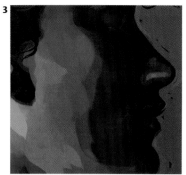

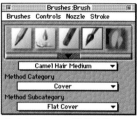

*Sculpting facial features with Stahl's custom Camel Hair variant*

**4a**

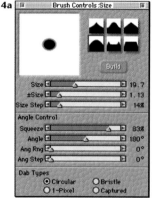

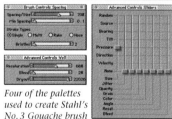

*Four of the palettes used to create Stahl's No. 3 Gouache brush*

**4b**

*Layering strokes using the No. 3 Gouache brush*

of paint. To create Stahl's surface for gouache, click on the Library button in the Papers palette to retrieve the Micro Grain paper texture from the More Wild Textures library. To make the surface even smoother, scale it to 25%. This surface is most noticeable when using Stahl's No. 5 Brush in step 5.

**2 Starting with a sketch.** After roughing a dark brown into the background with the Huge Rough Out brush, Stahl modified the Cover Brush variant and used it to create an outline sketch. To do this, select the Cover Brush variant of the Brush and reduce Size to 2.0 in the Brush Controls:Size palette. Choose a russet color and begin sketching.

**3 Sculpting teardrop shapes.** To paint teardrop-shaped high-lights in the hair and to sculpt the facial features, Stahl created a new variant based on the Camel Hair Brush variant of the Brush. Choose the Camel Hair Brush variant and change the submethod to Flat Cover; this will give your strokes the crisp edge that you would get using conventional materials. In the Size palette, increase the brush size to 9.6. Choose Brushes, Variants, Save Variant, name your variant (Stahl named hers Camel Hair Medium) and click OK. Stahl varied the size of her brush while she worked.

**4 Building Stahl's No. 3 Gouache brush.** To build Stahl's No. 3 Gouache brush, first take a deep breath—it's a complex brush. Start with the Camel Hair Brush variant and change the sub-method to Flat Cover.

Now start making choices from the Controls menu in the Brushes palette. In the Size palette: set Size to 19.7; set ± Size to 1.13; set Squeeze to 83% (giving the brush a slightly oval shape); set Angle to 180. Build your brush (you can do it now or later) by clicking the Build button. To make the brush faster and smaller, in Brush Controls:Spacing change the Stroke Type from Rake to Single. (Don't worry about the Bristles setting; after you've set the Stroke Type to Single, the program ignores this slider.) Set Spacing/Size to 70%, and move the Minimum Spacing slider all the way to the left. In the Advanced Controls:Well palette, reduce Resaturation to 66% (so brushstrokes run out of color sooner) and increase Bleed to 2% (to let colors mix a bit more). In Advanced Controls:Sliders, drag the Size slider to Pressure (this makes stroke size dependent on pressure, not velocity) and set Opacity to None (to make strokes more opaque). Whew! Save your variant as before. Stahl used this brush to make linear strokes in the hair and on the blouse.

**NOT JUST FOR GOUACHE**

If you use Painter to emulate oils or acrylics, you may find it beneficial to use brushes with slight modifications. For example, you can get a multi-colored, multi-bristle "oil" brush using these Color Variability settings (in the zoomed-out Color palette) for Stahl's No. 3 Gouache brush: ± H, 3%; ± S, 5%; ± V, 3%. Apply paint with short, dabbing strokes.

*Opacity and Grain settings for the No. 5 Gouache brush*

**5b**

*Stroking with the No. 5 Gouache brush*

**6**

*Pulling one color into another with the Coarse Smeary Mover variant*

**7a**

*Line work on the lips using the Cover Brush Small variant*

**7b**

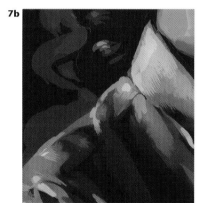

*Adding details with a modified Oil Paint variant*

**5 Building Stahl's No. 5 Gouache brush.** Stahl wanted a fast, sensitive, brush with grainy edges to use on the blouse and the background. To build her variant, start with the Huge Rough Out variant of the Brush. In the Size palette, change Size to 25.3; drag the ± Size slider all the way to the right; click the Build button. In the Controls palette, set Grain to 100%. Save the variant.

**6 Pulling color.** To blend the opaque colors in the background and in the shadows on the blouse, Stahl used varying sizes of the Coarse Smeary Mover variant of the Liquid brush. Since this brush uses a Grainy Hard Drip submethod, she was able to soften color transitions with texture.

**7 Finishing touches.** Using the same modified, small Cover Brush variant she used in step 2, Stahl enhanced detail on the woman's profile and hair. She used a low-opacity version of the Oil Paint variant to add texture on the blouse and collar.

*Stahl painted* Tennis Woman *with the same set of Gouache brushes used for* Woman with Braid. *To soften the background and focus more attention on the figure, she used the Smeary Mover variant of the Liquid brush on the background. To soften it further, she selected the background with the Lasso tool—and after feathering the selection a few pixels to create a smooth edge—she used Effects, Focus, Soften.*

# Painting with Oils

**Overview** *Create a sketch with a Pencils variant; add color to the underpainting with an Artist Pastels variant; use the Liquid brush to create the look of oils.*

DENNIS ORLANDO

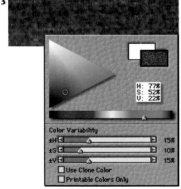

*Sketching the canoes and shoreline*

*Switching to Grainy Soft Cover submethod*

*Roughing in the beach with the Artist Pastel Chalk variant*

*Painting the water (detail) with the Artist Pastel Chalk variant, using Color Variability settings in the Colors palette*

ARTIST DENNIS ORLANDO CAPTURES an exquisite harmony between man-made and organic elements in his *Canoe Trip at Cedar Water.* A strong composition, deft modeling of shapes, sensitivity to light and shadow and his unique electronic oil painting technique all combine to give the piece its power. Orlando used a photograph taken on a camping trip in the New Jersey Pine Barrens as a reference.

**Open a new file.** Orlando set up a new 8.25 x 3.5-inch document with a resolution of 150 ppi and a white Paper Color.

**1 Sketching the canoes.** Orlando started by placing the reference photo under the clear plastic flap of his drawing tablet. He modified a Pencils brush variant and used it to trace the four canoes and the shoreline. To create his custom variant, select the Thick & Thin Pencils variant of the Pencils brush. Change to Cover method and Grainy Soft Cover submethod. In the Brush Controls:Size palette (under the Controls pull-down menu on the Brushes palette), drag the Size slider to 2.0. Select Basic Paper in the Papers palette, choose a color (Orlando started with a grayblue), and begin sketching.

**2 Beginning the underpainting.** To help define the exterior shapes of the canoes, Orlando roughed in the beach with a Chalk brush and a rough texture. To do this, select the Artist Pastel Chalk variant of the Chalk brush. Change the submethod to Grainy Soft Cover—this gives softer brushstrokes than Grainy Hard Cover. In the Paper palette, Grains library, choose Big Canvas paper texture (Orlando used this paper on the rest of the piece). He chose a creamy tan tint and quickly blocked in large areas of the beach around the edges of the canoes.

**3 Using Color Variability in the water.** One of Orlando's "electronic oil" trademarks is activity in the color. He achieves this by adjusting the Color Variability settings for certain brushes. To re-create the active color look he achieved in the water, start with the same Chalk brush that you created in step 2. Choose a dark gray-green, then zoom-out the Colors palette and adjust the

**4**

*Establishing values*

**5a**

*Choosing the Total Oil Brush variant*

**5b**

*Pulling color along the canoe with the Total Oil Brush variant*

**5c**

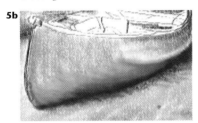

*Detail of the foreground sand painted with the Artist Pastel Chalk and Total Oil Brush variants*

**6**

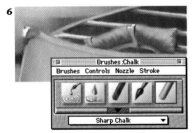

*Painting crisp, final details on the boat with the Sharp Chalk*

**7**

*Using the Grainy Water brush to blend areas of the water*

Color Variability sliders: set Hue (± H) to 10, Saturation (± S) to 5, and Value (± V) to 10. Name and save this variant (Brushes, Variants, Save Variant, enter a name and click OK) or you'll lose these settings when you switch brushes. Begin painting. Orlando changed to a smaller brush size when working close to the canoes in order to preserve their shapes.

**4 Establishing values and adding details.** Use a smaller version of the same Chalk brush (Orlando resized his to 7.1) to rough in color and value details. Keep the same Color Variability settings. Orlando used a blue-gray color to paint the dark, recessed areas inside the canoes, then switched to a lighter value of the same color to paint the metallic hulls of the boats.

**5 Simulating traditional oils.** Painter's Liquid brushes let you smear existing "pixel paint" to get the same look that you would get by pushing conventional oils around a canvas. The Total Oil Brush variant, which Orlando used, also paints with the current color in the Color palette. Choose the Liquid brush, Total Oil Brush variant. In the Brush Controls:Size palette, drag the Size slider to 18.5 (Orlando varied his brush size slightly as he painted). Sample a color from the area you want to paint with the Dropper tool, or hold down the Command key while you're using the brush to temporarily switch to the Dropper. To maintain the modulated color of the underpainting, give this brush the same Color Variability settings used in step 3. Save this variant.

Use this brush and short, crisp strokes to pull color from one area of your painting into another. Orlando switched between this brush and his Chalk variant to work over the entire surface of the painting, including the shadow areas on the sand and the detail in the canoes. He created the reflection of the sand on the canoes by sampling color from the sand and painting short, curved strokes on the canoes with the Total Oil Brush variant.

**6 Defining the details.** Orlando used the Sharp Chalk variant of the Chalk brush to define surface edges and to add color details on the sand and boats.

**7 Blurring the water.** The Grainy Water variant of the Water brush is perfect for blending and softening areas, making them appear to recede. Orlando dabbed this brush on the water, using short strokes to preserve the modulated color.

**Output.** Orlando typically makes proofs of several versions of a piece on a Canon Color Laser Copier with an EFI Fiery RIP. He then picks a favorite to send out to be printed with an Iris inkjet on archival paper. This image was printed by Cone Editions Press on Somerset, a softly textured, handmade English paper. ◆

# "Sculpting" a Portrait

***Overview*** *Create a collage for the portrait background using a cloning brush; sculpt the portrait out of the dark background with a custom airbrush.*

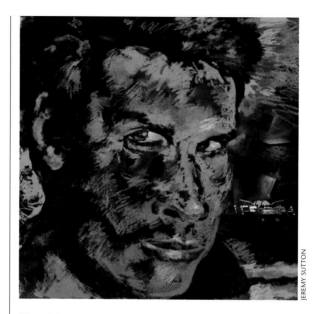

JEREMY SUTTON

Source images to be cloned into the background

Video frame image used as the background

Turning a crayon into a Cloning brush

Lowering the Cloning brush's opacity

NEW MEDIA MAGAZINE COMMISSIONED ARTIST Jeremy Sutton to create a series of portraits of influential software developers, including this portrait of CD-ROM game guru Bill Appleton of Cyberflix, Inc. Sutton used a custom Cloning brush to create a dark, electric background containing images from a Cyberflix game, then pulled the face out of the background with color.

**1 Preparing files for cloning.** Open the source images that you'll clone into your background, and use Canvas, Resize to change their size. Rotate the images using Effects, Orientation, Rotate, then click the Drop button in the Floater List palette (rotating the images turns them into floaters). Sutton began with video grabs from Appleton's CD-ROM game, *Jump Raven,* resizing and rotating the images.

**2 Preparing the background.** Open a new or existing document that will be used as the portrait's background. You'll be cloning source files into this image. For this portrait, Sutton used a video frame of a spaceship landing platform that he resized to 1009 x 998 pixels.

**3 Making a Cloning brush.** To get the waxy, grainy cloned images that Sutton achieved, choose the Waxy Crayons variant of the Crayons brush. Change the method to Cloning and the submethod to Grainy Soft Cover Cloning. Select the Rougher paper texture and lower the Opacity slider on the Controls palette to a value between 20% and 30% (for more sensitivity).

**4 Cloning elements into the background.** Click on one of the source images to make it active. With the Brush tool selected,

**4**

*Adding the Jump Raven logo to the background*

**5a**

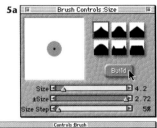

*Modifying the airbrush*

**5b**  **6**

*Beginning the sketch*   *Adding vibrant highlights*

**7**

*The finished portrait on the cover of* New Media *magazine. Sutton resized and cropped the original art to 8 x 10 inches and 300 ppi, then added more detail.*

hold down the Control key (use the Shift key on the PC). The cursor will change to a crosshair. Click on the area of the source image that you want to appear in the portrait. Now click on the portrait background window to make it active and begin sketching lightly with the stylus in the area where you want the clone to appear. The cloned image should emerge from the background. If the clone isn't appearing in the correct location, select Edit, Undo, and repeat this step, keeping in mind that the start of your sketching stroke establishes a direct relationship between the source image and the background. Using this method, Sutton added the Jump Raven logo and the game's control panel to the background image of the landing platform.

**5 "Sculpting" the portrait.** Once you've completed the background, it's time to "pull" the portrait out of it. Choose a color that complements the background—Sutton chose a neutral blue. To create a small, pointed airbrush similar to Sutton's, start by choosing the Airbrush, Thin Stroke variant. In the Brush Controls:Size palette, choose the top left brush tip profile. This tip will concentrate more color in the center of the brush. Drag the Size slider to 4.5, and the ± Size slider all the way to the right (to get maximum variance in stroke thickness). In Advanced Controls:Sliders, set Size to Pressure, and in Brush Controls: Spacing, set Spacing/Size to 30%. Sutton wanted his strokes to cover the background more completely, so he moved the Opacity slider (Controls palette) to 54%. Click the Build button (Size palette) to make a brush with those settings and begin sketching over the collage background.

**6 Adding highlights.** After you have roughed in the basics with a neutral color, choose more vibrant ones to add highlights and definition. If you want the underpainted color to show through, be sure to apply your new strokes with a light touch. After developing Appleton's facial features in blue, Sutton applied vivid greens and oranges as highlights for emphasis and balance.

**7 Illustrating the magazine.** A tightly cropped version of Sutton's completed portrait was used on the magazine's cover, and the complete composition was used on an opening spread. Sutton also created six other portraits for the feature story.

*Portrait of Greg Roach, author of* The Madness of Roland

# Colorizing Pencil Illustrations

***Overview*** *Scan a pencil sketch; clone it; tint it and add texture; restore from the original; add color with the Airbrush, Chalk and Water Color brushes.*

PHILIP HOWE

*The original pencil illustration, scanned*

*Adding a tint and a texture to the clone*

*Using a Cloning method brush to partially restore the gray tones of the original*

MUCH OF THE BEAUTY of illustrator Philip Howe's work lies in his seamless, creative blending of the traditional with the digital. In a spread for *Trailblazer* magazine—a detail of which is shown here—Howe used Photoshop to combine hand-drawn calligraphy, a photo of two slides, a photo of a watercolor block (for the background), and his own pencil sketches, colorized in Painter to simulate traditional watercolor.

**1 Starting with a sketch.** Howe began by sketching the various birds in pencil on watercolor paper. He scanned the images on a flatbed scanner, saving them as grayscale files in TIFF format. Each bird image was 4 to 5 inches square and 300 ppi.

**2 Modifying a clone.** Open a grayscale scan in Painter. Choose File, Clone, to clone your scan, giving you an "original" and a clone. Keep the original open—you'll want to pull from it later. Howe added a color tint and a texture to the clone of the scanned bird. To add a tint, choose a color in the Colors palette (Howe chose a reddish brown), then choose Effects, Surface Control, Color Overlay. Select Uniform Color from the pop-up menu, set Opacity to 30%, click the Dye Concentration button and click OK. To add a texture, select a Paper texture (Howe chose Basic Paper) and choose Effects, Surface Control, Apply Surface Texture. Select Paper Grain from the pop-up menu, set Amount to 50% and uncheck the Shiny button. Click OK.

**3 Restoring from the original.** Howe used Painter's cloning capabilities to replace most of the tint and texture in the bird's body with the light gray tones of the original. You could use a standard cloning brush to do this, but Howe chose the Fat Stroke variant of the Airbrush, changed the method to Cloning and the submethod to Soft Cover Cloning. Once you've changed methods, paint on the portion of your image that you want to restore. The original will automatically be revealed in the area covered by your strokes. Try lowering this cloning brush's Opacity in the Controls palette for more sensitivity.

*Applying color tints with the Fat Stroke Airbrush in Buildup method*

*Using a modified Chalk brush to add color to the background*

*Applying watercolor accents with the Spatter Water variant*

**4 Adding color tints with the Airbrush.** To achieve an effect of traditional airbrushing with transparent dyes or watercolor pigments, Howe used two versions of the Fat Stroke Airbrush variant. He switched back to Cover method, Soft Cover submethod, and reduced the Opacity setting in the Controls palette to between 5% and 10%. He used these settings to carefully lay in the golden brown tones on the bird's back. Next, he switched to the Buildup method, Soft Buildup submethod, and added the more saturated yellow and rust hues. The Buildup method allowed him to use a slightly higher opacity (between 10% and 20%) to achieve richer color while preserving the intensity of the pencil sketch.

**5 Cloning again and brushing with Chalk.** Howe uses the Clone feature like a flexible "Save As" command. When he's ready to move on to the next phase of an illustration, he often makes a clone and uses the original as "source material." Here, when he had colorized the bird to his satisfaction, he chose File, Clone and saved the clone.

**SWITCHING CLONE SOURCES**

When you choose File, Clone, the original image automatically becomes the "source image," indicated by a checkmark under File, Clone Source. You can override this and make any open image the source image by choosing a different file under File, Clone Source.

Howe switched to the Large Chalk variant of the Chalk brush and began to paint loose, gestural strokes on the image background behind the bird using two similar green hues. He made frequent adjustments in the Brush Controls:Size palette as he worked, changing Size, ± Size, Angle and Squeeze.

**6 Adding a watercolor look.** To add a finishing touch without muddying his existing color work, Howe used the Water Color brush. He used the Simple Water variant to add more depth to the color on the bird's head and other areas. He switched to the Spatter Water variant to add a "water drop" effect on the background, sampling color from the bird and background using the Dropper tool. When he finished, he chose Canvas, Dry to drop the color on the Wet Layer onto the background.

*Another spot illustration from the Trailblazer spread. Howe used the same brushes and technique for all illustrations.*

**Merging the file.** Howe opened the bird and 17 x 11-inch main image file in Photoshop. He drew a selection around the bird, feathered it to 30 pixels, then copied it and pasted it into the main image. He used Photoshop's Multiply compositing command to blend the two images.

# Lifelike Commercial Illustration

**Overview** *Sketch an object from life; add color; select the object to isolate it; add detail, shading, blending and type.*

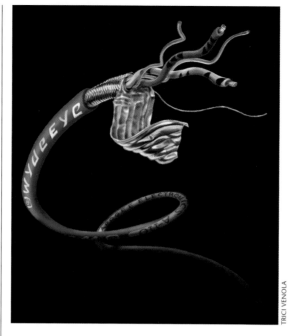

TRICI VENOLA

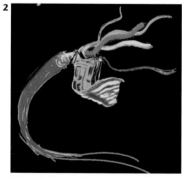

*The Photoshop sketch*

*Using the Rough Out variant to add color*

*Setting the selection's feather to 2.0*

WHEN TRICI VENOLA WAS COMMISSIONED BY APOGEE—a manufacturer of sound equipment for the music industry—to illustrate an audio cable, she sold the client on a realistic, painterly approach to the product rather than a flashy airbrush illustration with exaggerated metallic highlights. Inspired by the Dutch master Jan Vermeer's simple and direct treatment of common household objects, Venola paid special attention to the lighting, rendering and composition of this piece. The finished illustration was a hit with the client and the audience: The ad featuring it won "Best Return Ad" award in the industry publication *Mix*.

**1 Setting up the model.** Choose an object and place it near your monitor for easy viewing. Set the lighting so it won't change, and begin sketching in Painter. Since Apogee's president Bruce Jackson had told Venola that the cable looked like a striking cobra, she propped up the cable, cobra-like, next to her monitor. He also wanted to feature the cable's patented braid design, so she positioned it to emphasize that aspect of the product. She covered the windows in the studio and lit the subject. To create the sketch, Venola used Photoshop's Airbrush tool and a small brush size, paying special attention to the subject's proportions.

**2 Coloring with Soft Cover brushes.** After the client approved the sketch, Venola opened it in Painter and chose Effects, Tonal Control, Negative (to create a black background and a white cable) and brushed in color. To recreate the custom brush she used, select the Rough Out variant of the Brush and change the submethod to Soft Cover. Block in areas of color using this

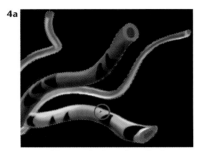

*Airbrushing inside the active selection*

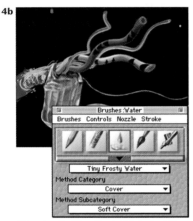

*Changing the Tiny Frosty Water to Soft Cover to blend areas of the foil*

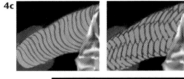

*Adding detail and form to the cable*

*Hand lettering with the Scratchboard tool*

brush. Venola also used the Artist Pastel Chalk variant of the Chalk brush to rough in the exposed wires.

**3 Selecting the cable.** To give the product a distinct edge and isolate it from the background, Venola selected the roughed-out cable, drawing around it with the Lasso tool. Then she switched to the Selection Adjuster tool so she could soften the selection by dragging the Feather slider (Controls palette) to 2. After you create a selection, Painter automatically switches to the far right Draw icon on the expanded Objects:Path List, enabling you to draw inside of the selection. Turn to Chapter 4 for more information about working with selections.

**4 Rendering the cable.** Starting with the exposed wiring and working down the cable, Venola rendered her image. Since every detail of the product was important to the client, she carefully studied the ends of the wire—even using a hand-held magnifying glass at one point—while zoomed in at 400%. To get the smooth look of Vermeer on the wiring and the rest of the cable, Venola used brushes with the Cover method, Soft Cover submethod. She added detail with the Scratchboard Tool variant of the Pens brush; added shading, highlights and reflected lighting with several variants of the Airbrush and the Dodge and Burn brushes (at 10–15% opacities); and blended the foil and other areas with a modified Tiny Frosty Water variant of the Water brush. To get a slightly coarser look in certain areas, she switched to the Artist Pastel Chalk. Venola changed brush sizes frequently as she worked.

**5 Adding type.** Mechanically setting curved lines of a custom typeface to fit the coiled cable would have been difficult and time-consuming; it was much easier for Venola to draw it by hand. She referred to a printout of the logo and sketched the type and the other lettering directly on the rendered cable using the Scratchboard variant.

**Finishing in Photoshop.** It's a rare client who's satisfied the first time around, and Venola's was no exception. He wanted the foil to look gold on both sides, he wanted to emphasize the hand lettering, and he wanted the tips of the wires to look less frayed. In Photoshop, Venola used the Airbrush in Color Only mode to tint the silver portion of the foil gold; she used a large, low-opacity airbrush to darken the lower right portion of her image; and she cleaned up the wire tips with a tiny airbrush. 🐾

■ Since buying her first Macintosh in 1984, **Trici Venola** has used the computer as her primary medium for fine art and commercial illustration. Her mastery of painting from life is evident in these cover illustrations for a series of comic books created to interest young readers in classic American novels. Venola's husband and her assistant frequently model for her artwork. To get the smooth look of the Dutch master Vermeer in Painter, she usually changes whatever brush she's using at the time to the Cover method, Soft Cover submethod.

To paint *Dracula* (top left), Venola started by scanning several photos of a Roman cathedral. She started a rough composition in Painter, then opened the scans and cloned portions of the images into her sketch with the Chalk Cloner and the Fat Stroke Airbrush switched to the Cloning method. Venola blended the texture into the image using the Artist Pastel Chalk variant and the Frosty Water variant of the Water brush. She roughly sketched the figures (posed by her husband and assistant) with the Fat Stroke Airbrush variant. She used the Chalk brush to model the form and color of the foreground arches, the stonework and the gargoyles, and added detail with the Crayon brush. Venola painted Dracula's face—based on the description in the book—using the Artist Pastel Chalk, and blended color with Frosty Water. The woman's diaphanous gown was painted using a tiny Thin Stroke Airbrush variant and the Dodge brush; the mist behind and below Dracula was painted with the Distorto variant of the Liquid brush and blended with Frosty Water.

Venola used a costuming book as a reference for *Tom Sawyer* (left), which helped her accurately depict the clothes, hair and body shapes of the 1850s. She began with a rough sketch while looking at her references, then built dimension in the forms using the Large Chalk and Artist Pastel Chalk variants (which she switched to Soft Cover submethods). She blended color with the Frosty Water variant. Venola saved several versions as she worked, enabling her to clone into overworked areas with an earlier version.

■ Art director, fine artist and nature-lover **Ben Barbante** had achieved a high level of skill with a traditional airbrush long before he discovered Painter. *Stalking on Still Water* is part of a series of wildlife illustrations that Barbante created for a show of his work. His inspiration for this piece came during a hike while he observed a Great Blue Heron stalking and fishing. He later made a detailed graphite pencil drawing of the heron and scanned

it at 16 x 20 inches and 200 ppi. He tinted the scan in Painter using the Simple Water Brush variant of the Water Color brush, switching occasionally to the Pure Water variant to blend and the Wet Eraser variant to remove color. His watercolor technique is similar to glazing with traditional watercolor: He "dried" the painting (Canvas, Dry) at various stages when he did not want color to mix. The water background was created

in a separate file using Kai's Power Tools and Painter's Dodge and Burn brushes. He selected the heron, then copied it and pasted it onto the background image. To create the bird's reflection in the water, Barbante copied the bird, flipped it, and reduced its opacity, then used the Distorto variant of the Liquid brush to give the reflection a ripple effect. Final output was to an Iris inkjet printer, 24 x 36 inches, on archival paper.

■ **Nancy Stahl** created *Premiere*—two celebrities caught in the glare of the paparazzi—for the cover of New York City's *Premiere* magazine. She started by photographing herself in all of the figures' positions, then assembled the photos into a rough composition in Photoshop. She used the composite image as a reference for her work in Painter and brushed a dark green color onto the background of a new document using one of her gouache brushes. (See pages 51–53 for a complete description of her custom brushes.) Stahl painted the lower left area first—without the photographers—then chose Effects, Surface Control, Apply Lighting to create a slight gradation over the entire image. She then painted the figures in the upper right. To get the flashbulb effects perfectly positioned underneath the photographers, she began by painting the photographers in another document. She selected them, dragged them into the Floaters palette, then dragged them into her main image and positioned them. She saved the image as a TIFF file, opened it in Photoshop, and created the flash effects by drawing paths and stroking them with the airbrush. (To accomplish this in Painter, make a circular selection, and switch to the Selection Adjuster tool to feather the selection using the Controls:Adjuster palette. Now choose the airbrush, and choose Stroke Selection from the P.List pull-down menu on the Objects palette.) Stahl opened the image in Painter, and again dragged the photographers from the Floaters palette. She positioned them precisely atop the original photographers (now covered by the glowing circles), gave them a low feather setting to soften the edges, then dropped them to the background.

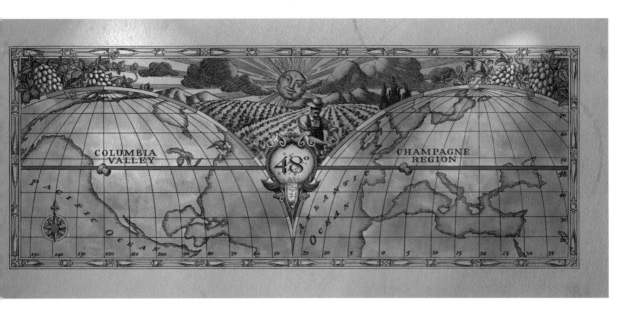

■ Although he has been a successful commercial illustrator for 20 years using conventional materials, **John Fretz** has happily set them aside for Painter's more exciting electronic tools.

Fretz created the *Domaine St. Michele Champagne Winery Map* (above) for an ad campaign. He began by drawing a detailed pen-and-ink map which he scanned along with a painted, distressed piece of Arches cold-pressed watercolor paper. (He scratched the paper and made marks on it to make it look "aged.") Fretz pasted the line drawing into the paper background image, then used the Broad Water Brush, the Simple Water, and the

Pure Water variants of the Water Color brush to paint and blend tints of color on the map. Other color was added with the Fat Stroke Airbrush, and spotlights were created with Apply Lighting. To further blend the pen-and-ink illustration with the background, Fretz used Color Overlay (Paper Grain, Mottled Paper texture).

Fretz created the *Microsoft Natural Keyboard Package* (below) using three layers of scanned images: a background of wood-flecked oatmeal-colored paper, a pen-and-ink line drawing of the hands and keyboard, and a pencil schematic. Fretz pasted the pen and ink drawing onto the background as a floater,

changed its compositing method to Gel (Controls palette) and painted the keyboard and hands using a low opacity Fat Stroke Airbrush and the Fat Bleach variant of the Eraser (to remove color and create highlights). Fretz made the soft, irregular edges around the keyboard using a large, low opacity Fat Stroke Airbrush, and added texture around the edges of the vignette using the Scratchboard Rake variant of the Pens. He added the pencil schematic as a floater (also composited with the Gel method), then added Color Overlay (Paper Grain, Mottled Paper texture) to unify the piece.

■ Intense, late-afternoon sunlight on a Northern Californian hillside provided the inspiration for *Coastal Meadow* (above) by **Cher Threinen-Pendarvis**. She made a series of color sketches on location that she later used for reference. In Painter, she used the Colored Pencils variant and Big Canvas texture to sketch a rough composition. She blocked in loose areas of color with a modified Artist Pastel Chalk variant, then applied directional strokes on top with a smaller brush size. She finished the painting by alternating between the Artist Pastel Chalk and Grainy Water variants, first adding, then smudging color.

Threinen-Pendarvis used dynamic strokes on *Mesa San Carlos* (right) to capture the energy of wild surf and atmosphere after a stormy night in Baja California. She painted the cliffs pushing up from the sea with a Felt Marker variant, switching the submethod to Grainy Hard Buildup to show the Watercolor 2 paper texture. She began painting the hills with the Felt Marker, then added Sharp Chalk over the top, blending the two with Frosty Water. The sky was painted with Felt Marker and Artist Pastel Chalk, and the water was painted with the Medium Tip variant of Felt Pens and blended with Grainy Water.

■ To create the vibrant look of oil paints, **Dennis Orlando** uses the Artist Pastel Chalk and the Total Oil Brush variant of the Liquid brush. He modifies the brushes by increasing their Color Variability settings (in the zoomed-out Color palette), allowing him to paint with modulated color.

Inspired by a gift of flowers, Orlando painted *Chair with Tulip Tree Flowers* (right). This piece was begun with a modified Artist Pastel Chalk. Orlando used the Grainy Water variant to blend the underpainting, then he used the Total Oil Brush variant of the Liquid brush to add color and blend colors into each other.

*Lancaster Farm* (bottom right) is based on a photograph Orlando took of an Amish farm while traveling through the Pennsylvania countryside on an autumn day. He blocked in colors with the Artist Pastel Chalk (with increased Color Variability settings), then finished by applying layers of color with the Total Oil Brush variant.

■ To paint *Still Life* (above), **Chelsea Sammel** took full advantage of Painter 3's "digital oils." Sammel began by applying Surface Texture using Paper Grain and the Canvas 2 texture. She loosely sketched the composition on this surface using the Colored Pencils variant. To establish a warm, dark tone in the underpainting, she used the Coarse Hairs variant, Grainy Soft Cover submethod (to allow more brush interaction with the canvas). To create a more opaque layer of paint, Sammel painted with the Loaded Oils variant, switching back to her custom Coarse Hairs variant where she wanted to add texture. For a dramatic effect, she used Apply Lighting, then added more strokes with the Coarse Hairs variant. She finished the image with another application of Surface Texture (again using the Canvas 2 paper texture) and added a few more brush strokes using the default Coarse Hairs brush.

Sammel created a soft look in her commissioned portrait *Kim Reading* (right) using Painter's Water Color brushes. She started by applying Surface Texture (using Paper Grain, Watercolor 2 paper), then blocked in the composition with a light blue Colored Pencils variant. She added color in broad washes with the Simple Water variant of the Water Color brush, applying neutral and medium tones first, then adding detail and contrast. She used the Wet Eraser to pull color out of areas where needed. Sammel dried the Wet Layer (Canvas, Dry), then added definition to Kim's hair, the chair and walls with Artist Pastel Chalk, blending the color with the Frosty Water and Grainy Water variants. Final pencil strokes were added using Colored Pencils switched to Grainy Hard Cover submethod.

■ **Chelsea Sammel's** vivid pastel work is also at home in the commercial world. She created *Kodak Skier* (right) for the 1994 Winter Olympics to demonstrate Kodak's digital cameras and dye-sublimation printers. Sammel started with a scan of a photograph of a skier. She selected the figure and floated it. She filled the backgound of the document with a blue gradation to create the sky, and then filled two curved selections with white to create the hills. She added depth and dimension to both areas with a modified Sharp Chalk variant and the Basic Paper texture. She cloned her image, deleted the clone, then used the Hairy Cloner variant to bring the original image into the clone. Sammel used the Chalk brush to create a sense of movement on the sky, skier and hills, then blended color with Frosty Water. She used a small tapered Sharp Chalk to draw the hair, trees, clouds and bits of snow. The Kodak logo was scanned in, rotated, distorted, and composited onto the skier's suit. She finished with expressive neon accent strokes using the Colored Pencils, Grainy Hard Cover submethod.

COLOR PROOFED ON A KODAK XL7700 DYE-SUBLIMATION PRINTER

■ As a freelance illustrator for the past 13 years, **Rick Kirkman** divides his time between cartoons for commercial clients and creating the King Feature Syndicate comic strip *Baby Blues* (with partner Jerry Scott). Kirkman began *Laundry Chase* (above left) and *Wanda* in Painter with black linework using Colored Pencils on Cotton paper texture. He switched to Medium paper and added color washes using the Simple Water variant of the Water Color brush.

■ Commercial illustrator and fine artist **Kerry Gavin** frequently paints from memory, using no reference material. He first creates a loose pencil sketch, then uses the Pastel and Water brushes to create an oil pastel look. He typically adjusts color density with Effects, Surface Control, Dye Concentration to complete and unify a piece.

*At the Beach* (left) began as a sketch with a Pencils brush in Painter. The book, letter and envelope were initially created larger in another document to accommodate the writing and postage details; each of them was copied and pasted into the final file, then reduced and rotated. After positioning, the floaters were dropped, and edges were painted over to merge them into the image. To complete the piece, Gavin increased contrast (Brightness/Contrast) and used Dye Concentration to create the effect of a glaze.

*Piano Man* also began as a pencil sketch in Painter. Gavin loosely selected areas of the image—like the ashtray and the musician's shirt—with the Outline Selection tool. He roughed color into the selected areas and the background with a Chalk brush, then smudged the color with Water brushes to give volume to the flat color shapes. Gavin floated the selections surrounding the ash tray, drink and sheet music so he could paint beneath them. He dropped the floaters and used the Water brush to blend them into the composition, then intensified the color with Dye Concentration. To create the rough vignette around the image, he drew a loose selection with the Outline Selection tool. He feathered it 15 pixels, copied the area and pasted the image into a new picture.

■ When he's not creating art for TV commercials (for clients like Nike or Coke), polishing an animation, drawing innovative characters (like Jessica in *Roger Rabbit*) or directing, **Dewey Reid** dusts off his traditional art tools and attends a life drawing class. Here are two images from his "still" portfolio.

Reid began *Totts Midnight* (above), an illustration for Gallo International, by scanning a photograph supplied by the client. He painted over most of the photo with Artist Pastel Chalk, then blurred and mixed the color with Grainy Water. He added highlights with the Small Eraser variant of the Eraser brush and blended them into the composition with Grainy Water.

The expressive characters in *Haircut* (left) originated in Reid's fertile imagination. He started with a sketch using the Pencil brush and added color with the Pastel brushes. He used Grainy Water to smudge the colors and the Small Eraser to create the highlights. As a final touch, he selected the Watercolor 2 paper texture (More Paper Textures) and used Apply Surface Texture with Paper Grain.

■ Although fine artist and illustrator **Francois Guerin** still works with conventional media, most of his commercial illustrations are created in Photoshop, Painter, or a combination of the two. Guerin painted *The Strawberries* using Painter's Water Color brushes exclusively. He used a modified Simple Water for most of the piece, adjusting the size of his brush as he painted. Guerin started with large areas of wash, then built volume and added detail. He liked the look of color pooled along the edges of his strokes, so as he blended the image with the Pure Water variant, he left a few areas untouched. Guerin switched submethods frequently as he worked: To pull color out of tones that had become too dark, he changed to Wet Remove Density. He switched to Grainy Wet Buildup to add crisp details.

■ Fine artist **Anna Stump** began the life drawing study *Peter 1* (above) by sketching from a live model using Painter on a Macintosh Powerbook and a Wacom tablet. She created a grayscale image using the Artist Pastel Chalk variant. Back in her studio, she used her desktop Mac to add subtle touches of color and value using a low opacity Fat Stroke Airbrush variant.

■ **Cher Threinen-Pendarvis** created *Water Lilies* (left) for a book cover illustration. Using a personal photograph as a reference, she made a sketch and blocked in flat color with the Artist Pastel Chalk variant. She built up the underpainting and created form and dimension using several custom oil brush variants that she had created to emulate conventional oil brushes. She used Apply Lighting, then painted back into her image. To add a richer look to the lily, she selected it (using Color Mask), then used Apply Surface Texture with Image Luminance. She softened the effect by painting tiny brushstrokes onto the flower using a custom "soft" oil brush. To create the reflections in the water, she sampled color from the lily and lily pads and dabbed short brushstrokes in the water with a low opacity custom brush.

# SELECTIONS, SHAPE PATHS AND MASKS

*The selection and shape tools are grouped on the right side of the Tools palette. The Selection Adjuster tool is selected here. It shares a space in the palette with the Floater Adjuster tool.*

**CHOOSE A TOOL**

If the choice of tools for drawing selections and shapes seems overwhelming—the Lasso, Pen, Quick Curve, Oval and Rectangular Shape Design tools, and Oval and Rectangular Shape Selection tools—choose a tool that you are already comfortable with. You can always convert the selection to a shape, or vice versa.

IF YOU WANT TO GET THE MOST FROM PAINTER, you need to invest some time in understanding how the program isolates portions of images so that you can paint them, apply special effects or otherwise change them without affecting the rest of the image. Much of the program's power is tucked into the complex area of *outline selections*, *shape paths* and *masks*.

Painter has two very different methods of isolating areas. The first method uses *outline* (vector-based) information—a way of describing the perimeter of objects in mathematical terms. Painter lets you view and work with these vector-based outlines as either *outline selections* (or, more simply, *selections*) or as *shape paths*.

Outline selections exist in two different conditions: *active selections* display a black or red marquee (the marching ants) and are ready to limit the application of paint and effects to the area within their boundaries. An *inactive selection* (or, more accurately, *inactive outline*) will not show up on your document at all. But its name will appear in the Path List (described on page 80). Inactive selections don't affect brushstrokes or other effects. But they provide a way of storing selection information until you need to activate a selection.

If you used Painter 3.1 you're probably familiar with paths drawn using the Outline Selection tool (Pen) in Bézier drawing mode (a series of anchor points, straight lines and curves). This function and others have been added to Painter 4's new Pen tool, with which you can draw precise paths for shapes. Painter's shapes combine the vector outlines of selections with attributes such as stroke, fill and transparency. Shapes and their attributes are Postscript objects; the paths are displayed as a series of points and curves. Shapes exist in a layer above the image canvas; their names appear in the Floater List (covered in Chapter 5).

*Type on a curve is most easily set in a drawing program. Convert the type to paths and save the file in either EPS or Illustrator format. To import the outlines into Painter, copy them to the clipboard in your drawing program, and paste them into your Painter image, or choose File, Acquire, Adobe Illustrator file.*

*These shapes were created with the Text tool. The shape path (top, with no fill and line) shows selected Bézier anchor points and curves. The lower letter shape, not selected, has a white fill.*

*For this image we extruded type using Adobe Dimensions; imported it into Macromedia Freehand; duplicated, flopped and skewed the face of the type to make the shadow; saved the face, the sides and the shadow as separate documents; imported each set of outlines into Painter; and painted inside of the active selections with Airbrush and Liquid brush variants.*

In contrast to vector-based selections, Painter's second method of isolating areas doesn't involve outline information at all. Instead it uses an orange-tinted protective mask that you can "thin" or even completely remove, pixel by pixel. Because it's an 8-bit mask, it allows 256 levels of thinning, from fully opaque (which completely protects the pixels underneath from change) to fully clear (which fully exposes them to brushstrokes).

Although the outline and mask methods have entirely different origins, there is some degree of interchangeability. For instance, you can turn a mask into a *mask representation selection* (see the "Masks" section later in this introduction) and then into an outline selection. But converting a mask turns its pixel information into outline information, so transparency effects will be permanently lost. Because selections and shape paths come from outline information, we'll discuss them together first, then talk about masks later.

## CREATING SELECTIONS AND SHAPES

You can make outline selections and shape paths in a number of ways: Create them with one of the selection tools (the Lasso, Oval or Rectangular Selection tool) or the shape design tools (Pen, Quick Curve, or Oval or Rectangular Shape tools) or with the Text tool; drag an existing path from the Paths palette into your image; import EPS paths from a Postscript drawing program; or convert masks to selections.

Outline selection and shape information is interchangeable. To convert a selection to a shape, choose the Objects palette, and Convert to Shape from the Path List menu. Conversely, after you draw a shape using one of the shape design tools, it's easy to convert it to a selection using Shapes, Convert to Selection, or by clicking the Make Selection button on the Controls:Shape Design palette.

The Path List and Floater List palettes store selections and shapes and control operations such as choosing them and making them active. (The Path List is described on page 80 and the Floater List is described in Chapter 5.) When you convert a shape

---

**CONVERTING SHAPES TO SELECTIONS**

You can convert a shape to a selection by clicking on it (or clicking its name in the Floater List) and then choosing Shapes, Convert to Selection. But the result you get depends on the tool you click with:

• If you want to fill the selection or apply an effect within its boundary, click the shape with the Floater Adjuster tool.

*Clicked with the Floater Adjuster tool, converted and ready to fill*

• If you want to scale or rotate the selection, click the shape with the Selection Adjuster tool.

*Clicked with the Selection Adjuster tool, converted and ready to scale*

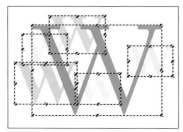

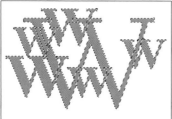

These type shapes were selected with the Floater Adjuster tool (top), and converted to active selections and then filled (bottom).

The Tools palette with selection and shape design tools (top, from left to right): Lasso, Selection Adjuster, Pen, Rectangular Shape Design tool; (bottom, from left to right), Rectangular Selection tool, Text tool, Direct Selection tool and Scissors tool.

## SPEEDY PATHWORK

Working with shapes and outlines can be slow with higher-resolution files. Try importing outlines into a low-resolution (72 ppi) version of your final image. Scale, position and group the shapes and selections as necessary, then resize your document to its final resolution. Shapes and outline selections are resolution-independent and will scale up with the document.

to a selection, its name moves from the Floater List to the Path List palette. Likewise the name of a selection converted to a shape moves from the Path List palette to the Floater List palette.

**Lasso tool.** The lasso tool is good for making quick, freehand selections. Begin by dragging with the Lasso to create a shape path. To close the path and make it an active selection, drag the Lasso precisely to the origin point or press the Close button in the Controls:Lasso palette. (See page 92 for Steve Campbell's work with freehand selections.)

**Oval and Rectangular selection tools.** These tools share a space in the Tools palette. To constrain the oval or rectangular selection tools so they select perfect circles or squares, hold down the Shift key and drag with the tool. Oval selections can be converted to shapes using Objects, P. List, Convert to Shape.

It probably wouldn't take you long to figure out that the Rectangular Selection tool is not like the other selection tools, but it might take you a while to figure out *how* it's different! It makes transient selections, without leaving path information on your document. You can edit the size of a rectangular selection numerically using the Edit Rectangular Selection dialog box found under Objects, P. List. To adjust the size of a rectangular selection intuitively, press the Control key and drag. Typically you would use a rectangular selection to temporarily highlight an area so you could apply one of the commands under the Effects menu or float the area. (Chapter 5 tells more about working with floaters.)

You can't directly convert a rectangular selection to a shape, feather it (see "Feathering" on page 79), skew it or perform any of the other tricks that you can on regular selections. But, there *is* a work-around: To create a rectangular outline from your rectangular marquee, float and drop your selection (using the Drop button on the Objects:Floater List palette); then it will perform like other outline selections.

**Rectangular and Oval Shape tools.** These tools share a space in the upper right corner of the Tools palette and are for creating rectangular and elliptical shape objects. Press the Shift key and drag with the tool to draw a perfect square or circle shape.

**Text tool.** As you type with the Text tool, each letter appears as an active shape; the name of each letter also appears in the Floater List palette. Make corrections as you type by using the Delete key, and press Return or Enter to start a new line of type. If

## GOOD PATH HOUSEKEEPING

Every time you make an outline selection, the outline is left on the image canvas. To remove outlines you no longer need, choose the Selection Adjuster tool and Shift-select them (or Shift-select their names in the Path List) and press the Delete key (or click the Clear button in the Path List).

The hexagon shapes above show two ways to select a shape. The hexagon on the left was selected with the Floater Adjuster tool and displays the black and yellow bounding box that's characteristic of shapes and floaters. (Because no path is visible when the bounding box is showing, we chose a black fill in the Set Attributes dialog box so the hexagon would show up.) The shape path on the right shows line segments and control points that are visible when a shape is selected using the Whole Shape Selection tool or the Direct Selection tool. This hexagon displays a precise skeletal line (Attributes were set at 0 fill and 0 line.) Toggle the eye icon closed and open to hide and show a shape.

## DON'T SPEND THE TIME

Don't worry about grouping shapes in the Floater List if you intend to convert them to selections—groups will not make the transition from the Floater List to the Path List.

## UNEXPECTED NAME CHANGES

If you convert a shape to a selection, the name of the shape will be retained when the item moves to the Path List. Not so the other way around (as of this writing)—if you convert a selection to a shape, the name will be lost and the item will be renamed as a shape (Shape 1, 2, and so on). You may want to rename a shape right away after moving it—giving it a name similar to its original selection name—so you won't get confused later.

you convert text shapes to selections, their letter names will move from the Floater List to the Path List palette. But if you move them back to the Floater List, their counters may be lost (as of this writing).

**Pen and Quick Curve tools.** The Pen and Quick Curve tools are shape design tools that share a space in the top row of the Tools palette. Choose the Pen tool for precision drawing using a combination of straight lines and curves. Click to create straight line segments; to draw curves, press and drag to pull out handles that control the curves. Drag with the Quick Curve tool to draw freehand shapes. To complete a boundary drawn by the Pen or Quick Curve tool, close the shape by connecting to the origin point or by pressing the Close button on the Controls:Shape Design palette. To convert a shape drawn with the Pen or Quick Curve tool to a selection, click the Make Selection button on the Controls: Shape Design palette.

**Shape Selection tools.** The Whole Shape Selection tool (solid arrow) and the Direct Selection tool (hollow arrow) share a space in the Tools palette. The Whole Shape Selection tool is used to select an entire shape so that it can be duplicated or transformed. The Direct Selection tool allows you to select and adjust individual anchor points and control handles to modify shapes. This dual tool works much like its counterpart in Illustrator or like the Pick and Shape tools in CorelDraw.

**Shape Edit tools.** The Scissors, Add Point, Remove Point and Convert Point tools will also be familiar to Illustrator users. They share a space in the bottom right corner of the Tools palette and (like the Direct Selection tool) are used for changing shape paths. The Scissors tool allows you to cut a line segment of a shape path selected with the Whole Shape or Direct Selection tool.

**Selection Adjuster and Floater Adjuster tools.** These tools share a space in the top row of the Tools palette. Use the Selection Adjuster to move or transform selections, or use it in conjunction

## PRECISION DRAWING SETUP

When you're drawing shape paths and you find the default stroke and fill on the path make it hard to see your path outline and to draw precisely, change the Shape Attributes to a skeletal line. In the Shape Attributes dialog box, uncheck the Stroke and Fill checkboxes. Under Edit, Preferences, Shapes, check the Big Handles drawing option. (Fill and stroke preferences can also be specified here.) You'll be able to see the path outline with anchor points and handles so you can draw more precisely. To view and manipulate a shape path with these attributes after drawing it, choose the Whole Shape or Direct Selection tool.

## AUTOMATIC SELECTIONS

To automatically convert a shape path drawn with the Pen or Quick Curve tools into an active selection, press the Make Selection button immediately after drawing.

*Choosing a heart-shaped path in the Painter Paths library in the Objects:Paths palette*

*When these fish, drawn in Adobe Illustrator, were copied and pasted into Painter, they came in as compound shapes. To recreate this look, turn to "Dropping a Shadow" in Chapter 5.*

with the Controls:Adjuster palette to feather selections. Read more about this tool on page 79.

The Floater Adjuster tool is useful for working with shapes and floaters. Read more about it in the introduction to Chapter 5. Use the buttons on the Controls: Adjuster palette to switch tools when you convert a shape to a selection (Selection Adjuster), or to float an active selection (Floater Adjuster).

**The Paths palette.** In Painter 4, the Paths palette can be chosen from the Objects palette, P. List pop-up menu. Choose Paths to open the palette. To choose a stored path, drag items from the front of the Paths palette, or from the Paths palette drawer into your image. If you use a lot of custom paths in your work, use the Path Mover to create custom libraries (see the "Libraries and Movers" section in Chapter 1).

**Importing EPS outlines.** Painter 4 supports two ways to import paths, such as type on a curve created in Postscript drawing programs, or preexisting EPS clip art. The first option (File, Acquire, Adobe Illustrator file) creates a new file. To do this, copy and paste outlines from the new file into your working composition. The second option (our choice) allows you to copy outlines from a Postscript program to the clipboard and paste them into your Painter file. The outlines will paste into your document and will appear in the Floater List palette. Objects such as the letters "O" and "A" have a *counter*, or hole, cut in them and will come into Painter as compound shapes.

### EPS IMPORTING ALERT!

A word of warning: As of this writing, we encountered problems when importing some EPS files created in earlier versions of Freehand and Illustrator using both of the import methods. When importing compound objects, we obtained the best results with drawings completely created in Illustrator 5 or newer (simply resaving an older file created in the new format resulted in some compound objects not making the transition).

## TRANSFORMING SELECTIONS

An important concept to understand when working with selections and paths is that of *active* vs. *selected*. These words are synonymous in most programs, but not in Painter.

An *active* selection displays an animated marquee, resembling "marching ants." As soon as you've drawn a complete boundary with a selection tool, or dragged a selection into your image from the Paths palette, you will see a marquee letting you know it's active. The area within the boundary can now be painted into, filled or treated with an effect. If you convert a shape into a selection and don't see a marquee, open the Path List palette, select the selection name and press Enter to activate it.

An *inactive* selection is invisible, does not affect brushstrokes, and can't be filled or treated with special effects.

### ACTIVE VS. SELECTED

Here's an outline in an image and its corresponding appearance in the Path List palette:

*Active, unselected selection*    *Active, selected selection*

*Option-dragging a selection to make a copy*

*Dragging a side handle to scale horizontally*

*Shift-dragging one of the corner handles to scale proportionally*

*Using a corner handle and the Command key to rotate*

The lower portion of the expanded Path List palette

*To create these concentric stars, drag one from the Paths palette and scale it up to the size you want for the outermost star using the Selection Adjuster tool. Then click on the Widen button in the Path List palette and enter a negative value (such as –10). Do this several times to create smaller, perfectly centered stars. Make alternating selections negative in the Path List. With all selections active, fill (Command-F) with a gradation.*

A *selected* selection displays eight bounding box handles around its edges—the handles are visible only when the Selection Adjuster tool is selected. You select selections in order to group them, move them, rotate them, or prepare them to be activated.

The distinction between "active" and "selected" gives you great flexibility. Both Painter and other image editors let you convert selections to paths in order to modify individual Bézier control points, *but Painter lets you scale, rotate and skew the outline without affecting the pixel information within it.* You can do these operations and more by applying the Selection Adjuster tool to the interior or to the bounding box handles of a selected path or selection.

**Working with the Selection Adjuster tool.** Since outline selections are based on mathematical information rather than pixels, they can undergo all of the following transformations with no loss of edge quality and without moving the pixels within the selection boundary. To *move* a selection, position the Selection Adjuster over it and press; when you see the four-arrowed cursor, it's safe to move the selection. To *duplicate*, hold down Option, then move the item and release. To *scale*, first select a path or selection by clicking on it once; position the tool over one of the corner handles; when the cursor changes, drag the handle. Use the Shift key to *resize proportionately*. If you want to *resize only horizontally or vertically*, drag on a side handle. To *rotate*, use a corner handle, adding the Command key as you position the cursor before dragging. To *skew*, press Command while positioning over a side handle, then drag.

**Feathering.** Feathering a selection softens its edge. To see feathering at work, drag a selection from the Paths palette into your image. Choose the Selection Adjuster tool, then set the Feather slider in the Controls:Adjuster palette to 20. Now choose Effects, Fill, select one of the options and click OK. Note the soft edges of the filled selection. The feather is always built inward and outward from the object-oriented outline.

You can change the feather setting as many times as you want with no loss in quality: the feather always refers to the original outline to rebuild itself. It takes longer for Painter to calculate a change made to a feathered selection than to an unfeathered one, so if you're arranging or modifying selections, you can speed your work by setting the Feather slider back to 0; then Painter won't have to refeather the selection every time you move or modify it. You can't feather a closed group of outlines (see "Grouping and activating" on the next page). Instead you'll need to open the group and feather each selection individually, or Shift-click to feather more than one at a time.

**Modifying outlines in the Path List.** In the zoomed-out Path List palette (described on page 80), you can click on the *Widen*

*Multiple clicks with the Smooth button (Path List palette) can turn a perfectly good typeface (Stone Sans, left) into a trendy, avant-garde one.*

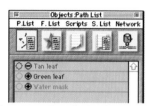

*A mask representation selection (in green), a positive selection (blue), and a negative selection (red) in the Path List palette*

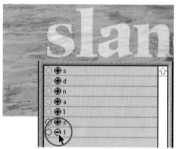

*Here's how a series of type selections appear in the Path List and on the image. We applied a Dye Concentration effect within the type selections. The "l" and "s" selections are active (animated marquee); the other selections are inactive (no marquee). The negative selection (red marquee) protected the letter "l" from the effect application.*

### QUICK LIST ACCESS

To quickly open the Path List (to work with selections), double-click on the Selection Adjuster tool in the Tools palette. To open the Floater List (to work with shapes), double-click on the Floater Adjuster tool, Whole Shape Selection, Direct Selection or Pen tool.

button to create a bevel for type (see page 85, "Creating Beveled Cast Metal") or other selections. Use the *Smooth* button to round the sharp corners of a selection. You can delete outlines (or groups of outlines) by selecting or Shift-selecting their names in the Path List and pressing the *Clear* button.

## ORGANIZING WITH THE PATH LIST PALETTE

The Path List palette lists all the selections in your file by name. If you'll be doing a lot of work with outlines, it's a good idea to get on friendly terms with this palette. Here are some basics:

**The little icons on the far left.** Click on the circle icon to the far left of an item's name (or press Enter when that item is selected) to toggle an outline selection either active or inactive. You can turn a selection positive or negative by selecting it and toggling the Plus/Minus icon at the left of the selection name.

**What the colors mean.** In the Path List, *blue* is the standard color for positive outlines, although in your image, the corresponding marquee or path appears black. A *red* item in the Path List palette and a red marquee or path in your image means that it's *negative*. (Negative selections are used to punch holes in positive ones, or to protect an area from painting or from an applied effect.) *Green* items that appear in the Path List are masks that have been temporarily turned into selections. These *mask representation selections* are described on page 83.

### DRAWING-ORDER BLUES

If you've made a selection negative but it doesn't punch a hole in the positive selection that surrounds it, it's probably positioned below the positive selection. Remedy this by dragging the name of the negative selection above the positive one's name in the Path List.

**Selected items.** If an item is highlighted in blue in the Path List and its name is in also bold, it means the item is selected and is ready to be moved, rotated, grouped and so on. Make sure to click on the item's *name* to select it and not the circle icon.

**Grouping and activating.** If you're working with a lot of outline selections, it's wise to group items that need to stay together—all of the letterforms in a headline, for instance. Shift-select the items in the Path List and click the Group button. Use the Enter key to alternatively activate and deactivate selected individual outlines in an open group, or all of the outlines in a closed group. You can close a group by clicking on the arrowhead to the left of its name.

## SELECTIONS AT WORK

Once you've activated selections, you can choose to draw outside of them instead of inside. You can also choose whether to keep them visible or not. These functions are controlled by the Drawing and Visibility icons—the Pencil and Eye—found in two places:

*Use Objects, P. List, Stroke Selection to stroke a selection (we dragged this one in from the Paths palette and resized it two times larger; then used the Image Hose, "Candy" nozzle, and the top left Drawing icon). Try feathering the selection, choosing a different Drawing icon, or using a Cloning brush instead of the Image Hose.*

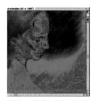

*Using Edit, Mask, AutoMask, we made a luminosity mask for this painting. The color view, with the center Visibility icon chosen, shows the background mask; the black-and-white view appears when you switch to Mask Edit Mode.*

in the zoomed-out Path List and in the bottom left corner of an active document's window. Several of the techniques in this chapter demonstrate how these icons work, and you can refer to Painter's *User Guide* for a detailed explanation.

Take the name "Drawing icons" literally; they affect drawing and painting actions only, not fills or other effects. A fill or effect is always constrained to the inside of an active selection, regardless of which drawing icon you choose. If you want to apply a fill or effect to the *outside* of your active selection, use Invert Mask (described on page 83).

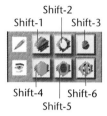
### SAVING OUTLINES

Use the Selection Adjuster tool to drag outlines to the Paths palette to store them. If you want to save shapes into a library, first convert them to selections (Shapes, Convert to Selection) and drag them to the Paths palette. If you're very organized, you might create multiple Path libraries for different jobs. To swap outlines between libraries or to set up a new, empty palette, you can use Objects, P. List, Path Mover.

Exporting selections to Postscript drawing programs using the File, Export Adobe Illustrator file was not successful at this writing. The result can be Postscript error messages or previewless images that don't look like the originals when printed.

### MASKS

You can create masks in Painter in several ways: by rendering outline selections to the 8-bit mask layer, by painting them directly with Masking brushes or by generating them with Auto Mask or Color Mask.

**Rendering selections into the mask.** Every time you make a selection active, you're actually rendering it to make what's called the *background mask* in Painter parlance, meaning the currently active, working mask. To see what this means, draw an oval with the Oval Selection tool. It will be active when you finish drawing. Click on the right Drawing and center Visibility icon (the one with the orange mask oval) in the expanded Path List to see how the oval "cuts" a hole in the orange mask. Everything covered with solid orange (orange is the default color for the mask layer) is protected from your brushstrokes; anything less than solid orange will allow your brushstrokes to penetrate to some degree.

To turn the background mask into black-and-white, so you can paint on it, choose Canvas, View Mask, or toggle the Mask Edit

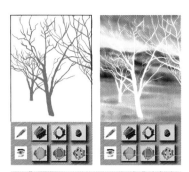

*Painting a resist for the trees with the Masking Pen (top left); painting washes on the background using a Water Color brush (top right); and the finished artwork, including brushstrokes inside of the mask (above)*

**MOVING MASKS**

Shuffle masks between images with identical pixel dimensions using Auto Mask, Original Mask. For instance, if you made a mask for an image and then cloned the image (Edit, Clone), the mask would not appear in the clone. To move the mask to the clone, make the clone's window active, choose Edit, Mask, Auto Mask, choose Original Mask from the pop-up menu and click OK. (To make any image an "original," select its name under Edit, Clone Source.)

Mode button (above the vertical scroll bar) from color view to a black circle for mask view. You can use any Painter brush to alter the background mask in Mask Edit Mode, without changing that brush's method to masking method. Photoshop users will find working in default Mask Edit Mode similar to a black and white Photoshop channel with the values reversed. (To invert the values, choose Invert Mask.)

**Painting a resist with Masking brushes.** Instead of making masks by using Bézier curves to draw selections, artists with experience in drawing often feel more comfortable using Masking brushes to paint the areas they want to isolate. One of the best ways to get acquainted with Masking brushes is to paint a resist.

A traditional resist involves applying a protective substance to define an area and to prevent paint from being applied to it. To create a resist in Painter, begin with a new file and choose any Masking brush. Choose the center Drawing icon and begin painting on the background. (The center Visibility icon is chosen automatically when you choose a Masking brush.) Choose black to paint a solid mask, white to erase your work, and any color in between if you want varying levels of mask transparency. Keep in mind as you work that you're painting the areas that will either reject paint (black) or accept paint (white). When you're done, choose a non-Masking brush and begin painting broad strokes across the background. All orange areas that you painted with the Masking brush and black paint are protected from these strokes. To "reverse" the mask so you can paint with a non-Masking brush on the areas covered by your masking strokes, select the far right Drawing icon. To view your work without the mask layer, choose the far left Visibility icon.

**Auto Mask and Color Mask.** Choose Edit, Mask to use these two "automated" methods of generating masks from existing images. Many artists often begin the process of isolating complex areas of an image using one of these two tools, then finish their mask by adding to or subtracting from it with Masking brushes.

Use Auto Mask, Image Luminance to generate a mask based on the brightness values in the image. Try this: Choose black and the Scratchboard Tool variant of the Pens brush and make a sketch in a new document. Turn your sketch into a mask by choosing Auto Mask (Command-Shift-M) using Image Luminance. Click on the center Visibility and Drawing icons to see the mask. For an example of Auto Mask using Current Color—the only one of these automated masking methods that produces an aliased, rough-edged mask—turn to page 96, "Isolating Color with Auto Mask."

Color Mask is a great way to select areas of color that would be tedious to select by hand—for instance, to select the white background behind a head in a portrait photo. Turn to page 94, "Using Color Mask," for a Color Mask demonstration.

## TINY MOVES

Use arrow keys to nudge selected selections or shapes one screen pixel at a time. Since the distance moved is a screen pixel and not a fixed width, zoom out from the selection or shape if you want to make coarse adjustments and zoom in for fine adjustments. Arrow-key nudging is especially handy for kerning type.

## NO TWO FEATHERS ALIKE

You must use
Edit:Mask:Feather Mask to
feather the mask now.

OK

If you see the dialog box above, you just tried to feather a mask or a mask representation selection using the Controls palette's Feather slider. Since feathering a mask (pixel information) is a different proposition than feathering an outline selection, you'll need to choose Edit, Mask, Feather Mask instead. The good news is that Feather Mask lets you specify a much higher Feather setting than you can get using the Controls palette (up to 126 instead of 50).

## DON'T WASTE A FEATHER

If you're going to convert a mask to an outline selection, use the Controls palette to feather it *after* the conversion process. If you do it beforehand, Painter will discard the feather along with all of the mask's other transparency information when it converts the mask to an outline selection.

**Mask representation selections.** If you want to apply any of the commands under the Effects menu to unmasked portions of your image, you'll need to view your mask as a *mask representation selection* by clicking on the far right Visibility icon. The orange masked area will change to a green-and-white marquee that shows that the mask information has been turned into an active, but temporary selection, and thus has become the operating background mask for the moment. Since Painter has only one background mask, if you activate another selection, the information represented by the first green marquee is lost! The solution to preserving those masks: Convert the pixel-based mask representation selection into an object-oriented outline selection (black marquee) by selecting the mask (or closed mask group) in the Path List and pressing the Enter key.

**Invert Mask.** Since Painter applies non-painting effects only to the interior of active selections, here's a great way to flip-flop a selection, making everything outside of it active. Starting with an active selection, choose Edit, Mask, Invert Mask; an inverted mask representation selection (the green and white animated marquee) appears. This command works similar to Photoshop's Select, Inverse command, and if you're viewing selection marquees (the right-hand Visibility icon), you don't need to switch to mask view (the center Visibility icon) for Invert Mask to work.

## INVERT MASK ALERT!

The Invert Mask command converts all active selections into a single, inverse selection and there's no way to get the original individual selections back! (You can Invert Mask again, but you get a single selection instead of your multiple originals.) Work around this limitation by dragging selections into the Paths palette, then return them in register by double-clicking on their icons on the front of the Paths palette's drawer after Invert Mask has deleted the original selections.

**Magic Wand.** Although Painter's Color Mask feature eclipses most of the Magic Wand's capabilities, the Wand is still a good tool for selecting large areas of flat color. Choose Edit, Magic Wand, click in your image on a color you want to isolate, and Shift-click on nearby colors to add them to the selection. You can also adjust the HSV sliders in the Magic Wand dialog box to select a narrower or wider range of colors. Although it appears that you're building an orange-colored mask, when you click OK, Painter generates an outline selection group complete with negative selections, based on the selected orange area. Selections made by the Magic Wand are aliased and rough-edged; if you want to soften their edges, use the Smooth button in the expanded Path List or choose Edit, Mask, Feather Mask and apply a 1–3 pixel setting.

# Creating a Bas Relief

***Overview*** *Open a new file with a colored background; create a type shape; convert the shape to a selection; fill the selection with color; apply a paper grain to add texture; use a feathered mask and Surface Texture to create a three-dimensional look.*

*The top portion of the Floater List palette showing the selected shape*

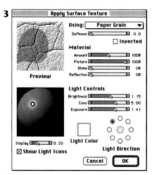

*Scaling the selection*

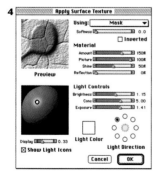

*Applying Surface Texture with Paper Grain*

*Applying Surface Texture using Mask to create the bas relief effect*

PAINTER HIDES POWERFUL FEATURES for creating textured, 3D artwork under Effects, Surface Control. You can get results much more quickly than if you added highlights and shadows using brushes.

**1 Setting type and converting to a selection.** Create a new file with a light background color, then open the Floater List palette so that you can see the type shape appear in the list. Click in the image with the Text tool and type a letter. (Using a 950-pixel-wide file we set an ornament using the Adobe Wood Type Ornaments font.) Before you can use the shape to apply effects to the image background, you'll need to convert it to a selection. Choose the Selection Adjuster tool, select the shape in the Floater List (or click on it in the image) and choose Shapes, Convert to Selection.

**2 Moving, scaling and feathering.** Press inside the active selection with the Selection Adjuster tool and when you see the four-arrow cursor, it's safe to move your selection without distorting it. To scale, drag on one of the selection handles; to scale proportionately, press Shift and drag one of the corner handles. For a softer transition between colors in the next step, move the Feather slider in the Controls:Adjuster palette to 1–2 pixels.

**3 Filling and applying a paper texture.** Select a darker color from the Color palette and fill the selection with the color (Effects, Fill, Current Color). Deactivate the selection by pressing Enter in preparation for applying a texture to the entire image. Select a texture in the Papers palette (we used Big Crackle from the Nature texture library, scaled to 150% using the Scale slider on the front of the Paper drawer). Next, add a 3D texture using Effects, Surface Control, Apply Surface Texture using Paper Grain.

**4 Creating the bas relief effect.** A wider feather is the key to achieving a 3D look. Choose a moderate feather in the Controls: Adjuster palette. (We used 10 pixels.) Choose Effects, Surface Control, Apply Surface Texture again—and this time choose Mask from the pop-up menu. Experiment with the settings. 🖌

# Creating Beveled Cast Metal

***Overview*** *Make a dark background; set type; widen the type to make bevels; apply color and texture to the type and bevels.*

TO BUILD BEVELED CAST METAL LETTERFORMS that appear to hover above a soft fabric background, we set type in Painter, kerned it and created a drop shadow. Widened selections were generated from the type to create a bevel. We filled the type with a creamy gold tint, then applied a series of Surface Control effects—Color Overlay and Surface Texture—and painted airbrush highlights and shadows to make the metal casting look real.

**1 Making a background file.** For a soft background that won't compete with the gleam of the type effect, choose a dark color in the Color palette. In the Paper palette, choose a texture. We started with a 3.6-inch wide file at 72 ppi, chose Swirly from the Nature paper library and scaled it to 400%. To apply your texture, choose Surface Control, Color Overlay, using Paper Texture, and click the Dye Concentration button. We then increased the file's resolution to 266 ppi using Canvas, Resize.

**2 Setting the type.** Choose the Text tool and pick a font in the Controls:Text palette. We chose 85-point City Bold. To accommodate a bevel, you'll need to give the type additional letterspacing. You can do this by moving the Tracking slider to the right before setting the type, or by kerning individual letters after it's set (see below). Decide how wide you want the bevel to be (we chose 5 pixels) and set the type. Painter knows the identity of the letters typed, and brings named, individual letter shapes into the Objects:Floater List. To kern, deselect your letters, then choose the Floater Adjuster tool and click on an individual letter to reselect it. (Or click on its name in the Floater List to highlight it.) Move the active shape with the left and right arrow keys; each key press moves the shape one screen pixel.

**3 Making the shadow.** After kerning the type shapes, we created a soft shadow to add dimension. Since shapes do not accept feathering, convert the text shapes to selections using Shapes, Convert to Selection. Next, position your selections where you want the shadow to fall using the Selection Adjuster tool, then use the slider in the Controls:Adjuster palette to feather them (we set a feather of 26.1). Choose black, then Effects, Fill (Command-F),

**1**

*Creating a fabric-like background with the Swirly paper texture, scaled to 400%*

**2a**

*Sizing type in the Controls palette*

**2b**

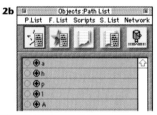

*Letterform selections in the Path List*

**3**

*The soft shadow, filled with black*

**4a**

*An active, widened text selection*

**4b**

*Opened groups in the Path List. Close each group by clicking on its green arrowhead.*

**5**

*Sampling a gold color from a photo reference (left), and filling the active selection*

**6**

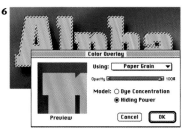

*Applying Color Overlay to all selections*

**7a**

*Moving a group of negative selections above positive selections in the Path List*

**7b**

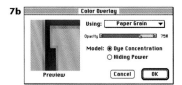

*Using Color Overlay to darken the bevel*

**8**

*Spraying highlights on the bevel with the Feather Tip Airbrush*

using Current Color and 70% Opacity (for a softer, more transparent shadow).

**4 Positioning and widening the text selection.** Now that you've used the selections to make the drop shadow, you can use them to set up the letterform faces and bevel. You'll need to unfeather your selections (do this now by dragging the Feather slider to 0) and move them. Use the Selection Adjuster tool to select all of the selections and move them up and to the left about 8 pixels. Click the Widen button in the Path List palette and type 5 to create a 5-pixel bevel. (If you're using smaller type, check your bevel width so the letterforms don't overlap each other.)

Widening the letterforms will create a new set of selections, and each selection will appear directly above its original in the Path List. You can double-click on the current names of the widened selections to rename them if you like.

It's a good idea to group the two sets of text selections so you can turn them on and off easily. Shift-click to select all of the original selections in the Path List. When they are all highlighted in blue, click on the Group button. Follow the same process to create a group for the widened selections. We named our groups "Letterform Faces group" and "Bevel group," respectively. Close the groups by clicking the green arrow.

**5 Filling the selections.** Choose a gold color. A realistic gold can be difficult to mix, so we sampled color (Dropper tool) from a photo of gold bars for a natural look. Use your creamy gold to fill all selections with flat color, covering the faces and bevels with a base coat (Command-F, Current Color at 100% opacity).

**6 Adding a gold texture to the letterforms.** Select the Driven paper texture from the More Wild Textures library and scale it to 400%. Keeping the same gold color and with all selections active, choose Effects, Surface Control, Color Overlay, using Paper Grain at 100%. Click on the Hiding Power button.

**7 Darkening the bevel.** A darker bevel adds to the 3D illusion. Choose a darker gold in the Color palette. Select the Letterform Faces group by clicking on its name in the Path List. Open the group and Shift-select its members and turn all of them negative by clicking on each Plus button to toggle it to a Minus: this isolates the bevel and protects the letterform faces from editing. In your image, the Bevel group should be positive (black marquees), and the original Letterform Faces group should now be negative (red marquees). For a negative selection to work, it must be on top of any positive selection that surrounds it. Close the Letterform Faces group and drag it above the Bevel group in the Path List.

It's time to apply the new color to your bevel. Select Effects, Surface Control, Color Overlay, using Paper Grain, but this time use Dye Concentration instead of Hiding Power. We used an

**9**

*Airbrushing soft strokes across the letterform faces*

**10**

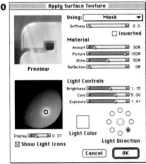

*Adding more emphasis to the bevel with Apply Surface Texture*

**11a**

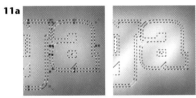

*Creating the soft glow behind Omega, and airbrushing across the letterforms*

**11b**

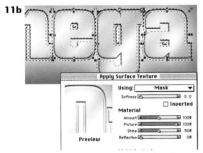

*The first of three applications of Surface Texture using Mask*

**11c**

*Omega with final pass of Surface Texture*

opacity of 75% and scaled the Driven paper texture to 300% so the resulting lines would add to the illusion of a receding bevel.

**8 Adding highlights and shadows to the bevel.** Use the same negative and positive selection setup to fine-tune the bevel. We used the Dodge brush to lighten some areas of the bevel and the Burn brush to darken other areas. We painted tiny white highlights with the Feather Tip variant of the Airbrush.

**9 Painting soft detail on the letterform faces.** We painted subtle highlights and shadows on the letterform faces, planning our strokes to complement the light that already appeared to be falling on the diagonal folds of the fabric background. To paint on the letterform faces, open the Letterform Faces group in the Path List, Shift-select items in the group and turn the selections from negative to positive by toggling the button from a Minus to a Plus, then select the closed Bevel group and press Enter to deactivate the bevel. Now only the faces are active. Choose the Fat Stroke Airbrush variant and reduce its opacity in the Controls palette to 10–15%. Paint soft strokes across the gold letterforms.

**10 Popping the bevel.** After airbrushing the highlights and shadows, we applied a small amount of Surface Texture using Mask to make the metal look more realistic. Painter can't feather a closed group of selections, so open the Bevel group, Shift-select each selection, choose the Selection Adjuster tool, then drag the Feather slider to exactly the same number of pixels you used for the bevel. We used 5 pixels to match our 5-pixel bevel. Press Enter to reactivate all of the selected Bevel letterforms. Choose Effects, Surface Control, Apply Surface Texture; set Using to Mask, Amount to 30%, Picture and Shine to 100%. Choose a Light Direction button that complements your airbrush work. Click OK. We heightened hot spots and darkened some of the shadows with the Thin Stroke Airbrush. The result is shown at the top of page 85.

**11 Building a debossed bevel variation.** We began Omega with a purple background, then built letterform faces and bevels in a process similar to Alpha, in steps 1–10 above. To create the glow, we activated all the selections and applied a feather of 50 and a fill of white. A recessed bevel works best using a small Feather setting to emphasize the edge of the mask—just enough to remove the jagged edges on the curves when Surface Texture is applied—so we gave all selections a 1.3-pixel feather. We sprayed diagonal strokes across the letterforms with the Fat Stroke Airbrush for a metallic look, then made the faces negative and the bevels positive and applied Surface Texture using Mask three times: first with Amount, Picture and Shine set to 100% with the top Light Direction button; next with Amount lowered to 30% with the right Light Direction button; and finally with Shine slider moved to 0% to accentuate the recessed, stamped-metal look.

# Working with Bézier Paths and Selections

**Overview** *Use the Pen tool to create shape paths of straight and curved lines; convert the shape paths to selections; use a custom pencil to draw inside and outside of selections.*

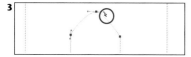

The logo sketch, including a rough grid

Pulling a handle from an anchor point to prepare for a curved path segment, then pressing and dragging to create the curve

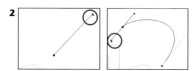

Dragging on a control handle to change the path's shape

## CHANGING DIRECTION

While drawing with the Pen, Option-click on an anchor point to create a cusp and establish a new direction for the following curve. A cusp is a corner point between two curved line segments, such as the "dent" at the top of a heart shape.

JOHN FRETZ

TO DESIGN A LOGO FOR THE 100-YEAR-OLD Bethany Church in Seattle, John Fretz used a custom pencil to draw inside and outside of outline selections to create a hard-edged, graduated look similar to his conventional colored pencil illustration style.

**1 Sketching the logo.** Fretz created a 4 x 4-inch pencil drawing of the logo that included a rough grid aligning the roofs of the houses. He scanned the sketch at 300 ppi and opened it in Painter to use as a template.

**2 Creating a path with Bézier curves.** The most efficient way to create a combination of curve and straight-line path segments is with the Pen tool. (If your drawing is very complex, you may want to consider creating it in a full-featured Postscript drawing program and then importing it rather than drawing from scratch in Painter; see "Importing EPS outlines" on page 78.) Set up shape attributes (with no fill and stroke) to produce a skeletal line that will help you see precise lines and curves while you draw. Choose the Pen tool and click to place anchor points for straight-line segments, and press, hold and drag to create anchor points with control handles that control curve segments. When you want to close a path, place the cursor over the starting anchor point, and click when you see a small circle designating the origin point, or press the Close Button in the Controls:Shape Design palette.

**3 Changing the path shape.** You can fine-tune a path during or after the drawing process with the Direct Selection tool. (While drawing with the Pen tool, press the Command key to temporarily change from the Pen to the Direct Selection tool.) Move the Direct Selection tool over an anchor point or a control handle and drag to reposition it.

**4a**

*Click on the Make Selection button to change the shape path into a selection.*

**4b**

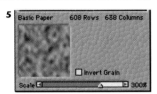

*The active clouds selection in the Path List*

**5**

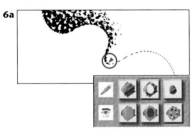

*Scaling the Basic Paper texture in the Papers palette*

**6a**

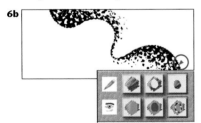

*Painting outside of the cloud selection using the custom black pencil*

**6b**

*Painting inside of the cloud selection*

**7**

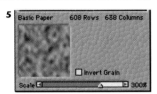

*An active negative selection (the red marquee) around the windows keeps them black when the house is filled with white. Fretz used his custom pencil to add black texture over the white fill.*

**4 Changing the path to a selection.** Shape paths must be turned into selections before you can paint inside or outside of them on the image canvas. You can convert a path drawn with the Pen or Quick Curve tool to a selection immediately after drawing it by pressing the Make Selection button in the Controls: Shape Design palette. You can also change a shape path into a selection by selecting the shape in the Floater List and choosing Shapes, Convert to Selection. In your image, the Bézier curves will turn into a black-and-white selection marquee and the path name will move from the Floater List to the Path List.

**5 Creating the pencil and surface.** To re-create the graduated effect he gets with conventional colored pencils on rough illustration board, Fretz built a heavy, grainy pencil based on Painter's 500 lb. Pencil variant. He modified the variant by switching to the Grainy Hard Cover submethod and increasing Size to roughly 200 pixels in the Brush Controls: Size palette. (You might also experiment with a brush that uses Grainy Edge Flat Cover method with a 7% Opacity setting in the Controls palette; it will give you an even coarser texture—black-and-white, with no grays.) Fretz chose Basic Paper because of its even texture, and scaled it to about 300% using the Scale slider in the front of the Papers drawer.

**6 Drawing in and out of selections.** With a selection active, zoom-out the Path List palette to reveal the icons that control Drawing (pencil row) and Visibility (eye row). To protect the area inside the outline, click on the middle Drawing button; to protect the area outside the outline, click on the far right Drawing button. Fretz switched back and forth between these two options as he rendered a graduated, even texture using his custom pencil.

**7 Using negative selections.** To fill each house with white and leave the windows black, Fretz used the Selection Adjuster tool to select the rectangular window selections, then made them negative by toggling the Plus button to a Minus in the Path List. The selection's name turns red when you do this and in your image the negative selection appears as a red marquee. Fretz selected white in the Color palette and chose Effects, Fill. He selected Current Color and clicked OK, turning the houses white. He added black texture to the houses with his custom pencil, then switched the negative window selections to positive and painted inside a few of them with a white pencil. He filled other shapes in the image with black and used a white pencil to add texture.

**Finalizing the composition.** Fretz continued to add textured, even tone with the black and white pencils until he completed the logo. The finished image was saved in TIFF format and to eliminate all grayscale information, Fretz opened the image in Photoshop and converted it to a 600 ppi bitmap image.

# Selections and Airbrush

**Overview** *Create a pencil sketch; add Postscript outlines in a drawing program; import outlines and template into Painter; add texture and gradient fills within the selections; use the Airbrush to create a metallic look.*

JOHN DISMUKES, CAPSTONE STUDIOS

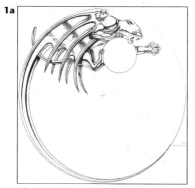

The original pencil sketch

Copying the selected and grouped panther outlines to the clipboard in Illustrator

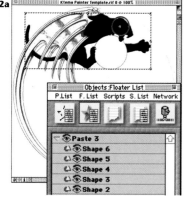

The pasted shapes selected with the Floater tool on the image and their names in the Floater List palette

ARTISTS USING TRADITIONAL AIRBRUSH technique cut friskets out of paper, film or plastic to protect portions of their artwork as they paint. For complex jobs this can become quite a task. That's one of the reasons why John Dismukes of Capstone Studios traded in his traditional tools for electronic ones. For this logo for Ktema, a manufacturer of promotional clothing for the entertainment industry, he started with a pencil sketch from memory, added Postscript paths and brought both into Painter. He painted inside and outside of the selections as he would with traditional friskets by turning them on and off using Path List palette controls.

**1 Creating the EPS paths.** Dismukes scanned his pencil sketch and used it as a template as he drew the elements to fit using Adobe Illustrator. He drew Postscript outlines for the panther, the wing ribs and membrane, the large and small globes, and the Ktema nameplate. Painter 4 can recognize fill and stroke attributes and groups when Postscript art is imported, so you may find it helpful to fill and group certain elements as you draw them. This will help you identify elements so that you can move and scale them. To prepare a document for importing into Painter 4, save a version in Adobe Illustrator 5 or EPS format.

**2 Importing, positioning and scaling.** Dismukes opened the original pencil sketch in Painter and begin importing the paths into the document. There are two ways to import Postscript outlines into a Painter file: Using File, Acquire, Adobe Illustrator file (which creates a new file) or copying from the Postscript program to the clipboard and then pasting into Painter; for this second method to work, both applications have to be running. Both alternatives import the outlines as shapes into your Painter file, but pasting through the clipboard is faster. To do this, select the

**2b**

*The Floater Adjuster tool changes to an arrow cursor when scaling the panther shapes to fit the template*

**3**

*Naming and grouping selections*

**4**

*Cloning texture into the membrane selection*

**5**

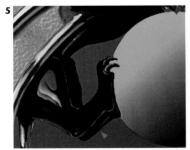

*Airbrushing highlights on the panther*

**6**

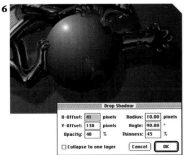

*Applying the shadow*

outlines in Illustrator and copy, then switch to Painter, and paste. You'll see a closed group of shapes appear in the Floater List palette. Move the shape group into position on the template using the Floater Adjuster tool or the arrow keys on your keyboard. To scale shapes proportionally, choose the Floater Adjuster tool, hold down the Shift key and drag on a corner handle.

**3 Converting, naming and grouping the paths.** To convert shapes to selections, so that you can paint or fill them, select the shapes in the Floater List and choose Shapes, Convert to Selection. The selection group will move from the Floater List to the Path List and the outlines will appear in the Path List selected and ungrouped. To help identify paths in the Path List so you can name them, first choose Edit, Deselect (Command-D). Select the circle icon to the left of the name for the first path in the list. This changes the path to an active selection; an animated marquee will appear around the chosen selection, helping you identify it. To name it, double-click on its current name. Type a name for the path in the Path Attributes dialog box and click OK. Do this for each of the paths in the list. When you find items you wish to group, Shift-select them, then click the Group button at the bottom of the palette. Name the group the same way you would name individual items, then close the group by clicking on the arrowhead to the left of its name.

**4 Filling selections.** Dismukes created texture within the membrane selection using a Cloning brush and a modified paper texture from a second document. He filled the large globe with a maroon gradient and the small globe with a green gradient.

**5 Airbrushing.** Dismukes' template showed good shadow and highlight detail. Using it as a guide, he began by laying down dark colors, gradually building forward to the white highlights. He used the Airbrush, Feather Tip variant, adjusting only the Size and ± Size in the Brush Controls palette. His digital airbrush techniques are identical to traditional ones, with selections serving as friskets.

**6 Floating a shadow.** Dismukes used floaters to create the panther's drop shadow on the maroon globe. Use the Create Drop Shadow command to do this. Activate the selections, either in the image with the Selection Adjuster tool or in the Path List palette by clicking on their circle icons. Float the selections by clicking on them in your image with the Floater Adjuster tool. Choose Effects, Objects, Create Drop Shadow. Use the default settings or experiment with other settings (unfortunately, there's no Preview window), then click OK to create the shadow.

**Finishing touches.** As a final touch, Dismukes opened the image in Adobe Photoshop and applied the Lens Flare filter to the green globe. The 40 MB logo was output to a 4 x 5-inch color transparency at 762 ppi.

# Working with Freehand Selections

**Overview** *Open a scanned image as a template; select areas of the image using the Lasso tool; add fills and effects to the selections; finish with brushwork and more effects.*

STEVE CAMPBELL

*The original pencil sketch*

*Choosing the New selection button*

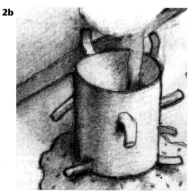

*An active selection on the front of the pot*

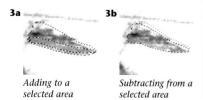

*Adding to a selected area*     *Subtracting from a selected area*

TO ISOLATE AREAS FOR FILLING, PAINTING AND LIGHTING effects in the whimsical *Go, Little Pot, Go!*, artist Steve Campbell used the Lasso tool. After applying multiple effects to each selection, he unified the piece by applying a number of filters—in both Painter and Photoshop—to the entire image.

**1 Sketching and scanning.** Campbell started with a pencil sketch, which he scanned and opened in Painter.

**2 Creating selections.** Select the Lasso tool, and click the New button in the Controls:Lasso palette. In your image, drag carefully around the area you want to select, dragging the Lasso precisely to the origin point. You may find it helpful to zoom in on your image while making detailed freehand selections. If you do not see a marquee indicating an active selection when you release the mouse or let up on the stylus, press the Close button on the Controls:Lasso palette. When the selection is complete, you will see its name appear in the Objects:Path List. Campbell created selections for every object in the drawing except the figure's head, neck and legs and the baseboard along the wall.

**3 Modifying the selected area.** The Lasso tool does not allow you to reshape your original selection outline, but you can add to or subtract from the currently *selected area* of your image. To add to the currently selected area, press the Add to Selection button on the Controls:Lasso palette. Drag with the Lasso to add a new selection marquee. To subtract from the currently selected area, press the Subtract from Selection button and drag with the Lasso tool to create a negative selection that will cut a hole in the currently selected area. Each new active selection will appear as an item in the Path List. It's often useful to group selections that

**4**

*Filling and fading within a selection*

**5**

*Adding a paper texture to the wall*

**6**

*Brushwork added to the face and skirt*

**7**

*Lighting within selections*

pertain to a particular object so that you can turn them on and off easily using the Enter key.

**4 Filling selections.** To tint each selection, yet allow the detail of the pencil sketch to come through, Campbell used a combination of Painter's Fill and Fade commands. To do this with an active selection, choose a color and then select Effects, Fill (Command-F). Select Current Color and click OK. Now choose Edit, Fade, and drag the Undo Amount slider until you get the transparency effect you want in the Preview window. Click OK. (You can eliminate the Fade step by adjusting the Opacity slider in the Fill dialog box.) Campbell faded his fills 30% to 50%.

**5 Adding effects.** Campbell used Surface Control to apply various paper textures to the skirt, the floor and the wall. To do this, start with an active selection and choose Effects, Surface Control, Apply Surface Texture. Choose Paper Grain from the pop-up menu and view the effect in the Preview window. If you want, you can choose a different paper texture from the Papers palette with this dialog box still open. Experiment with various settings and click OK.

**6 Adding brushwork.** To add detail and texture in the image, Campbell started by choosing Basic Paper texture. He used the Sharp Chalk (the marks on the skirt), the Artist Pastel Chalk (on the chin) and the Fat Stroke Airbrush (on the cheek).

**7 More effects.** Campbell turned the floor a deep red by filling the selection with red, fading it back, then choosing Effects, Surface Control, Dye Concentration, choosing Paper Grain from the pop-up menu and dragging the Maximum slider to 200%. To get

*A later version of the piece that Campbell imported back into Painter to apply effects overall and on individual selections*

the smooth gradations in the floor and wall, he selected Effects, Surface Control, Apply Lighting. He selected the Drama lighting effect and clicked OK.

**Will he ever stop?** To give the image a sense of motion, Campbell imported it into Photoshop and applied the Twirl filter to the entire file. He also applied the Motion Blur filter to the figure's head. 🖐

# Using Color Mask

**Overview** *Use Color Mask and Masking brushes to mask an area of an image; convert the mask to a selection; use Adjust Color to shift the color of the selected area.*

CTP/PHOTO: PHOTO DISC/FRACTAL DESIGN EXTRAS CD

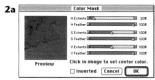

Isolating the center leaf using the Rectangular Selection tool in the original photo

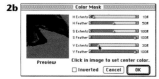

The default Color Mask dialog box

*Adjusting the sliders to isolate the leaf*

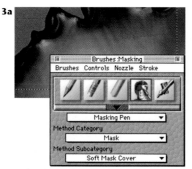

*Using the Masking Pen to clean up the mask*

COLOR MASK IS ONE OF PAINTER'S most powerful features, letting you create a mask based on a specific color in an image. In the example above, we used a combination of Color Mask and Masking brushes to create masks for individual leaves. We converted the masks to selections, then used Adjust Color to change the hue and saturation of the individual leaves and the background.

**1 Using the Rectangular Selection tool.** Open an image and decide which colored element you want to mask. To limit the extent of the mask, choose the Rectangular Selection tool from the Tool palette and drag a marquee around the subject you want to mask. This keeps "mask debris" from appearing throughout the entire image. (The technique of restricting the Color Mask to a selected area will not work with selection tools other than the Rectangular Selection tool. Also, don't click inside the rectangular marquee: it will turn the selected area into a floater.)

**2 Sampling color and adjusting the mask.** Choose Edit, Mask, Color Mask, then click in your image (*not* in the preview) on the color you want to sample (the "center color"); the arrow will momentarily turn into a dropper as you do this. We selected a color on the tan leaf in the center of the image. To narrow the range of selected colors, drag the H (Hue) Extents slider to the left (we set ours to 10%). Press and drag to scroll the image in the Preview window so you can see how your settings are affecting other parts of the image within the marquee. Experiment with the S (Saturation) and V (Value) Extents sliders; we got the best results when we reduced the V Extents to 30% to isolate the leaf from darker tan colors in the background water. You may also want to adjust the three Feather sliders to create softer transitions in your mask. When you're satisfied with the preview of your mask, click OK. Painter will generate a mask based on the sampled color.

**3 Cleaning up the mask.** To view the mask, click on the center Visibility (Eye) icon in the zoomed-out Path List palette. To edit

**3b**

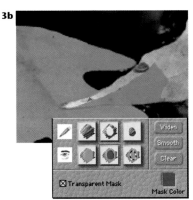

*Using a Masking Pen to erase the mask from an overlapping leaf. The Transparent Mask box is checked, making both the mask and the image beneath it visible.*

**3c**

*The finished mask of the center leaf*

**4**

*Opening the group after converting the mask representation selection to an outline selection*

**5**

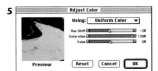

*Adjusting color within the center leaf selection*

the mask, first choose a Masking brush variant from the Brushes palette; we chose the Masking Pen. Choose black and paint on your image to add to your mask; paint with white to remove portions of the mask. The interior of your mask must be opaque to completely cover your subject, so unless you want some degree of transparency, use the Masking brush to paint over any thin spots.

You can make it easier to identify subtle overlapping color—in this example the tip of the leaf on the far right—by clicking the Transparent Mask checkbox in the Path List. This displays your mask at 50% opacity so you can see better during the "cleanup" process. When you're finished, click the checkbox again to view the mask at full opacity and give it another inspection.

As a final check for your mask, click on the far right Visibility button to turn the mask into a mask representation selection—the green marquee. The mask representation selection appears in the Path List as a green masking group. Open the group (click on the triangle to the left of its name); if you have a lot of items in the group, you may need to convert back to a mask (click the center Drawing and Visibility icons) and repair any holes in the mask with more Masking brush work. When you're finished, click on the far right Visibility icon again. Painter generates a new mask representation selection group that replaces the old one.

**4 Converting to an outline selection.** Converting the mask from pixel information to outline information will allow you to make another mask without losing your existing work. To do this, select the closed group in the Path List and press Enter. In your image, the green marquee will turn black.

**5 Colorizing with Adjust Color.** With the selection active, choose Effects, Tonal Control, Adjust Colors. Use this feature to change the hue and increase saturation in your selection. If you prefer more radical changes, you can also paint within your selection or apply any of the commands under the Effects menu.

**Making and storing multiple masks.** Repeat steps 1–5 to mask, convert and adjust other areas of your image. As an alternative to storing outlines in the Path List, drag them from your image into the Paths palette, which resides under the P. List pull-down menu on the Objects palette. The copy of the path in the Paths palette remembers its original location in your image; you can return it to that exact position by moving the path's icon to the front of the Paths drawer, then double-clicking on its icon on the front of the drawer. 🖌

# Isolating Color with Auto Mask

***Overview*** *Use Auto Mask to generate a mask based on a selected color; change the mask to a selection; fill the selection with a color.*

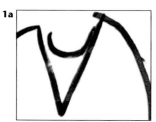

**1a**

*Detail of the Smooth Ink Pen sketch*

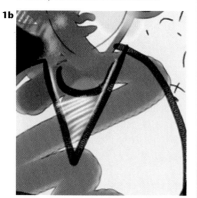

**1b**

*Adding multiple media to the sketch*

**1c**

*Woman 2 ready for Auto Mask*

LEVAN/BARBEE STUDIO

PAINTER'S AUTO MASK FEATURE IS A QUICK WAY to isolate an area of an image; once the mask has been created, you can fill the area with color or paint into it. Susan LeVan of LeVan/Barbee Studio did both while creating *Woman 2*, one in a series of paintings entitled *Woman: She Writes*. She used Auto Mask's Current Color setting to create jaggy white "halos" around the background scratch marks, giving her piece more lightness and air.

**1 Establishing the composition.** LeVan began a new document with a white paper color. She chose Basic Paper from the Papers palette, then used the Smooth Ink Pen variant of the Pens brush and a dark green color to sketch the basic shape of the image. (LeVan liked the Smooth Ink Pen for this job because it uses the same Brush Tip Profile—one that creates more dense color on the stroke edges—as the Water Color brushes she would use next.) She added color and form using various other media: transparent washes of purple, pale red, tan and gray with varying sizes of the Simple Water Color brush; soft color to the face and sweater with the Fat Stroke Airbrush variant; the Sharp Chalk on the sweater and fine lines with the 2B Pencil; the Soft Charcoal variant for the black background; and white highlights using the Ultrafine Eraser.

**2 Generating and viewing a mask.** To create a mask that would allow her to fill all white areas in her image, LeVan used Auto Mask's Current Color option. To do this, first sample a color from your image with the Dropper tool, making that color your Current Color. (LeVan clicked the Dropper on a white area in her image.) To generate the mask, choose Edit, Mask, Auto Mask (or

**2a**

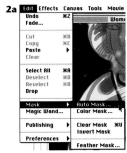

Selecting Auto Mask in the Edit menu

**2b**

Viewing the mask using the center Visibility icon in the Path List palette

**3**

Preparing to fill the masked area by viewing it as a mask representation selection

**4**

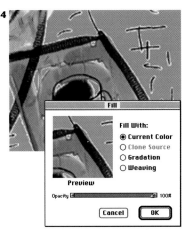

Filling the selection with orange, the Current Color

press Command-Shift-M), using Current Color and click OK. To view the mask, select the center Visibility icon (in the bottom row) in the zoomed-out Path List palette. In your image, you'll see all instances of the current color masked in orange.

Since Auto Mask using Current Color lacks the feathering capabilities of Painter's Color Mask (see "Using Color Mask" on page 94), you'll notice rough, aliased areas around the unselected portions of your image. LeVan liked these white "halos" because they accentuated the scratch marks on the background.

**3 Viewing the mask as a selection.** If you want to apply an effect to a masked area or fill it with a color, you must view it as a mask representation selection—the green marquee. (You can, however, use brushes to paint on an image while viewing it as a mask.) To change viewing modes, click on the far right Visibility icon in the Path List palette.

**4 Filling the selection.** To fill the mask representation selection with a color, first choose a color by sampling with the Dropper tool. (LeVan used the Dropper tool to sample an orange from the woman's sweater.) Then choose Effects, Fill, and when the dialog box appears, click the Current Color button and OK. The color you've chosen will fill the selected area. 🐾

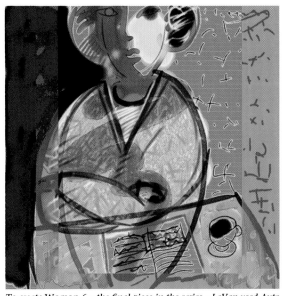

To create Woman 6—the final piece in the series—LeVan used Auto Mask on the left side of the image, then added blue strokes using the Large Chalk. She finished by pasting an earlier version on top of the image (as a floater) set to 50% Opacity.

■ To create the cheerful urban scene *Taxi* (above), **Susan LeVan** of LeVan/Barbee Studio began with a white background and made a loose drawing of the man, speech balloon and buildings using the Simple Water Water Color variant and the Smooth Ink Pen. After drying the Wet Layer (Canvas, Dry), she applied a mask to the white background with Edit, Mask, Auto Mask, using Current Color. She filled the background selection with an orange-tan color which left white "halos" around the existing color. The rest of the image was drawn with the Simple Water Color variant to give the piece a bleeding, watery look. LeVan set the street off from the rest of the image by sketching on it with a light gray Large Chalk using Rougher paper texture.

In *The Agreement* (right), LeVan created a black background using Edit, Select All and filling with black. She added multiple textures and contrasting, bright color to paint the two businessmen. LeVan used the Rectangular Selection tool to isolate the areas of both heads, inverted them using Effects, Tonal Control, Negative to create a boxy, digital look, then painted over the areas to soften the effect. As a last step, LeVan selected, copied and dropped the image into a larger file with a white background. She added rough edges with the Large Chalk and Grainy Water brushes.

■ For an interactive children's book commissioned by Josten's Learning, **Beth Shipper** started *Castle* (left) with a tight line sketch, then colorized the image using Water Color brush variants. She used the Lasso tool to isolate areas and applied various textures using Apply Surface Texture. To add a sense of depth to the image, she scaled up textures to use in the foreground and scaled them down for use in the background. Shipper increased contrast in her image and emphasized the texture using the Dodge and Burn brushes and the Ultrafine Bleach variant of the Eraser brush. Finally, she activated specific selections again, and applied low-opacity Airbrush strokes in saturated hues, taking care not to cover the texture.

■ The occasion of Richard Nixon's death was the inspiration for **Steve Campbell's** *Nixon and Checkers* (below), which "roughly depicts Checkers rescuing Nixon from Hell." Campbell built many of the larger shapes of the image in Adobe Illustrator, rasterized the file by opening it in Adobe Photoshop and added video grabs of images relating to Nixon and the Vietnam war. He then opened the file in Painter and used the Lasso tool to create new selections (like the infinity loop across the center) and to isolate the images he had added in Photoshop. He created several new textures using type and video grabs, then applied them within selections using Apply Surface Texture. The Apply Lighting command was used to emphasize the texture and add dimension. Campbell used only a small amount of brushwork with the Chalk and Airbrush; the piece was created almost entirely by applying effects within selections.

■ Although **Sharon Steuer** still works with traditional oils on canvas, she has used the computer as her primary illustration tool since 1984 because of its unlimited editing capabilities. *Eagle and Chick* (right) is one of a series of wildlife illustrations that Steuer created for a book proposal for the Smithsonian Institution. Starting in Macromedia Freehand, she drew the shapes that make up the larger eagle using the variable stroke Freehand tool and filled the shapes with colored gradients, then rasterized the file by opening it in Photoshop, where she roughed in the rest of the composition. Steuer opened the file in Painter and applied various lighting effects to the eagle. She used a custom Masking brush to paint masks (which she later turned into selections) for the sky, the water, the hills and the foreground grass. She worked within individual selections, applying lighting effects and painting with the Brush, Airbrush, and Dodge and Burn brushes to add detail and create a dramatic, sculptural look.

■ **James D'Avanzo** created *Deep Love* (right) using saturated, complementary colors to help communicate the powerful healing of love. To create the background, he used the Lasso tool, then feathered and painted into the selection to create the illusion of a horizon. He used the same technique for the hand and figure. D'Avanzo worked from background to foreground, painting into the selections with low opacity Thin Stroke and Fat Stroke Airbrush variants.

■ To create *Airbrush Head* (left), an illustration for her portfolio, **Nancy Stahl** began by importing EPS outlines of the woman and background from Adobe Illustrator into Painter. She resized the paths to fill her image. She loaded the Mountains texture from the Nature paper library and chose the Fat Stroke Airbrush, Grainy Soft Cover submethod. Working with one selection at a time, she used various sizes and opacities of the Airbrush to fill each selection with soft, textured color. Stahl edited one path to make a change to the woman's lower lip, then repainted that area.

■ **John Fretz** began *Man at Crossroads* (below), an illustration commissioned for an investment brochure, on conventional black-and-white scratchboard using a very fine croquill pen for the hatching and line work. He scanned the scratchboard art, opened it in Painter and used the Pen tool to make curved and straight line selections on the scan. Using a low-opacity Fat Stroke Airbrush, Fretz painted colored tints into the selections. He used the Scratchboard Rake variant of the Pens brush in various sizes to add color and texture to the image and to weave the traditional scratchboard pen work smoothly into the digital illustration.

# 5

# USING
# FLOATERS
# AND SHAPES

*This editorial illustration was created by Rick Kirkman for* Professional Speaker *magazine. He drew the shapes in Painter using the Pen tool and converted them to floaters, then added airbrush spray, texture and special effects to the floaters to add dimension to the image.*

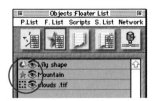

*Recognizing items in the Floater List: A shape is designated by a circle and triangle, an image floater by a star, and a reference floater by a dotted rectangle.*

FLOATERS AND SHAPES are elements that hover above Painter's background layer. These floating elements give you a lot of flexibility. You can move them without affecting the background layer and you can try multiple layout possibilities by repositioning the various elements. When they're exactly as you like them, you can drop them, blending them with the background canvas.

Painter 4 uses three types of hovering elements: *image* (or standard) *floaters, reference floaters* and *shapes*. The layering hierarchy of all three, as well as controls for organizing them (for instance, grouping and naming) are managed by the Floater List (described on page 106). Each floater or shape has a Composite Method that affects how it interacts (or blends) with the background and with other floaters and shapes. To preserve floaters and shapes, save your file in RIFF format.

To create an *image floater*, you can float any portion of your image background—including freehand selections made with the Lasso, Bézier paths drawn with the Pen tool and converted to selections, images with masks, and so on. Like the background layer, an image floater includes an 8-bit mask layer that accompanies the 24-bit image, so you can blend images with exciting transparency effects.

You'll want to use *reference floaters* if you regularly assemble large images from several separate source files. A reference floater is a 72 ppi screen proxy (or "stand-in"), for a standard floater in the current image, or for a placed image that exists outside of the document. Converting an image floater temporarily to "reference state" allows you to do rotation, skewing and other transformations much more quickly than if Painter had to manage the full-size original.

*To create this poster comp we layered Helvetica Black Condensed type shapes, scaled to various sizes over a colored background. To quickly view a variety of color combinations, we used Painter 4's interactive Shape Attributes dialog box. Select the Fill (or Stroke) color square in the dialog box. (Make sure the checkbox is checked.) When you click on a new color in the Color palette, the color of the selected type shape will update in your image. Drag the Color Ring and watch the color of the shape change.*

---

### USE THE OPTION KEY TO COPY

If you don't hold down the Option key when you click with the Floater tool, you'll leave a hole behind where your image used to be. Occasionally this is desirable, but most of the time you'll want the Option!

*Floating a selection without using the Option key*

---

### READY TO COLLAPSE

If you're finished making changes to a group of floaters but you still want to keep the group floating, consider using the Collapse button in the expanded Floater List. This feature merges a selected group of floaters into a single floater and can be a real memory-saver.

---

*Shapes* are essentially a resolution-independent type of floater; they combine paths displayed as a series of anchor points, straight lines and curves with attributes such as stroke, fill and transparency. Shapes and their attributes are Postscript objects. But if you paint on a shape, adding pixel information, it stops being a shape and becomes an image floater.

Image floaters and shapes take up extra disk space and RAM (see Chapter 1). You can work around this, though. Float only what's necessary, and drop and combine floaters when possible.

## WORKING WITH IMAGE FLOATERS

Make an image floater by clicking on an active selection using the Floater Adjuster tool. This process cuts the selected area out of the background layer and floats it. Option-click to float a copy of an active selection or to duplicate a floater. This leaves the original selection in place and floats a copy. All elements pasted into a Painter document come in as floaters, and you can also drag a floater from the Floaters palette into your image.

### FLOATER TOOL SHORTCUT

You can use the Rectangular Selection tool to float an area that you've selected with that tool: Move the crosshair cursor over the just-selected area (the crosshair changes to a pointer) and click. Option-click to float a copy.

Here's how to work with floaters once you've created or imported one:

**To paint or to apply an effect to an image floater**, make sure it's selected by clicking on it with the Floater Adjuster tool or by selecting its name in the Floater List palette. (If no floaters are selected, your strokes or effect will be applied to the background.) To deselect the floater, use the Floater Adjuster tool to click on the background or in the blank area below the floater's name in the Floater List.

**To move an image floater**, click and drag on it with the Floater Adjuster tool. To adjust a floater's position a screen pixel at a time, click it with the Floater Adjuster and use the arrow keys on your keyboard.

**To drop an image floater** onto the background, select it and click the Drop button in the Floater List. If you want to drop all of your floaters—much like Photoshop's Flatten Image command—click on the Drop All button. Another option is to choose File, Clone; a duplicate of the image will appear with floaters dropped.

**To scale, rotate, distort or flip an image floater**, click it with the Floater Adjuster and choose the appropriate command under Effects, Orientation.

**To change the opacity or the feathered edge of an image floater**, choose the Floater Adjuster tool and reset the values in

If you'll be making several adjustments to a single floater—like rotating it several times until you get the angle you like—you need to know that the quality of an image floater degrades with every rotation. Consider converting the floater temporarily to a reference floater by selecting it and choosing Effects, Orientation, Free Transform. Rotate the floater under reference as many times as you like without loss of quality. When you arrive at the angle you like, choose Effects, Orientation, Commit Transform.

*A selected reference floater has a yellow-and-white striped bounding box with eight handles.*

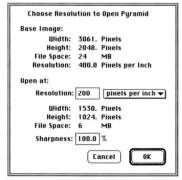

*Opening a pyramid file using a new resolution*

the Controls:Adjuster palette. Turn to page 113, "Backlighting 3D Text," to see an example of feathered floaters.

## USING REFERENCE FLOATERS

If you work with large images and your computer slows to a crawl when you try to reposition a big floater, consider converting it to a reference floater. Reference floaters let you manipulate faster-moving 72 ppi proxy images in real time, instead of dragging huge 300 ppi images around your screen. To temporarily convert a floater in your image to a reference floater, select it and choose Effects, Orientation, Free Transform. Because you are working with a proxy—and not the original—you can perform multiple rotations, scaling, and skewing very quickly without

loss of quality. When you have all of your images in place, convert reference floaters back to image floaters.

**To make a reference floater**, select a floater in your image and choose Effects, Free Transform. You can also import a reference floater (an outside image with its mask, if you like) into your working file using File, Place.

**To scale a reference floater proportionately**, press the Shift key and drag on a corner handle to adjust the size as many times as needed to get just the result you want.

**To rotate a reference floater intuitively**, press the Command key and drag a corner handle.

**To skew a reference floater intuitively**, press the Command key and drag a side handle.

**To scale, skew or rotate a reference floater numerically**, choose Effects, Orientation, Set Transform and type specifications into the fields.

**To turn a reference floater back into an image floater**, choose Effects, Orientation, Commit Transform, or paint or apply an effect to the reference floater, or drag it into a Floater library.

**Using the pyramid data structure.** Painter's pyramid data structure is a way of getting the best possible speed and quality out of a reference floater. When you ask Painter to build a pyramid file, it creates a file that includes several sizes of the image. (If you're familiar with Kodak's PhotoCD file format, you can think of a pyramid file as a similar, but more flexible structure.) Painter uses the multiple versions stored in the pyramid file to calculate when you perform a resize (Canvas, Resize). We made a comparison, importing a hi-res reference floater into a composite image

*These type shapes were set in Painter using the Text tool. We specified color fills using Set Shape Attributes, and used Saturation and Multiply composite methods to blend colors where the shapes overlap.*

and also importing the same image that had been saved as a pyramid file. Because the pyramid file was saved with multiple resolutions already calculated, when we chose File, Place, it loaded much faster, and any rotations and scaling that were applied to the pyramid file were achieved with better quality. To build a pyramid data structure, save an existing file in Pyramid file format (File, Save As), or import an image as a reference floater and check the Create Pyramid checkbox.

## WORKING WITH SHAPES

Shapes can be drawn using any of the Shape Design tools, or made from a selection (converted from a selection using the Objects: P. List, Convert to Shape command), or imported from a Postscript draw program such as Adobe Illustrator (this process is described in Chapter 4).

Before modifying a shape, you need to select it. There are three ways to select shapes: The first selects the entire shape and displays a bounding box with a black-and-yellow striped border with eight handles around its edges; the second also selects the entire shape, but displays anchor points without a bounding box. These first two selection methods allow you to duplicate, move or transform the shape. The third method displays the Bézier path with its anchor points and handles and permits manipulation of the path.

**To drag off a copy of a shape**, select the shape with the Floater Adjuster tool, press Option and drag.

**To duplicate, move or transform a group of shapes**, select the group with the Floater Adjuster tool.

**To move an individual shape within a closed group**, click on the shape with the Whole Shape Selection tool and drag the shape; or move it using the arrow keys.

**To move a shape within an open group**, click and drag it with the Floater Adjuster tool.

**To scale a shape proportionately**, press the Shift key and drag a corner handle.

**To rotate a shape**, press the Command key and drag a corner handle.

**To skew a shape intuitively**, press the Command key and drag a side handle.

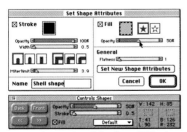

*Setting the opacity of the shape fill in the Set Shape Attributes dialog box (top), and the corresponding Controls:Shapes palette (bottom), which is visible when the Floater Adjuster tool is selected*

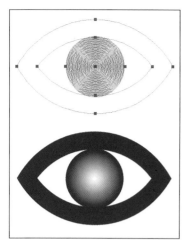

*Viewing shape paths (top) and finished objects (bottom). To create this filled compound outer object with blended interior object, we first made a compound of the two outer shapes by selecting them both with the Whole Shape Selection tool and choosing Shapes, Make Compound. (The compound cuts a hole with the smaller eye shape, allowing only the outer fill to be visible.) The interior blue circle was blended with a very small white circle in its center, by selecting both circles, then choosing Shapes, Blend and specifying 50 steps.*

*This Floater List palette helped Rick Kirkman organize nearly 100 shapes and floaters while creating the editorial illustration on page 111.*

**To scale, distort, rotate or flip a shape**, select it and use one of the choices found under Effects, Orientation.

**To transform a duplicate of a shape**, use the commands under the Shapes menu. Set up specifications in the Set Duplicate Transform dialog box. When you choose Shapes, Duplicate, the transformation will be applied to the copy.

**To modify the stroke and fill attributes of a shape**, select it and choose Shapes, Set Attributes, or double-click on the name of a shape in the Floater List to open the Set Shape Attributes dialog box (or highlight its name and press Enter).

**To change the fill or stroke of a shape to the current color**, chosen while using the Shape Attributes dialog box, click in the Stroke or Fill color field and click on the color ring in the Color palette. (This method selects the current color without displaying the color wheel.) A word of warning: If you paint on, or apply an effect to a shape—rather than simply changing its stroke and fill—it will be automatically converted into an image floater. When this happens, shape attributes are lost.

**To blend between shapes.** Here's a useful application for Painter 4's new Blend command: If you've imported an image created in Illustrator that has blends and they don't make the transition successfully into Painter, zoom-in and delete the interior objects inside the blend using the Direct Selection tool. Select the two outside objects, choose Shapes, Blend and specify the number of steps to regenerate the blend.

**To make a compound.** To cut a hole in a shape and reveal the underlying image, make a compound using two shapes: Place a small shape on top of a large one, select both of them, and choose Shapes, Make Compound. The top shape will cut a hole in the bottom shape to reveal the underlying image. Compounds are made automatically to create counters in letters when the type is set or type outlines are imported.

**To apply automatic drop shadows.** Selecting a closed group of shapes and choosing Effects, Objects, Create Drop Shadow will apply an automatic drop shadow to each of the individual shapes in the group, and will convert the shapes to image floaters as well!

## ORGANIZING FLOATERS AND SHAPES

In the Floater List palette, Painter assigns sequential names to floaters and shapes (such as Floater 1, Floater 2 and so on) in the order they were created. *Rename* them by double-clicking on a name (or select the name and press the Enter key) to bring up the appropriate Attributes dialog box. Enter the name and click OK. *Grouping* floaters is an ideal way of connecting related elements—for instance, grouping a floating image and its drop shadow. To group floaters or shapes, Shift-select the elements in the Floater

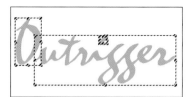

For this restaurant logo, we drew black calligraphy letters using the Calligraphy variant of the Pens brush. We made a luminosity mask using Edit, Mask, Auto Mask, then converted mask representation selections to shapes (Objects, P.List, Convert to Shape). The client planned to use the logo in a variety of ways, so it made sense to build the logo with compound shapes that could be layered easily over other images (or converted easily to selections). To make counters transparent in the letter "O," the two descending "g" shapes and the "e," we selected each individual counter and compounded it with the outer shape, then compounded the other letters in the same way. (For best results, create only one compound at a time.) The selected compounded filled shapes (top), and the logo applied onto Koa wood (bottom).

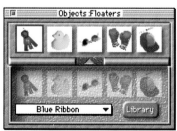

Create an empty Floaters palette by choosing Objects, F. List, Floater Mover. You can fill it with floaters while you're in that dialog box, or open it via the Library button in the Floaters palette. Drag floaters from your image directly into it, or drag floaters out of the Floaters palette into another image.

List and click the Group button (or press Command-G). If you want to apply effects (other than Scale and Create Drop Shadow) to a group of floaters or shapes, you'll need to open the group, select individual items, then apply the effect. If you're working with a lot of layered items in a document, *hide* floaters or shapes by clicking to close the Eye icons next to their names, so that you can more easily work with underlying items. Click the Eye open to show an item again. For the ultimate in floater grouping and management, see how Rick Kirkman did it in "Organizing Floaters in an Illustration" on page 118.

**Floaters palette.** To store floaters for later use or for use in another document, drag them into the Floaters palette. Hold the Option key if you want to leave a copy in your document. For a look at Rhoda Grossman's innovative use of the Floaters palette, turn to page 117, "Putting Floaters to Work."

> ### A HIDDEN RASTERIZER
>
> You can rasterize Postscript art from Illustrator (without complex blends and masks) in Painter. Choose File, Acquire, Adobe Illustrator file. Select the shapes and convert them to floaters using Shapes, Convert to Floater. Use the Drop button on the expanded Floater List palette to flatten the image. And a bonus: Outlines (from the shapes) are dropped to the canvas and appear in the Path List, should you need to use them as selections.

> ### REALIGNING IMAGE FLOATERS
>
> If you want to be able to return a floater to its precise original position, *before* you move it double-click on its name (or select the name and press the Enter key), to bring up the Floater Attributes dialog box. Name the floater, including in the name the information in the Top and Left boxes. When you want to return the floater to its original position, double-click on its name and enter the recorded values in the fields. Click OK, to return the floater to its original position.
>
>

## FLOATERS AND THEIR MASKS

Just as the background has an 8-bit mask layer (see Chapter 4's introduction), floaters have an 8-bit mask layer that allows for transparent effects. If you float an area that contains a background mask, you also float that portion of the background mask. You can also create masks directly on a floater, using either Masking brushes or automatic mask-generating commands (Edit, Mask, Auto Mask/Color Mask). View a mask on a selected floater using Mask Edit mode (Canvas, View Mask). To read about painting with Masking brushes on floaters, turn to page 115, "Melting Text Into Water."

**Importing a reference floater with its mask.** Because it's faster to work with small files than to manipulate large files, many

We made a luminosity mask in the cloud image source file and imported the reference floater with its mask into the composite image—creating semi-transparent clouds over the letters.

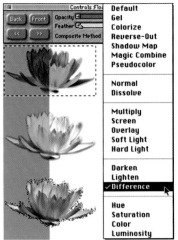

We applied three of Painter's Composite Methods (borrowed from Photoshop's blending modes) to these three lilies floating over a green-and-white background. The top lily uses Difference; the middle one uses Luminosity; and the bottom one uses Dissolve.

artists assemble source files, then import them into a final composite file. Consider preparing a mask in a smaller source file that you plan to import as a reference floater (using File, Place). In the Place dialog box, check the Retain Mask checkbox, and click OK to place the reference floater in your document.

## DROPPING A FLOATER MASK

If you want to drop a floater and its mask layer, check the Drop with Mask checkbox in the expanded Floater List palette. If there is already a background mask in your image when you drop a floater and its mask, the two masks will be combined. Clear the background mask first (Command-U) if you want only the dropped floater's mask to appear on the background mask layer.

## PAINT IT, BLACK

A good analogy to help you remember whether to use black or white with a Masking brush, at least when the upper right Visibility icon is selected in the Floater List, is to think of using white as an eraser on the mask and black as applying paint to the mask. To actually view and edit the floater mask in black-and-white (using Mask Edit Mode), select the floater and choose Canvas, View Mask.

## COMPOSITE CONTROLS

Painter's composite controls can give you nifty special effects with very little effort. With a floater and the Floater tool selected, choose from the Composite Method pop-up menu in the Controls palette. The scrolling list includes Photoshop's blending modes underneath Painter's native ones. The opposite page shows all of the Composite Methods in action.

## WORKING WITH PHOTOSHOP

If you save your Painter 4 image with floaters in Photoshop 3.0 format, Photoshop will open it and translate the floaters to layers. The opposite is also true: Photoshop layers open as floaters in Painter. Here are a few pointers:

• When Photoshop encounters a Painter native Composite Method (like Pseudocolor), it converts that layer to Normal.

• A Photoshop document made up of transparent layers only— that is, without a Background layer—opens in Painter as floaters over a white background.

• If a document contains floaters that extend beyond Painter's live image area, and that document is opened in Photoshop, areas outside of the live area will be permanently clipped.

• Shapes cannot be imported into Photoshop with their object-oriented information intact—saving a file with shapes in Photoshop 3.0 format converts shapes to Photoshop layers, which appear in the Layers palette using the compositing (blending) method you specified for the shapes in Painter. ◆

## FLOATER MASK VISIBILITY

You can use the top row of Visibility buttons in the zoomed-out Floater List palette to determine which part of the floater is masked. To see how they work, drag a floater out of the Floaters palette onto a colored background. Since the floaters in the Floaters palette have had masks already created for them, in the zoomed-out Floater List palette, the Masked Outside (the top right Visibility button) should be active, meaning that everything in the floater outside of the mask is invisible. To reverse the effect, click the top center Visibility button. Now the masked area is invisible and the surrounding area is visible. To see both areas, click on the top left Visibility button. Keep in mind that these modes affect visibility only; any painting or effect applied to the floater will be applied to the entire floater, not just the visible areas.

## IMAGE MASK VISIBILITY

To see how the Image Mask Visibility buttons work, start with any image in the background and create a mask for it by choosing Edit, Mask, Auto Mask, Paper Grain, and choose Ciphertext from the Painter Textures library. Click OK. (Press Shift-5 to see the mask, Shift-4 to return to the image.) Now drag a floater from the Floaters palette into your image and enlarge it (so you can see the effects better) using Effects, Orientation, Scale. In the expanded Floater List palette, choose the bottom center Visibility button. The background mask will be visible within the shape of the floater's mask, taking its color from the floater. Click the bottom right Visibility button to see the background mask within the shape of the floater's mask using the background color. Experiment with the use of Masking and non-Masking brushes on both background and floater.

## A VISUAL DISPLAY OF THE COMPOSITE MODES

We applied a different Composite Method (from the Controls:Adjuster palette, with the Floater Adjuster tool selected) to each of these leaves floating over a two-part background. The Default and Normal methods give the same results, as do Shadow Map and Multiply. For complete descriptions of what the modes are doing, refer to Painter's *User Guide, The Photoshop 3 Wow! Book* or Photoshop's *User Guide.*

*Default / Normal*

*Gel*

*Colorize*

*Reverse-out*

*Shadow Map / Multiply*

*Magic Combine*

*Pseudocolor*

*Dissolve*

*Screen*

*Overlay*

*Soft Light*

*Hard Light*

*Darken*

*Lighten*

*Difference*

*Hue*

*Saturation*

*Color*

*Luminosity*

# Dropping a Shadow

***Overview*** *Convert a shape to a floater and fill the floater; make the shadow by copying the floater, filling the copy, feathering it and reducing its opacity.*

**1**

*Background modified with Apply Surface Texture and Apply Lighting*

**2**

*Converting the pasted shapes into a floater*

**3**

*Filling the fish floater with a color*

**4a**

*Filling the shadow floater*

**4b**

*Controls palette settings for the shadow floater in the finished art*

THERE ARE A NUMBER OF WAYS to create a drop shadow in Painter; here's one that uses floaters, feathering and transparency.

**1 Preparing a background.** Create a new document: Ours was 788 pixels wide with a tan background. To add a "cave wall" appearance, in the Art Materials:Paper palette choose the Rock paper from the Nature library. Select Effects, Surface Control, Apply Surface Texture using Paper Grain, and experiment with the settings until you get a look that you like. Click OK. To create a spotlight effect, choose Effects, Surface Control, Apply Lighting. Choose Side Lighting, lower the distance and spread settings and increase the brightness. Click OK.

**2 Importing and converting.** You can float any active selection or convert any shape to a floater. For this image, we imported fish drawn in Adobe Illustrator. With both Illustrator 6 and Painter 4 running, we copied the fish from Illustrator to the clipboard and pasted them into the cave wall image in Painter. Objects that have holes cut in them in Illustrator, such as the openings in the fish, or letters such as "O" or "A" converted to outlines, will import into Painter as compound shapes. Select the shape with the Floater Adjuster tool and choose Shapes, Convert to Floater.

**3 Filling the floater.** To apply a fill to the floater, choose a color from the Art Materials:Color palette, then select Effects, Fill, Current Color (100% Opacity) and click OK.

**4 Creating the shadow.** Use the Floater Adjuster tool to duplicate the floater to use for the shadow. Hold down the Option key, click and drag on the floater, and release when the copy is slightly offset from the original. In the Floater List, double-click on the copy's name (or press the Enter key) and rename it "shadow;" then drag its name below the original floater's name. Fill the shadow as you did in step 3, using black or a dark color sampled from the background image. In the Controls:Adjuster palette, lower the Opacity setting to make the shadow more transparent, and increase the Feather setting to soften the shadow's edge.

# Working with Shapes and Floaters

***Overview*** *Draw Bézier shape paths in Painter; fill and name the shapes; convert the shapes to floaters; paint details on the floaters with brushes; apply textured special effects with Color Overlay and Glass Distortion.*

**1**

*Kirkman's pencil sketch*

**2**

*Dragging with the Direct Selection tool to adjust a control handle on a path*

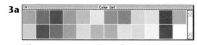

**3a**

*The custom magazine color set*

RICK KIRKMAN

SHAPES BRING NEW POWER to Painter, saving many illustrators a trip to a draw program to create Bézier paths for import. With the expanded Pen tool (now similar to Illustrator's), you can completely create and edit Bézier paths—add a stroke and fill, name them—and organize them in the Floater List. After you draw shapes, you can convert them to floaters and add paint and special effects. Rick Kirkman created the above illustration—one in a series of editorial illustrations for the "Ideas That Work" column in *Professional Speaker* magazine—entirely within Painter.

**1 Setting up a template.** Kirkman began by scanning a client-approved pencil sketch and saving it as a TIFF file. He opened the scan in Painter and cloned it (File, Clone).

**2 Creating shape paths.** Working in the clone (with the original clone source image still open), Kirkman turned on tracing paper (Command-T) and traced his sketch, using the Pen tool to draw Bézier shape paths. To make adjustments on the fly while drawing a path with the Pen tool (like adjusting a control handle or anchor point), press the Command key to temporarily switch to the Direct Selection tool. To create your outlines, work either

### WHERE'S THE PATH?

If you switch from the Pen to another tool (such as the Brush), and your paths seem to disappear, choose the Pen, the Whole Selection or Direct Selection tool or a Shape Edit tool to see them again.

**3b**

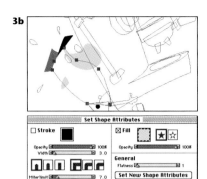

*Preparing to fill the selected Head shape with a flesh color (selected here using the Whole Shape Selection tool)*

**3c**

*The layered floaters in the Floater List*

**4**

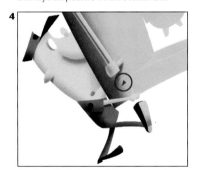

*Shading the left side of the machine (under the long stem) using the Spatter Airbrush*

**5**

*Detail showing the filigree design*

in Painter or in a Postscript drawing program. If you plan to trace a template—as Kirkman did—set up shape attributes so that you can draw with a precise skeletal line. Choose Shapes, Set Attributes, and uncheck the Fill and Stroke checkboxes.

**3 Coloring, naming and converting.** Kirkman built a Color Set containing favorite basic colors for the series of magazine illustrations. (Read more about color sets in Chapter 2.) To name and add a colored fill (or stroke) to a shape, double-click on its name in the Floater List. Rename the shape in the Set Shape Attributes dialog box and check the Fill checkbox. With the Fill field active, click in the Color palette, or click a color in your Color Set to update the color in the Fill field. After he had filled shapes with basic colors from his color set, Kirkman Shift-selected them in the Floater List and chose Shapes, Convert to Floater.

**4 Shading individual floaters.** To paint on an individual floater, select it in the image with the Floater Adjuster tool. To create a nice grainy look—similar to colored pencil on kid-finish illustration board—Kirkman chose Basic paper texture and added shading to the machine and clothing using the Spatter Airbrush variant, switching between the Cover and Buildup methods (Brushes palette). He also added strokes with the Fat Stroke Airbrush for a smoother look on the skin and eyes.

Layering the floaters helped Kirkman visualize how the cast shadows would fall. For example, to paint the shadow under the gauge and long stem, he deselected them and selected the underlying machine body floater and airbrushed directly on it.

**5 Adding details and texture.** To see the template as he drew the delicate filigree design, Kirkman temporarily reduced the opacity (Controls:Adjuster palette) of all the floaters. Then, using a tiny Feather Tip Airbrush variant, he added the dark gold and white filigree design to the sides and nozzle of the espresso machine and carefully painted the black notches on the gauge.

To create the subtly textured blue background, Kirkman selected the floater and applied a blue color with Effects, Surface Control, Color Overlay using Paper Texture and Dark Cork texture from the Sensational Surfaces CD-ROM. Before applying a second application of Color Overlay (using a greenish-gray color), he checked the Invert Grain checkbox in the Paper palette. Next, he added a swirly, marbled effect to the colored background using Glass Distortion and Nature Spots (Wild texture library). To build the textured edge of the soft, irregular background shape, he created a luminosity mask (Edit, Mask, Auto Mask) on the background floater, feathering the mask to 16 pixels. He switched to Mask Edit mode (Canvas, View Mask) and applied Express Texture using Paper Texture to the floater mask only, with Halftone 2 texture from the More Paper Textures library. Finally, he dropped all floaters (Drop All button, Floater List).

# Backlighting 3D Text

**Overview** *Set type shapes and convert them to selections and floaters; layer floaters over backlighting to create a 3D effect with type.*

1a

*Choosing a yellow fill in the Set Shape Attributes dialog box*

1b

*Dragging on a top handle with the Floater Adjuster tool to scale a letter shape taller*

1c

*Selecting the shapes in the Floater List*

2

*The backlight floater and shape group*

TODAY'S MULTIMEDIA AND PRINT DESIGNERS need quick, unique solutions for titles, and Painter is just the tool for the job. To create a glowing 1920s Art Deco effect for *Gatsby*, a title comp, we applied a number of effects to each of four layered type floaters.

**1 Setting up the file and creating the type.** This technique's glowing effects require a feather setting larger than the 16-pixel "factory" default. To change the setting, choose Edit, Preferences, General and type 50 (the maximum allowed) in the Floater pre-feather box. For the change to take effect, you'll need to quit the program and relaunch it. Once the program is up and running, create a new file (ours was 788 pixels wide) with a black background. (Neon looks best at night!)

In preparation for creating the yellow backlight floater—and in order to see the text easily as we typed, scaled and kerned it—we set Shape Attributes to a yellow fill. To specify a colored fill, choose Shapes, Set Attributes, click once on the color fill square and click on a yellow color in the Color palette. Click OK. In the Set Shape Attributes dialog box, check the Fill checkbox.

You can create type shapes using Painter's Text tool, or import type outlines from a Postscript drawing program. Choose a typeface with thick, even strokes. We set type in Painter and used 90-point Monoline Script, scaling the "G" taller and narrower and kerning the letterforms tighter. To scale a letter shape, select the Floater Adjuster tool and drag on a side handle. To kern individual letter shapes in Painter, select a shape in the Floater List (or click on it with the Floater Adjuster tool) and use the arrow keys to move it horizontally. When you've finished kerning, Shift-select all the shapes and group them by clicking the Group button in the zoomed-out Floater list palette, or by pressing Command-G.

**2 Duplicating and converting the shapes.** To create the first of the four floaters that will serve as a crisp-edged backdrop for the neon effect to follow, we began by making a duplicate of the closed shape group. To duplicate the type shapes, choose the Floater Adjuster tool, press the Option key and click on the selected type shape group. With the duplicate selected, choose

**3a**

*Darkening the text via Dye Concentration*

**3b**

*Applying a second pass of Surface Texture*

**3c**

*Using Color Overlay to quiet the hot spots*

**4**

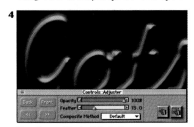

*Creating a 15-pixel first glow*

**5a**

*The hierarchy of items in the Floater List*

**5b**

*Creating a 45-pixel soft red glow*

Shapes, Convert to Floater. Double-click on the floater's name in the Floater List palette (or press Enter) and rename it "backlight." Toggle the Eye icon shut to hide the yellow floater to protect it from being selected in the next step.

Next, convert the original yellow shapes to outline selections. (When you float an outline selection, you can repeatedly change the feather setting without loss of quality because the feather refers to the outline when it rebuilds.) Select the Floater Adjuster tool, close the shape group, and choose Shapes, Convert to Selection. (As of this writing, the group name will be left in the Floater List while the outlines move to the Path List.) Shift-select the outline selections and group them by clicking on the Group button in the expanded Path List. Close the group, and press Enter to activate it. Choose the Floater Adjuster tool and Option-click on the selections to float them. You'll see your new floater appear in the Floater List. Name the floater "text."

**3 Building a third dimension into the text.** To create a convincing 3D effect, set the feather (Controls:Adjuster palette) for the text floater to 8, choose a bright red and fill it (Command-F). Now choose Effects, Surface Control, Apply Surface Texture, using Mask. Set Picture to 100%, click the top Light Direction button and click OK. Darken the type floater by choosing Effects, Surface Control, Dye Concentration, using Image Luminance. Set both Maximum and Minimum settings to 225% and click OK.

To make the letters "pop" even more, again choose Effects, Surface Control, Apply Surface Texture using Mask. Set Picture to 80%, Shine to 100%, click the top left Light Direction button and click OK. (Switching from the top to the top left button gives the effect of multiple light sources.) Next, apply a transparent tint of color to the text floater to tone down the hot spots. Choose a gold color and select Effects, Surface Control, Color Overlay, using Image Luminance and Hiding Power at 100% Opacity.

**4 Creating the first glow.** A soft glow close to the type helps increase the illusion of neon. Start by Option-clicking the text floater using the Floater Adjuster tool (making a third floater), then rename it "top text." Reselect the text floater (it should be underneath the top text floater in the Floater List palette), and make the glow by giving it a 15-pixel feather in the Controls: Adjuster palette.

**5 Creating a soft background glow.** Make a fourth floater (it will become a red background glow) by Option-clicking on the top text floater. Rename it "soft glow," and drag it beneath the other items in the Floater List. Choose a warm red color, fill the floater (Command-F), and set the Feather slider to 45 pixels.

**Offsetting the top text.** To complement the lighting, activate the top text floater and use the arrow keys to move it 3 screen pixels down and 3 to the right (while viewing at 100%).

# Melting Text into Water

*Overview* Use the Text tool to set text shapes over a background; convert the shapes to selections; float two copies of the text; use feathering and Dye Concentration to add dimension to the type; paint with Masking brushes to "melt" the bottoms of the floaters.

**1**

*Selected text shapes on the background and in the Floater List palette*

**2a**

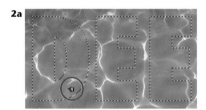

*Option-clicking with the Floater Adjuster tool on the text selection to make the two floaters*

**2b**

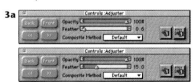

*The Floater List palette after naming the two floaters*

**3a**

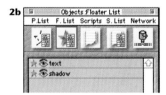

*Feather settings in the Controls:Adjuster palette for the text (top) and shadow floaters*

YOU CAN ACHIEVE A DRAMATIC TRANSLUCENT EFFECT using Painter's Masking brushes to partially remove the mask layer of a floater. In the image above, we used a Masking Airbrush on the lower part of two floaters—the text and the feathered shadow behind it—to create the illusion of type melting into water. You can get a similar result using a background of clouds, stone or wood.

**1 Setting type shapes and converting to selections.** Open an image to use as a background; our photo was 3 inches wide and 225 pixels per inch. Choose the Text tool and select a font in the Controls:Text palette. We chose 90-point Futura Extra Bold Condensed. Click in the image and begin typing. If the Floater List palette is open, you'll see each letter shape appear as you type. Use the Floater Adjuster tool to select individual letterform shapes and use the arrow keys on your keyboard to kern the type. To achieve the result in the above image and use the text outlines to float portions of the background, it's necessary to convert the text shapes to selections. With the Floater Adjuster tool chosen, choose Shapes, Convert to Selection. The text shapes will disappear from your image and will reappear as black-and-white animated marquees; and they'll move from the Floater List to the Path List.

**2 Using selections to make floaters.** To turn the type selection into the two floaters needed for this technique, choose the Floater Adjuster tool, press the Option key and make two separate clicks on the active text selection. (Holding the Option key makes a copy of the selection, leaving the background intact.) Open the Floater List palette. You'll see two items named Floater, followed by a number. Double-click on the top name (or select the name and press the Enter key) and rename it "text" in the Floater Attributes dialog box. Do the same for the floater below it, naming it "shadow."

**3 Distinguishing the floaters.** Use feathering and Dye Concentration to make the floaters stand out from the background

**3b**

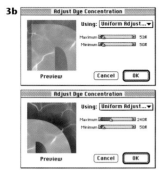

*Using Dye Concentration to lighten the text (top) and create the shadow*

**4**

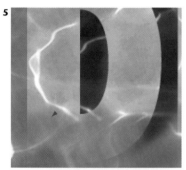

*Skewing the shadow to add a look of depth*

**5**

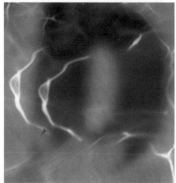

*Using the Masking Airbrush variant on the text floater (top) and the shadow floater (with the text floater hidden) to reveal the underlying image*

and from each other. In the Floater List palette, click once on the text floater to make it active. Set the Feather slider in the Controls:Adjuster palette to 0.6 to slightly soften the text's edge, then choose Effects, Surface Control, Dye Concentration, using Uniform Adjustment and drag the Maximum slider to 53%. Click OK. To create a soft, saturated shadow, select the shadow floater in the Floater List. In the Controls:Adjuster palette, set the Feather slider to 15. Again choose Dye Concentration, and this time experiment with setting the Maximum slider to a high value (we chose 240%). When you like the result you see in the Preview window, click OK. A dark shadow should now surround the lightened type.

**4 Offsetting the shadow.** Give a greater illusion of depth to the type by nudging the shadow up and to the right using the up and right arrow keys on your keyboard. If you want to make the type appear to stand at an angle to the background, as we did, skew the shadow. Select the shadow floater and choose Effects, Orientation, Distort. Drag the top center handle of the bounding box down and to the right, check the Better box (if you don't mind waiting a little longer) and click OK. There's no preview of this effect, so it may take a few tries to get the look you want.

**5 Painting into the floater masks.** To "melt" the lower portions of the letterforms into the water, use a Masking brush to partially erase the mask layer of both the text and shadow floaters. Choose the Masking Airbrush variant of the Masking brush, and reduce its opacity in the Controls palette to 10% for more sensitivity. Choose white in the Color palette, select the text floater in the Floater List and begin brushing along the bottom of the letterforms. The lower part of the text floater will begin to disappear, revealing the shadow floater. Complete the effect by choosing the shadow floater in the Floater List and brushing along its bottom, revealing the background.

You may find it easier to work on the shadow without seeing the text floater. To temporarily hide the text floater, select it in the Floater List and click to shut the Eye icon next to its name. When you're done, click the Eye icon open again.

If you erase more of the text or shadow than you'd like, you can recover the mask by choosing black and painting back into the area you want restored. Painter won't restrict your restoration to the inside of the type, however, so you'll need to change to a smaller brush size. (Choose the Brush Controls:Size palette from the Controls pull-down menu on the Brushes palette, and adjust the Size slider.) With your smaller brush, work carefully to keep from restoring portions of the mask outside of the letterforms. Sometimes it's easier to start over with a fresh mask by clicking on the Restore button in the expanded Floater List.

# Putting Floaters to Work

***Overview*** *Drag items into the Floaters palette to store them; drag them out to start your image; use brushes to unify the elements.*

RHODA GROSSMAN

*Grossman's portfolio of facial features*

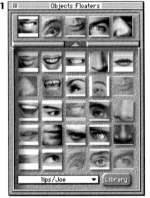

*The reference photo (left); floaters positioned on top of the photo's clone*

*Sampling color and painting on the image*

RHODA GROSSMAN'S CARICATURES—usually created on the spot at trade shows—begin with scanned bits of faces that she enhances with freehand painting. Her traveling Floaters palette holds 5 MB of facial features.

**1 Building the palette.** Create a new, empty Floaters palette by choosing Objects, F. List, Floater Mover, clicking on the New button and naming your palette. Open the new palette by clicking on the Library button in the current Floaters palette (Objects, F. List, Floaters). To add a floater to the palette, select an area of an image, choose the Floater Adjuster tool, and Option-click to copy the selected area. Drag the selected copy into the Floaters palette.

**2 Starting with floaters.** Drag items from the Floaters palette into a new document and arrange them. For *Portrait of Joe,* above, Grossman started with a photo of her subject. She cloned it (File, Clone), then deleted the image from the clone (Command-A, Delete key). She chose Canvas, Tracing Paper, enabling her to use the photo to position the floaters. She dragged a mouth and two eyes from the palette, resized and positioned them, then dropped each one (Drop button, Floater List) when she was satisfied.

**3 Painting and smudging.** Grossman used the Dropper tool to sample color from the imported images to paint the rest of the portrait. She used a variety of brushes, then smudged color with the Grainy Water variant of the Water brush. As a last touch, she used Effects, Surface Control, Apply Surface Texture to enhance several areas of the portrait.

# Organizing Floaters in an Illustration

***Overview*** *Import Postscript outlines into source files in Painter; convert shapes to selections; float each selection and fill each one with a flat color; paint details on floaters with brushes; copy and paste finished floater groups into a final composite file.*

RICK KIRKMAN / © 1995 BIC CORPORATION

**1**

*Kirkman's Paths palette, containing five groups of outlines*

**2a**
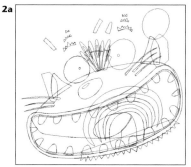

*Outlines for the BICtopus head in the source file*

**2b**

*The Floater List for the head source file*

PAINTER'S FLOATERS OFFER GREAT FLEXIBILITY—you can change any detail without affecting the rest of the image. In addition, Rick Kirkman takes advantage of the ability to organize and group floaters: Every element in his "BICtopus" character (featured on the BIC Pen Back to School campaign poster) is a floater, even the pen caps!

**1 Beginning the illustration.** Create several groups of outlines either in Painter or in a Postscript drawing program. Kirkman started by scanning a client-approved pencil sketch of the BICtopus. He opened the scan as a template in Adobe Illustrator and traced it with Bézier curves. Since the illustration was complex—the head alone, for instance, consisted of nearly 50 separate outlines—he split the drawing into five parts to make it easier to work with: the head, the body, the base (or "earth"), and the right and left arm groups. He imported each group of outlines into Painter (as shapes) using File, Acquire, Adobe Illustrator file and converted the shapes to selections using Shapes, Convert to Selection. Using the Selection Adjuster tool he dragged each group into the Paths palette and named it (double-click on the existing name).

**2 Making floater groups.** Drag a group of outlines from the Paths palette into a new file. To float the group, Option-click with the Floater Adjuster tool. Rename the floating item in the Floater List palette (by double-clicking on its name).

Kirkman saved time by working with the groups separately in four smaller source files, rather than dragging all of the selections into a final, full-sized

> **SAVE TIME AND SPACE**
>
> If you're working on a file that involves several source images with imported Postscript outlines, you'll save time and disk space by converting the shapes to selections and storing the outlines in a Paths palette instead of storing them as floaters.

**3a**

| Color 1 | Color 2 | Color 3 | Color 4 | Color 5 | Color 6 | Color 7 |
| Color 8 | Color 9 | Color 10 | Color 11 | Color 12 | Color 13 | |

*Kirkman's custom Color Set*

**3b**

*Using the Fat Stroke Airbrush to shade the flat color fills*

**3c**

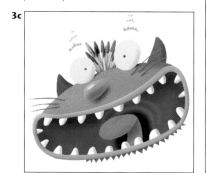

*The finished shaded head, after Kirkman applied Surface Texture*

**4**

*Adjusting the feather for the throat rings*

**5**

*Grouped floaters in the final composite*

image for floating and organizing. He created a new document just large enough for the head outlines, and dragged them from the Paths palette into the new file. Kirkman started the floating process with the smallest outlines and moved to the larger ones, since once the larger outlines are floated, it's difficult to float the smaller selections. (Painter thinks that you want to use the Floater Adjuster tool to move the larger floater, not float other selections.)

**3 Coloring and shading.** To color individual floaters, choose a name in the Floater List and select Effects, Fill, Current Color. Restack floaters by dragging them up in the Floater List to move them forward, or down to move them back. Paint on the floaters to add color, texture or dimension.

Kirkman created a marker comp of the image to help visualize color. He built a Color Set based on the colors in the comp and used the comp as a reference while he filled the floaters with color. Kirkman used the Fat Stroke Airbrush and Feather Tip Airbrush variants to add dimension to the floaters. He also added a bumpy texture to the orange face floater with Effects, Surface Control, Apply Surface Texture using the Basketball paper texture from the Wild Textures library at 65% of its original size (using the Scale slider on the front of the Papers palette drawer).

Layering the floaters helped Kirkman visualize how the shadows would fall. To paint the shadows under the whiskers and nose, for example, he selected the face floater and airbrushed strokes directly on it. The whiskers and nose were unaffected (since they were deselected floaters), and since they were floating above the face, they served as a kind of mask that gave a crisp edge to the brush work by hiding any excess airbrush spray.

**4 Adjusting opacity and feather.** To change the Opacity or Feather of a floater, select it with the Floater Adjuster tool and adjust the appropriate setting in the Controls:Adjuster palette. Kirkman decreased the opacity of the eyebrows farthest from the head. He applied a feather of 24.1 to the black throat hole and 13 to the surrounding throat rings.

**5 Pasting floater groups into the final file.** Group individual floaters by Shift-selecting them in the Floater List and clicking the Group button. Copy the group (Command-C), open a new file (Command-N), and paste (Command-V). Kirkman gave his new document a black background color. It was large enough to contain the entire illustration—24.5 x 28 inches at 75 ppi. He copied and pasted the groups of floaters from his five files into this composite image. At first he dropped only the "earth" to the background (using the Drop button in the Floater List) so he could make finishing touches to the image while the groups were still floating—such as adding a shadow on the body under one of the arms. He dropped all floaters (Drop All button, Floater List) before preparing the file for output. ✍

# Adding Dimension to Flat Color

**Overview** *Create basic colored shapes in a Postscript drawing program; rasterize the files in Photoshop; open the files in Painter and create selections using the Magic Wand; float the selections and position the floaters in a new document; paint on the floaters.*

BEN BARBANTE

*Filling shapes with flat color in Illustrator*

*Opening the Illustrator file in Photoshop*

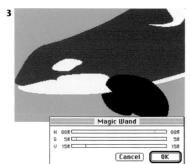

*Clicking or dragging with the Magic Wand creates an orange area that becomes an outline selection. You can fine-tune the coverage by clicking and dragging on the individual H, S and V bars.*

BEN BARBANTE RELIED ON THE FLEXIBILITY of floaters to create *Orcastration*, and used the Airbrush, Dodge and Burn brushes to transform flat color shapes into a silent, mysterious environment.

**1 Preparing shapes in Adobe Illustrator.** Use a Postscript drawing program to create the individual elements of the image. Barbante scanned a pencil sketch and opened it as a template in Illustrator. He drew and colorized the basic shapes for each element of the scene: a large and small whale, the foreground water, the water surface, the rocks, and the foreground and background trees. He copied each element and pasted it into its own file.

**2 Rasterizing files with Adobe Photoshop.** One of the definitions of *rasterize* is to turn draw-based images (like EPS files) into pixel-based ones. This is a handy way to retain the color of art created in a drawing program, especially if the objects contain masks and complex blends that do not currently import into Painter 4 successfully as shapes. Barbante rasterized each image in Photoshop at 200 ppi, then flattened and saved each one as a PICT file for opening in Painter.

**3 Creating selections with the Magic Wand.** Barbante used Painter's Magic Wand to create selections for each of the individual files. Open one of your files and choose Edit, Magic Wand. Click with the Magic Wand tool in an area of flat color, or drag to select a wider range of color. The dialog box will show values for Hue (H), Saturation (S) and Value (V) as you drag. Release to display the selected pixels in the current mask color (the default is orange). When you are satisfied with your selection, click OK. The orange area will become a selection group.

The Path List, showing positive and negative Wand selections for the large whale

Adding form with the Dodge and Burn brushes

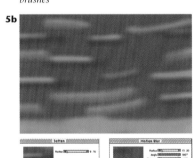

Softening and blurring the water

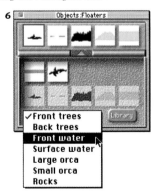

Making and storing floaters

**4 Naming the selections.** To see the individual elements in the selection group, open the Objects:Path List palette. You'll see your selection group named "Wand Group" followed by a number. To rename each selection in the group, open the group and double-click on each "Wand Selection" in turn. Type a name when the dialog box appears and click OK. Barbante turned a few selections negative—such as the white patches on the whales—by toggling the Plus button (to the left of its name) to a Minus in the Path List. This allowed him to protect those areas from his brushwork. (Areas completely surrounded by the Magic Wand selection—like the orca's eye patch—automatically appear in the Path List as negative selections.)

**5 Building volume in the shapes.** Make a selection active by clicking on the dotted circle icon to the left of its name in the Path List. Use the Dodge brush to lighten areas within the selection and the Burn brush to darken areas. Barbante used these brushes to create an illusion of dimension by shading or tinting areas of color in each of the separate files. To blend colors in the images, he temporarily switched off selections by choosing the left Drawing (Pencil) icon in the expanded Path List palette, then painted with the Just Add Water variant of the Water brush and a low Opacity setting (Controls:Brush palette). Barbante created texture on the water's surface by painting horizontal streaks of varying shades of green using the Pencils brush, Colored Pencils variant, Cover method and Soft Cover submethod. To blur the streaks he used Effects, Focus, Soften and Effects, Focus, Motion Blur.

**6 Floating and storing the selections.** When you've finished painting on the images, float and store each of them for later use. Start by creating a new, empty Floaters palette: Choose Objects, F. List, Floater Mover. Click on the New button, then name your palette, click Save and Quit the Floater Mover. Open the Floaters palette (Objects, F. List, Floaters), click the Library button and choose your palette. To store the elements in the Floaters palette, make sure that the selection is active only for the items you want grouped as a floater. Make any negative selections positive—unless you want the image to have a hole in it when it's floated. Choose the Floater Adjuster tool, hold down the Option key (to leave your original intact), click on the item in the document and drag it into

**USE COLOR MASK**

The Magic Wand is the fastest way to select an area of flat color, but Edit, Mask, Color Mask allows you to feather between colors using Hue, Saturation or Value, giving a soft-edged mask.

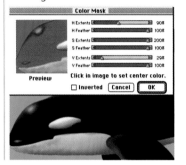

**7**

*Painting the sky using a low-opacity Fat Stroke Airbrush*

**8**

*The Floater List palette with all floaters*

**9**

*Revealing a portion of the large whale using Colored Pencils, Soft Mask Cover submethod*

**10**

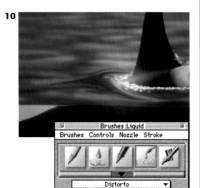

*Pushing the water with the Liquid brush, Distorto variant*

the Floaters palette. Name it when prompted. Barbante used this method on each file to create a new Floaters palette.

**7 Preparing the background.** Create a new document into which you'll drag all of the floaters. Barbante created a 16 x 20-inch image at 200 ppi (a 49 MB file) with a white background color. He painted a sky on the background using the Fat Stroke variant of the Airbrush with low opacity (Controls:Brush palette) and large size (Brushes palette, Controls, Brush Controls:Size palette).

**8 Arranging and painting on the floaters.** Drag items one by one from the Floaters palette onto your background image. After they're in place, use the Floater List palette to bring items forward or back in the composition: Click on an item's name and drag it up the list to move it forward or drag it down to move it back. Barbante dragged a copy of each of the elements from the Floaters palette onto his background image. He dragged an extra copy of the background trees and two additional copies of the small whale, scaling and positioning all elements to match his original Illustrator layout.

Barbante selected each floater in turn and painted on it. He added detail on the rocks using the Colored Pencil variant, Cover method, Soft Cover submethod. He used that brush as well as the Feather Tip variant of the Airbrush to pull individual trees out of the solid blocks of color. He created the background haze with the Dodge brush and the Feather Tip Airbrush variant.

**9 Using a masking brush to reveal hidden elements.** To make the large whale's fin and back appear to break the water's surface, Barbante began by dragging a second copy of the water's surface from the Floater palette, placing it atop the original surface and the whale, but below the background whales. He selected it with the Floater Adjuster tool and adjusted the opacity of the copy to 50% using the Controls:Adjuster palette. This allowed him to see the part of the back and fin hidden by the water's surface. He selected the Colored Pencil variant in the Mask method, Soft Mask Cover submethod. He chose white in the Color palette and began "erasing" the water that covered the back and fin, revealing more of the whale as he proceeded. To correct any errors, he switched to black to "paint" the water back in.

**10 Adding finishing touches.** With all of the elements in position, Barbante dropped the floaters (the Drop All button in the expanded Floater List). This enabled him to more easily blend the edges of the various elements. He used the Distorto variant of the Liquid brush to create the bow waves in front of each whale and the fin reflections of the smaller whales. Barbante drew the white foam around the edges of the whales and the puffs of mist coming from the blowhole using the Feather Tip variant of the Airbrush.

E N T R O P Y

■ **Jeff Brice** began *Entropy*—an exploration of the similarities between manmade objects and nature—by selecting images from his photo archive. As a backdrop for these, he scribbled purple, beige and other hues (sampled from the photos) on the background using the Oil Paint Brush variant. He smudged colors using various Water brushes, then added more color using the Chalk and Water Color brushes with Medium paper texture.

In Photoshop Brice created masks for the photos. His masks are quite complex and frequently include gradients. The main bone image, for instance, has a gradient mask that allows the background to show through the less important areas. He also created a gradient mask for the flower image to make it blend more smoothly with the surrounding elements.

In Painter Brice positioned the floaters using the Default Composite Method in the Controls:Adjuster palette. When the arrangement was complete, Brice selected Drop All from the Floater List. He sampled dark colors from the image and used the Large Chalk variant—with very low Opacity and Grain settings (Controls palette)—to apply two custom textures that he had previously scanned: a crackled texture (applied to the instrument, skull and horns) and a crumpled-paper texture (to fade and blend the edges of the images). Finally, he created drop shadows on the sign and behind the instrument by making selections with the Lasso tool, then using the Fat Stroke Airbrush variant inside the selections.

For *Meteor Man* (above), **John Dismukes** of Capstone Studios began with a tight visualization of the typography on paper. The pencil sketch was scanned and used as a template in Macromedia Freehand to create Postscript outlines. The team at Capstone extruded the outlines in Adobe Dimensions and opened them in Painter using File, Acquire, Adobe Illustrator file. Dismukes converted the shapes to two floaters (the two words), by Shift-selecting the letter shapes in each word and choosing Shapes, Convert to Floater. He used the Thin Stroke and Fat Stroke Airbrush variants to illustrate the entire image.

To create the *Miami Dolphins program cover* (right), Dismukes began with a composition sketch, then built the graphic elements and typography using Freehand and Letraset Letrastudio (now the Envelopes plug-in filter for Freehand). All elements were brought into Painter as selections via File, Acquire, Adobe Illustrator file and converted to floaters. Dismukes painted on individual floaters using the Thin Stroke and Fat Stroke Airbrush variants. He applied texture to the background using Effects, Focus, Glass Distortion.

■ **Chet Phillips** creates his illustrations with the Scratchboard Tool variant of the Pens brush, then floats the art using the Gel Composite Method and uses an Airbrush to colorize the background. (See page 21 for a step-by-step description of his technique.) When he's finished colorizing, he drops the floater and adds more effects.

For *Lighthouse* (left), Phillips used the Text tool to create letter shapes, then rotated, resized and filled them with color. He used Shapes, Convert to Selection to create selections that he could use to modify the background image. With all text selections active, he clicked and dragged (without the Option key) with the Floater Adjuster tool to offset the letters slightly from the background, leaving a white "shadow" around the lower right side of each letter.

Once the colorizing for *Fractured Runner* (below) was complete, Phillips used the Pen tool to select curved areas. After activating the selections, he copied and pasted them into a new, blank image with the same dimensions as the original. Once all of these floaters were in the image area, he moved some forward and others back, dropped several of them and used the Fat Stroke Airbrush along the outside of the remaining floaters to give the image a greater feeling of depth. Finally, Phillips created smaller triangular floaters one at a time, and used Effects, Tonal Control, Brightness/Contrast to adjust the value of one, dropping it, and then creating, adjusting and dropping the next, and so on.

# ENHANCING PHOTOS

*We used several features to enhance this portrait: We painted with Masking brushes to isolate the dancers; and to create a shallow depth of field, we used Effects, Tonal Control, Adjust Colors to desaturate the background and Effects, Focus, Soften to blur it.*

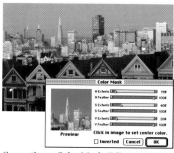

*Generating a Color Mask (Edit, Mask) for the sky in this photo helped to quickly isolate it from the buildings. We used the Big Masking Pen variant to remove masked areas in the photo's foreground that were also selected with the command.*

ALTHOUGH PAINTER BEGAN as a painting program, the features that have been added over the years have turned it into a powerful image processor as well. So when it comes to achieving painterly effects with photographs, Painter has no peer. If you're a photographer, a photo-illustrator or a designer who works with photos and you want to get the most out of Painter, you'll want to pay attention to the following areas.

**The Effects Menu.** Most of Painter's image-altering special effects can be found in the Effects menu. The features under the subheads Tonal Control, Surface Control and Focus are loaded with creative promise for the adventurous digital photographer.

**Selections and Masks.** To alter only a portion of an image, you'll need to become acquainted with Painter's shape paths, selection and masking capabilities. If you're not familiar with the Pen and Lasso tools, turn to "Working with Bézier Paths and Selections" and "Working with Freehand Selections" in Chapter 4.

Painter's powerful automatic masking features—Under Edit, Mask—give you a big jump on the tedious process of creating masks to isolate parts of your image. And since any of Painter's speedy brushes can be turned into Masking brushes (by changing their method to Mask), you can create custom Masking variants to finish the job. For an in-depth look at combining automatic and painterly masks, turn to Chapter 4, "Using Color Mask."

**Floaters.** Chapter 5 gave you a look at creative techniques using floaters; this chapter focuses on using floaters and Masking brushes for photo-compositing and other effects—for example, in "Creating a Montage Using Masks and Floaters" on page 141, and in "Selective Colorization" on page 132.

*Correcting the tonal range in an overexposed image using Effects, Tonal Control, Equalize*

*We applied Micro Grain (from the More Wild Textures libary) to this photo with Dye Concentration using Paper Texture with the Maximum slider set to 200%.*

*A classic solarization, created by merging positive and negative clones of the same image. The purple tone was added with Effects, Tonal Control, Color Overlay.*

**Cloning.** Although newcomers to Painter may have difficulty seeing the value of cloning (File, Clone), many Painter veterans wouldn't do without it. Among other benefits, cloning lets you make multiple copies of an image, alter each of them, then re-combine them in various ways while preserving access to the original. Several of the techniques described in this chapter use this or another kind of cloning method.

## IMAGE-PROCESSING BASICS

With its strong focus on *creative* image manipulation, Painter has left some *production*-oriented tasks such as color-correcting CMYK images to Adobe Photoshop. But there's no need to move an image from Painter to Photoshop to perform the basic image-processing tasks, because Painter has tools that can be set to emulate many of Photoshop's.

**Equalize.** Choosing Effects, Tonal Control, Equalize (Command-E) produces a dialog box with a histogram similar to Photoshop's Levels dialog box—except that the image is automatically equalized (an effect similar to clicking on the Auto button in Photoshop's Levels). Move the triangular sliders toward the ends of the histogram to decrease the effect.

**Stripping color from an image.** There are several ways to turn a color image into a grayscale one in Painter. The quickest way is to desaturate the image using the Adjust Colors dialog box. Choose Effects, Tonal Control, Adjust Colors and drag the Saturation slider all the way to the left.

**Changing color.** While you're using the Adjust Color dialog box, experiment with the Hue Shift slider to change the hue of all of the colors in an image (or a floater or a selection). You can get greater control in altering specific colors (turning blue eyes green, for instance) by using Effects, Tonal Control, Adjust Selected Colors. Click in the image to select a color, then drag the Hue Shift, Saturation and Value sliders at the bottom of the dialog box to make the changes. Fine-tune your color choice and the softness of its edge with the various Extents and Feather sliders.

**Adding film grain.** Photoshop's Noise filter is a good way to emulate film grain. To get a similar effect in Painter, choose a fine paper grain—like Fine Grain or Synthetic Super Fine from the More Paper Textures library—and select Effects, Surface Control, Dye Concentration. Scale the texture in the Papers palette until the grain in the Preview window is barely visible—try 50% as a starting point. Try minor adjustments to the Maximum and Minimum sliders in the Adjust Dye Concentration dialog box.

**Creating a shallow depth of field.** By softening the background of an image, you can simulate the shallow depth of field

*Using Effects, Focus, Glass Distortion and Fleece paper texture (Weaves library) to add a brushstroke look to this succulent image*

*Using Effects, Surface Control, Express Texture to get the effect of a line conversion using a straight-line screen*

*The original photo of a kelp frond had strong contrast, giving good detail for this embossing technique (created on a clone of an image using Effects, Surface Control, Apply Surface Texture with 3D Brushstrokes).*

that you'd get by setting your camera at a low *f*-stop. Select the area you want to soften, feather the selection (in the Controls: Adjuster palette) to avoid an artificial-looking edge, then choose Effects, Focus, Soften.

**Smudge and Blur tools.** To get an effect similar to Photoshop's Smudge tool, choose the Just Add Water variant of the Water brush, varying Opacity (in the Controls: Adjuster palette) between 70% and 100%. For a more radical effect, try the Distorto variant of the Liquid brush. To emulate Photoshop's Blur tool, use the Just Add Water variant set to a very low opacity (under 10%).

**Retouching.** The Straight Cloner or Soft Cloner variants of the Cloners brush works like Photoshop's Rubber Stamp tool in Clone Aligned mode; use the Control key like you would Photoshop's Option key to sample an area (even in another image), then reproduce that image (centered at the point of sampling) wherever you paint.

## ADVANCED TECHNIQUES

To get cool effects in-camera or in the darkroom, it frequently takes a lot of time, trial and error. Some third-party plug-in filters do an adequate job of replicating these effects, but Painter gives you more control than you can get with filters alone.

Here's a short guide on how to use Painter to re-create traditional photographic techniques, starting with simpler, in-camera ones and progressing to more esoteric darkroom maneuvers.

**Motion blur.** You can use the camera to blur a moving subject by using a slower shutter speed, or you can blur the background by panning with the subject. Check out "Simulating Motion" on page 133 to see how to "paint" a blur on an image.

**Lens filters and special film.** To re-create in-camera tinting effects achieved with special films (like infrared) or colored filters, use Effects, Surface Control, Color Overlay. If you want to mimic the effect of a graduated or spot lens attachment (partially colored filters), choose a gradation and fill your image (Effects, Fill) with the gradation at a reduced opacity. (You may need to add contrast to your image afterwards with Effects, Tonal Control, Equalize.)

We posterized this Craig McClain photo using a Color Set of "desert" colors and Effects, Tonal Control, Posterize Using Color Set.

### CREATING A VIGNETTE

To get a soft-edged look around an image, begin by using the Oval Selection tool to encircle your subject. In the Controls palette, set a high Feather value—we used the maximum 50-pixel setting for the 450-pixel-wide image below. (Keep in mind that in Painter, the feather extends equally on the inside and outside of the selection.) Cut or Copy your image and paste it into a new document with a white background (to fade the edges of the photo to white, as below) or a black background (to fade to black).

**Shooting through glass.** By selecting Effects, Focus, Glass Distortion, you can superimpose glass bas relief effects (using a paper texture or any other image) on your photo. A small amount of this feature adds texture to an image; larger amounts can make an image unrecognizable! Turn to page 144 to see Phil Howe's work with Glass Distortion.

**Lighting effects.** Use Painter's Apply Lighting feature (under Effects, Surface Control) to add subtle or dramatic lighting to a scene.

**Multiple exposures.** Whether created in camera (by underexposing and shooting twice before advancing the film) or in the darkroom (by "sandwiching" negatives or exposing two images on a single sheet of paper), it's easy to reproduce the effect using floaters or clones in Painter.

**Solarization.** Painter's Express Texture (Effects, Surface Control) command is a great way to re-create darkroom solarization. Read about a Painter version of a "classic" solarization on page 138.

**Line screen.** Instead of developing your image in the darkroom onto high-contrast "line" or "lith" paper, try getting a similar effect in Painter. Choose a lined paper texture from the Simple Textures library or make your own using the Make Paper Texture dialog box found under the Paper pull-down menu on the Art Materials palette. (Read more about the Make Paper Texture feature in Chapter 7's introduction.) Next, choose Effects, Surface Control, Apply Screen, using Paper Grain to get a two- or three-color effect with rough (aliased) lines. Or try Effects, Surface Control, Express Texture, using Paper Grain to get more subtle control and smoother, anti-aliased lines. Turn to "Toning with Textures," on page 136 to read about using Express Texture to apply colored, textured effects to an image.

**Posterizing an image.** Like other image processors, Painter lets you limit the number of colors in your image via posterization. Choose Effects, Tonal Control, Posterize and enter the number of levels (usually 8 or fewer). You can get creative effects by creating a Color Set (see "Capturing a Color Set" in Chapter 2) and selecting Effects, Tonal Control, Posterize Using Color Set. This is a great way to unify photos shot under a variety of conditions.

**Embossing and debossing.** To emboss an image, making its light areas "pop up," choose File, Clone; then Select All and delete, leaving a blank cloned image. Now choose Effects, Surface Control, Apply Surface Texture and choose 3D Brush Strokes from the pop-up menu. To get a debossed look—where light areas recede—use the Original Luminance pop-up menu choice. Images with a lot of contrast give the best results, and busy images work better if less important areas are first selected and softened using Effects, Focus, Soften. 🖌

# Putting Type Over a Photo

***Overview*** *Set headline type shapes and adjust their opacity; draw a rectangular shape and use it to lighten an area of your image to make the body copy on top of it more readable.*

**1a**

The settings in the Set Shape Attributes dialog box

**1b**

Scaling a shape group proportionally by Shift-dragging on a corner handle

**2**

Option-clicking on the active type selections to float a copy

**3**

Positioning the text bar using the Floater Adjuster tool

**4**

Reducing opacity of the floater and shape

PAINTER OFFERS MANY TECHNIQUES to make text and other objects stand out against a background. Here's one of our favorite (and fastest) methods, applied to a comp for a magazine layout.

**1 Preparing the type.** Open your photo and select the Text tool. Choose a typeface from the pop-up menu in the Controls: Text palette (we chose Isadora Bold). To automatically fill the type shapes with white as you set them, choose white in the Color palette and check the Fill checkbox in the Set Shape Attributes dialog box. Then click in your image and type your headline. Kern individual letterforms or groups by selecting them and using the arrow keys to move them. After you've kerned the letters, group the letters in each word to make them easy to select and reposition as a unit. Shift-select the letters in the Floater List palette and Group them (Command-G.) When you're finished, use the Floater Adjuster tool to move or scale the type shape groups. If your letters don't overlap, skip the next step and on go to step 3.

**2 Making Adjustments.** Our script letter shapes had overlapped when kerned and the overlap area looked too white when we reduced the opacity of the shapes (see step 4). To fill the letters evenly and hide the overlap, we converted the shapes to selections (Shapes, Convert to Selection) and Option-clicked on the selections to float a copy. Next, we filled the selected copy with white (Command-F).

**3 Adding the text bar.** We wanted to be able to reposition the text bar to try out different layout options, so we drew a white-filled rectangle with the Rectangular Shape tool. After drawing your rectangular shape, use the Floater Adjuster tool to move or resize it.

**4 Adjusting the opacity.** Finally, get the "screened back" look by Shift-selecting the items in the Floater List and lowering the Opacity slider in the Controls:Adjuster palette. We set ours to 45%.

# Creating a Sepia-Tone Photo

***Overview*** *Use gradation features to tint a color or black-and-white image; adjust the image's contrast and saturation.*

**1a**

*The original photo*

**1b**

*Choosing the Sepia Tones gradation*

**2**

*Applying the Sepia Tones gradation*

**3**

*Adjusting the contrast*

*Neutralizing the browns*

TYPICALLY FOUND IN IMAGES CREATED at the turn of the century, sepia-tones get their reddish-brown color cast in the darkroom when the photographer immerses a developed photo in a special toner bath. You can use Painter's gradation and tonal control features to quickly turn color or grayscale images into sepia-tones.

**1 Tinting the image.** Open a grayscale or color photo. Select the Art Materials:Grad palette and click on its pushbar to open the drawer. Select Sepia Tones from the pop-up menu. Choose Express in Image from the Grad pull-down menu on the Art Materials: Grad palette. (Read more about gradations in Chapter 2.) Your image will now be tinted with shades of brown. (You can also use a similar procedure to turn a color image into grayscale, but make sure the back and front Color rectangles in the Colors palette are black and white, respectively, and choose Two-Point in the Grad palette.)

**2 Adjusting the white and black points.** If you're working with an image that has poor contrast, you can adjust the white and black points by choosing Effects, Tonal Control, Equalize (Command-E). When the dialog box appears, the image will be automatically adjusted so that its lightest tones are pure white and its darkest ones are pure black. The automated contrast was too dramatic for our taste, so we decreased contrast by dragging the white point slider to the right to 22.7 and the black point slider to the left to 91.3. We also lightened the image by dragging the Brightness slider to 47.2 and clicked OK.

**3 Desaturating the image.** We wanted to emulate the mild tinting effect usually used for traditional sepia-tones, so we desaturated the image using Effects, Tonal Control, Adjust Colors, dragging the Saturation slider to the left to -45. Experiment with the Saturation slider until you see just the effect you want in the Preview window and click OK. 👋

# Selective Colorization

***Overview*** *Open a color photo and float a copy; desaturate the floater; paint with a Masking brush to erase the floater mask and portions of the underlying color photo.*

CTP / JB / PHOTO: PHOTO DISC

*The original color image*

*Using the Adjust Colors dialog box to desaturate the floater to black-and-white*

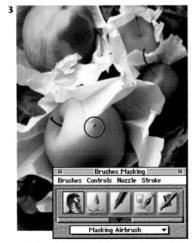

*Painting on the floater's mask to reveal the color image underneath*

IF YOU WANT TO FOCUS ATTENTION on a particular element in a color photo, you can turn the photo into a black-and-white image and then selectively add color back into it for emphasis. Here's a way to use Painter's floaters and Masking brushes to "paint" color on an image.

**1 Floating a copy of the image.** Open a color photo and choose Edit, Select All (Command-A). Choose the Floater Adjuster tool, hold down the Option key and click on the image. This creates a floater with the exact dimensions of the original image.

**2 Desaturating the floater.** Now use the floater to make the image appear grayscale: Choose Effects, Tonal Control, Adjust Colors, and drag the Saturation slider all the way to the left.

**3 Revealing color in the underlying image.** To allow parts of the color image to show through, use a Masking brush to erase portions of the floater's mask. In the Brushes palette, choose the Masking Airbrush variant of the Masking brush and choose white in the Color palette. As you erase the mask on the floater in the area you wish to colorize, the color will appear. If you want to turn a color area back to grayscale, choose black from the Color palette and paint on the area.

## FINE-TUNING YOUR MASK

It's difficult to tell if you've completely covered (or erased) areas when working on a mask with a Masking brush. To view the mask in black and white, switch to Mask Edit mode by choosing Canvas, View Mask. Choose any brush, and paint directly on the mask to clean up areas. (Black creates an opaque mask; pure white, no mask; shades of gray, a semi-transparent mask.) To switch back to Color View, click the Mask View icon (black circle) above the right scroll bar.

*Painting on the floater mask using Mask Edit mode*

# Simulating Motion

**Overview** *Create three clones of an image; add Motion Blur to two of the clones; use a Cloner brush to "paint" the blur onto the third, untouched clone.*

JB / PHOTO: PHOTODISC

**1a**

The original PhotoDisc image

**1b**

Arranging the clones on-screen for easy viewing

**2**

Adding Motion Blur to one of the clones

**3**

Adding blur with the Soft Cloner variant

CREATING A SENSE OF MOVEMENT on a subject *after* the film is out of the camera is easy with Painter's Cloners brush. We blurred two clones of an image, then "painted" the blur to a third, untouched clone of the original. The benefits of this method over applying effects to selections are that you can control the amount of the effect with brush pressure, you can simultaneously add effects other than a blur (such as lighting and texture) and you have easy access to your original image to restore any errors. The disadvantage: Working with big, multiple clones requires lots of RAM.

**1 Making multiple clones.** Open a photo. Choose File, Clone three times; this creates three clones (for a total of four images) on your screen. Size and move them so you can see all four at once; temporarily hide the palettes if you need to (Windows, Hide Palettes or Command-H). Save the clones, naming them "Blur," "Blur Heavy," and "Composite."

**2 Blurring the clones.** Select the Blur clone and choose Effects, Focus, Motion Blur. To get a moderate blur on our 1200-pixel-wide image, we set Radius to about 30, Angle to 64°, Thinness to 1%. (You'll want to experiment with different Angle settings for your particular image.) Click OK. Now select the Blur Heavy clone and repeat the process, increasing the Radius to about 60.

**3 "Painting" the blur.** To add a blur to selected parts of the Composite clone, first select the Soft Cloner variant of the Cloners brush and reduce its Opacity in the Controls:Brush palette to 13%. Select the Composite image. Choose File, Clone Source, and choose Blur. In the Composite image, begin painting where you want to give a sense of motion. To show more motion in some areas of your image (in ours, the red scarf), choose File, Clone Source, and Blur Heavy, then paint in the Composite image. To restore an area that you don't want blurred, make your original image the Clone Source and paint on the area of the Composite image that you want restored. 🖌

# Blending a Photo

**Overview** *Open a photo and clone it; use the Just Add Water variant to smear pixels in the image; restore a portion of the original with the Soft Cloner variant.*

ANDREW HATHAWAY

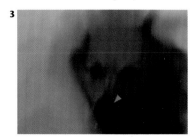

*Hathaway's original photo of the dogs*

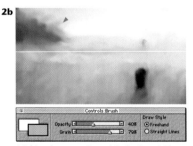

*Choosing the Just Add Water variant*

*Making loose strokes with the Just Add Water variant at 40% opacity*

*Partially restoring the dog's face using the low-opacity Soft Cloner variant*

TO CREATE THE EXPRESSIONISTIC *DOGS OF THE SURF*, Andrew Hathaway used Painter's Water brush to paint directly onto a clone of one of his photographs, transforming it into an intense, emotionally charged abstract painting. He gave the piece a touch of realism with a Cloners brush, using it to restore a hint of the original photo to the clone.

**1 Choosing a subject and making a clone.** Open your photo in Painter, then choose File, Clone to make a copy of your image to alter. Hathaway chose a PICT file from a PhotoCD—an image of two dogs running toward him on the beach—then cloned it.

**2 Blending with a Water brush.** Hathaway used the Just Add Water variant of the Water brush; since it uses the Soft Cover submethod and doesn't show paper texture, it's the smoothest of the blending brushes. You may want to adjust the brush Size or ± Size in the Brush Controls:Size palette (Brushes palette, under the Controls pull-down menu) or the Opacity in the Controls:Brush palette, for a more subtle smearing effect. Now, make some strokes on your clone. Hathaway painted aggressive, diagonal, smeary strokes on the clone to emphasize the focal point and perspective in the foreground, then he smeared the background into more abstract shapes. He modified his brush as he worked, varying Size between 10 and 30 pixels, increasing the ± Size setting, and lowering the Opacity to 30–40%.

**3 Partially restoring from the original.** As a last step, Hathaway used the Soft Cloner variant of the Cloners brush with a very low opacity (5%) to subtly restore the foreground dog's face. Try this on your clone. Use the Soft Cloner brush to bring the original back into the blurred areas of your image. Experiment with the Opacity slider until you find a setting that suits your drawing style and pressure.

# Overlaying Textures

**Overview** *Isolate several separate areas of a photo; apply color and texture with Color Overlay.*

CTP / PHOTO: PHOTODISC

**1a**

*The original PhotoDisc photo*

**1b**

*Making a color mask for the sky*

**2a**

*Applying a colored texture to the sky*

**2b**

*Applying texture to the inverted selection*

**3**

*Filling with the Clone Source to add detail*

TEXTURIZING IS A GREAT WAY TO ADD SPICE to an image that calls for more color or interest. To produce this "comp" for a children's book illustration, we added color and texture to a photo, giving it greater dimension and creating a playful mood.

**1 Making a clone and a mask.** Open a file with good tonal balance and contrast. Generate a clone by choosing File, Clone.

To isolate the sky from the windmills, we generated a color mask for the cloned image. For an in-depth explanation of creating a color mask, turn to "Using Color Mask" on page 94.

Before you apply a texture to a masked area, first convert the mask to a mask representation selection (the green selection marquee). Do this by clicking on the far right Visibility icon in the Path List palette.

**2 Applying the colored textures.** We sampled a blue color from the image sky (with the Dropper tool) and increased its saturation in the Color palette. After selecting a color, choose a texture from the Paper palette; for our 728-pixel-wide image, we used Vincent 1 from the New Textures library, scaled to 150%. Now choose Effects, Surface Control, Color Overlay, using Paper Grain, 100% Opacity and the Dye Concentration model. Next, to add pinpoints of light in the sky, we chose a white color and applied the Real Starry Sky texture (also from New Textures) using Hiding Power at 50% Opacity.

Now choose Edit, Mask, Invert Mask. In our image, this command protected the sky and let us apply texture to the windmills and ground. We sampled a dark brown color from the foreground, selected the Vincent 1 texture again (with 100% scaling), and applied Color Overlay, Dye Concentration at 80% Opacity.

**3 Restoring detail from the original.** Applying texture had flattened our image a bit, so we recovered detail from the original photo. To do this, choose Effects, Fill (Command-F), Clone Source and an Opacity setting of 25%. 🖌

# Toning with Textures

***Overview*** *Use Painter's Express Texture feature to make two line conversions of a color image; colorize the two images and merge them into a single file.*

CTP / PHOTO: PHOTODISC

*The original photo*

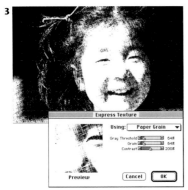

*Scaling down the Angle Weave texture*

*Express Texture settings for Light Exposure*

CONVERTING CONTINUOUS-TONE PHOTOGRAPHS into custom line art effects—like mezzotints, etch tones and straight-line screens—can be accomplished either in the darkroom or with a graphic arts camera using a screen made of film printed with a textured pattern. There are digital plug-in filters that give similar results, although they usually eliminate much of the original's fine detail. By using Painter's Express Texture feature on two separate, textured exposures and then "sandwiching" them, you can retain more highlight and shadow detail during the conversion process than through any other digital means.

**1 Selecting an image and cloning.** Open a file with good tonal balance and contrast. Make two clones of this file—choose File, Clone twice. Save and name one clone "Light Exposure," and the other "Dark Exposure."

**2 Choosing a texture.** Select a paper texture that resembles the screen effect you wish to achieve. To get a random line effect, we chose Angle Weave from the Wild Textures library; to preserve detail in our 738-pixel-wide image, we scaled the texture to 50%.

**3 Making a light exposure.** To create a light, "overexposed" image that brings out shadow detail, click on the Light Exposure clone to make it active. Choose Effects, Surface Control, Express Texture, using Paper Grain. Drag all three sliders to the left and experiment to see which settings bring out the most shadow detail: We got the best results in our image by setting Gray Threshold to 64%, Grain to 64% and Contrast to 200%.

**4 Making a dark exposure.** Next, create an "underexposed" image—dark, with texture visible in the midtones and highlights. Select the Dark Exposure clone and again choose Effects, Surface Control, Express Texture. Drag all three sliders farther to the right,

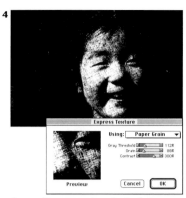

**4**

*Express Texture settings for Dark Exposure*

**5**

*Applying a brown-to-white gradation to Dark Exposure (left) and a brown-to-tan gradation to Light Exposure*

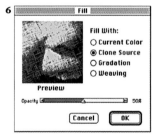

**6**

*Filling Dark Exposure with Light Exposure*

near their original (default) settings of 110%, 80%, 300%. We got good results by setting Gray Threshold to 112%, Grain to 88% and Contrast to 300%.

**5 Colorizing the clones.** Using Art Materials, Grad, Express in Image to tint the two clones before merging them gives richer tonal depth to the final image than colorizing it after merging the images. Start by selecting the Two-Point gradation in the Grad palette and choose colors for the front and back Color rectangles in the Color palette. Next, choose Express in Image from the Grad pull-down menu, and click OK. We applied a brown-to-white gradation to Dark Exposure, and a brown-to-tan gradation to Light Exposure.

**6 Combining the images.** Painter offers many ways to blend images; we got the best results on our example by filling with a Clone Source. Begin by making Light Exposure the Clone Source by choosing File, Clone Source, Light Exposure. Now fill Dark Exposure with Light Exposure: With the Dark Exposure window active, select Effects, Fill. Click the Clone Source button and experiment with a 40–60% Opacity setting. (We chose 50%.) Click OK.

As a final step to increase the color and tonal range, we selected Effects, Tonal Control, Equalize (Command-E). The effect was too strong, so we selected Edit, Fade at a 50% setting. 🖌

## TRADITIONAL LINE CONVERSION EFFECTS

Here's our best guess at the Painter textures required to mimic the look of a few traditional line conversions, using Express Texture on a single 410-pixel-wide color image. Use these examples as a launching pad for your own experimentation. To give your image a greater tonal range before using Express Texture, you may want to use Effects, Tonal Control, Equalize.

**Mezzotint:** *Micro grain (More Wild Textures library), scaled to 108%*

**Dry brush:** *Streaks (Wild Textures library), scaled to 50%*

**Etch tone:** *Medium (Paper Textures library), scaled to 100%*

PHOTO: PHOTODISC

# Solarizing

***Overview** Use Express Texture on positive and negative clones of an image; merge the images by filling with a Clone Source.*

**1**

*The original image after equalizing (left), and the negative clone*

**2**

*Creating black-and-white positive (left) and negative versions of the clones using Express Texture*

**3**

*Merging the positive and negative images*

**4**

*Adjusting the image's brightness and contrast*

IN THE DARKROOM, SOLARIZATION OCCURS when a negative is exposed to a flash of light during the development process, partially reversing the photo's tonal range. To achieve this effect digitally, we tested other image-processing programs and filters, and found that we got the most control and detail using Painter's Express Texture feature. Our technique gives you a lot of control over the image's value contrast and it frequently creates a glowing edge-line effect where contrasting elements meet.

**1 Making positive and negative clones.** Open an image with good value contrast, then choose Effects, Tonal Control, Equalize (Command-E) to increase its tonal range. Choose File, Clone twice. Make one of the clones into a color negative by selecting Effects, Tonal Control, Negative.

**2 Making black-and-white separations.** Use Painter's Express Texture feature to convert both clones to black-and-white: Choose Effects, Surface Control, Express Texture, and select Image Luminance from the pop-up menu. Experiment with the sliders and click OK. Repeat the process for the second clone. We set Gray Threshold to 72%, Grain to 72% and Contrast to 160%. These settings helped emphasize the gradient effect in the sky.

**3 Merging the two exposures.** Choose File, Clone Source and choose the positive clone. Now fill the negative image with a percentage of the positive (the "flash of light"): With the negative window active, choose Effects, Fill, Clone Source. Set the Opacity slider between 40% and 60%.

**4 Pumping up the tonal range.** To achieve a broader tonal range while maintaining a silvery solarized look, we selected Effects, Tonal Control, Brightness/Contrast. We increased the contrast (the top slider) and decreased the brightness. 🐾

# Hand-Tinting a Photo

**Overview** *Retouch a black-and-white photo; use selection and masking tools to isolate areas of the photo; tint the image using Water Color brushes.*

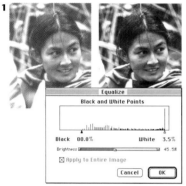

Using Equalize to adjust the tonal range on the black-and-white scan

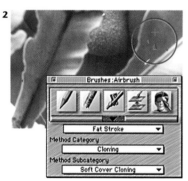

Repairing scratches with the Fat Stroke Airbrush, Soft Cover Cloning submethod

Image with the background mask visible

HAND-TINTING IS A GREAT WAY to give an old-fashioned look to a black-and-white print. It also gives the sensitive artist plenty of opportunities to add depth to an image using hues, tints and shades. To create *Rell with Bird's Nest Fern,* we hand-dyed a portrait of Hawaiian friend Rell Sunn using Painter's Water Color brushes, applying transparent color without disturbing the existing photo.

**1 Equalizing the image.** To preserve shadow detail during tinting, choose a light image without solid shadows, or lighten your image using the Equalize command. We scanned our 8 x 10-inch print at 100%, 150 pixels per inch. The print was slightly overexposed, so we used the Equalize command to darken it, taking care to preserve detail in the shadows. If your image needs tonal correction, select Effects, Tonal Control, Equalize (Command-E). Your image will be automatically adjusted when the dialog box appears. To obtain a more subtle result, experiment with spreading the triangular sliders on the histogram; move them closer together for a stronger effect. Use the Brightness slider to give the photo a brighter or darker exposure. Slider adjustments will be reflected in your image.

## STARTING WITH SEPIA

Before colorizing an image, try giving it a sepia-tone using Art Materials, Grad, Express in Image (see page 131) before equalizing. Use Edit, Fade for a subtle look (try 75%), then follow the tinting procedure in this story.

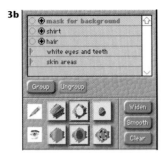

*The Path List palette, showing Mask Visibility settings for Figure 3a*

4a

*Tinting the background with the Large Simple Water variant. The mask (green marquee) protected the foreground.*

4b

*Flat transparent washes on the foreground*

5

*Adding color and highlights to the shirt*

**2 Retouching scratches.** To touch up scratches, first use the Magnifier tool to enlarge the area that needs retouching. Choose the Soft Cloner variant of the Cloners brush or switch the method on an existing brush (such as the Fat Stroke Airbrush) to Cloning method, Soft Cover Cloning submethod. Establish a clone source by Control-clicking (Shift-clicking on the PC) on your image near the area that needs touch-up, then begin painting. A crosshair cursor shows the origin of your sampling. If necessary, re-establish a clone source as you work. To retouch by painting with color sampled from a nearby area, switch to Cover method, Soft Cover submethod; sample the color with the Dropper tool; then paint.

**3 Making selections and a mask.** Before beginning the tinting process, make several selections to isolate areas of the image. Choose the Pen tool and draw a shape path around an area you want to isolate. When you've finished drawing the path, click the Make Selection button in the Controls:Shape Design palette. Switch to the Selection Adjuster tool and slightly soften the edges of the selection by setting a 1-pixel feather in the Controls: Adjuster palette. To isolate larger areas you may want to use a Masking brush; we used the Masking Pen variant to isolate the background from the figure. When you're finished making the mask, view it as a green selection marquee by clicking on the far right Visibility (the Eye) icon in the expanded Path List palette. Feather the mask 1 pixel (Edit, Mask, Feather Mask) to soften its edge.

**4 Applying transparent color.** Choose a color and the Large Simple Water variant of the Water Color brush. (Simple Water variants are the fastest Water Color brushes.) Activate a selection in the Path List (press Enter) and apply strokes to your image. The strokes are actually in the Wet Layer, which floats above the image. (The Wet Layer is turned on whenever you choose a Water Color brush.)

**5 Emphasizing the area of interest.** After you've added a layer of flat color, look at the overall balance and color density of your image. Add more or brighter color to the areas that you want to emphasize and apply darker or less saturated colors to make other areas appear to recede. Switch to the Simple Water variant for detail work. To remove color from oversaturated areas, use the Wet Eraser variant of the Water Color brush, adjusting its Opacity setting in the Controls palette as you work.

If you're coloring in more than one work session, save your image in RIFF format to keep the Wet Layer "wet," or separate from the canvas. Choosing Canvas, Dry drops the Wet Layer onto your image, so do this when you're finished tinting. After we "dried" our image, we wanted more color in the figure's shoulder and in portions of the foliage, so we added more Water Color brush strokes in those areas and chose Canvas, Dry again. For a complete example of this technique of layering colors, called *glazing*, turn to "Glazing with Watercolor" on page 48.

# Creating a Montage Using Masks and Floaters

***Overview*** *Create masks for photos in Photoshop or Painter; copy them into a single document; use a Masking brush to composite them; paint on the final image.*

*The original photos*

*The cut-and-pasted comp ready to be scanned and used as a template*

WHEN CONTINENTAL CABLEVISION asked John Dismukes of Capstone Studios to illustrate a direct-mail piece, he and his team turned to Painter. He combined photographs and splashy color with loose airbrush and chalk brushstrokes to illustrate the theme, "Can Summer in California Get Any Better?"

**1 Gathering illustration elements.** Begin by collecting all of the individual elements that you'll need for your illustration. Dismukes and his associates photographed separate images of clouds, a pair of sunglasses, ocean foam, palm trees, and a television on the sand. The photo negatives were scanned in Kodak Photo CD format.

**2 Making a template from laser prints.** Many experienced artists and designers who honed their skills without the aid of a computer prefer to assemble their "comps" by hand rather than digitally. Dismukes' team created a traditional comp by printing, then photocopying the individual elements at different scales and then assembling them using scissors and adhesive. They turned the completed comp into a template by scanning it at 72 ppi, opening it in Painter and sizing it to the final image size of 4 x 5 inches at 762 ppi. The template acted as a guide for Dismukes to accurately scale and position the various elements. If you choose to include this step, don't be concerned about the "bitmapping" that occurs when scanning the comp at a lower resolution; when

**3**

*Three of Dismukes' Photoshop masks*

**4**

*Bringing the floaters into the composite file*

**5**

*Hiding the background around the sunglasses using the upper right Mask Visibility icon in the Floater List*

**6a**

*Using the Masking Airbrush variant to erase the portion of the cloud floater's mask that covers the TV*

the composition is finished, the template will be completely covered by the source images.

**3 Masking unwanted portions of the source images.** Dismukes used Photoshop's Pen tool to cut masks for the sunglasses, ocean foam, palm trees and television on the beach. In Photoshop, he converted the path to a selection, saved the selection as Channel 4, then saved each image as an RGB TIFF file, including the alpha channel. You can accomplish the same result in Painter. Open one of your source photos and use the Pen or Quick Curve tool to draw a shape path around the desired portion of the image. When you're done, turn the path into an active selection by clicking the Make Selection button in the Controls:Shape Design palette. View the selection as a mask by clicking on the center Visibility button in the expanded Path List. You should see your image surrounded by a field of orange—the default color for the mask. To view only the mask in black-and-white, choose Canvas, View Mask.

**4 Compiling the source files.** When you've finished masking the images, bring them into a single document. Open either the template or the photo that will become your background image. Choose the Floater Adjuster tool, open the Objects:Floater List palette, then open each of the source images and choose Edit, Select All, and Edit, Copy. Make the background photo active and choose Edit, Paste. Each item's name—such as "Floater 1"—will appear in the Floater List. Rename each floater by double-clicking on the name and typing in a new name in the dialog box.

**5 Putting the masks to work.** To view the mask on a floater, select it in the Floater List and choose, Canvas, View Mask. To switch back to Color View, choose View Mask again. To hide the unwanted background around the masked image, zoom-out the Floater List palette to reveal the Mask Visibility buttons and click on the upper right button. A word of caution: Do this step before resizing or rotating the floater; otherwise, you may lose your mask.

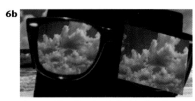

**6b**

*Compositing the clouds inside the glasses*

**6c**

*Revealing the cloud floater around the tree*

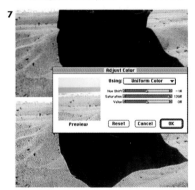

**7**

*Using Adjust Colors to increase saturation in the image*

**8**

*Adding squiggles and lens glare (top) and smudges and blurs*

**6 Using Masking brushes.** Painter's Masking brushes let you "paint" one element inside of another. To use them, first scale, rotate and position one floater atop another and make sure that the top floater is selected. Choose the Masking Airbrush variant of the Masking brush and choose white in the Colors palette. Begin painting around the edge of the top floater to erase part of its mask, making it appear "inside" of the floater beneath it. Paint with black to restore the mask. You may find it quicker and easier to work without the Selection Marquee visible; if so, uncheck the Show Selection Marquee box in the zoomed-out Floater List.

When you've completed all compositing, make a copy of your image with the floaters dropped to the background by choosing File, Clone. This step gives you a lot of flexibility—you have an "original" with floaters intact, and a "working image" (the clone) on which you can paint and make other adjustments.

**7 Shifting colors.** To make the image "pop" a bit more, Dismukes increased the color saturation. Choose Effects, Tonal Control, Adjust Colors, and experiment with the Hue Shift, Saturation and Value sliders to shift the colors in your image.

**8 Painting on the photo montage.** To transform the television into a lively caricature in vivid color, Dismukes first used the Feather Tip Airbrush variant to add glare to the glasses and other details. He switched to the Impressionist variant of the Artists brush to paint on the sand and water, and then painted spontaneous, textured squiggles around the TV and on the sand and water with the Artist Pastel Chalk variant and the Big Canvas paper (from the Grains library). As a final touch, Dismukes switched to the Water brush, Grainy Water variant, Cover method and Grainy Hard Cover submethod to add the smudges and blurs on the sand and television.

**Finishing the job.** Using the same style, technique, tools and colors, Dismukes created similar illustrations on a smaller scale that were used throughout the brochure, as well as a border around the edge of the piece. 🖌

---

**A TIFF-TO-RIFF LIFESAVER**

If you save a floater-filled file in TIFF format (a format that doesn't support floating elements), Painter is smart enough not to automatically drop your hard-earned floaters in your working image. A dialog box will appear, and when you click OK, the program saves a copy of your document with floaters dropped in TIFF format, but the floaters stay alive in your working image. Make sure to save in RIFF format before quitting to preserve the floaters.

⚠ The floaters in this image are merged with the canvas layer when saving to this format -- save as RIFF to save the canvas and floaters as independent objects.

[ OK ]

# "Crystallizing" a Montage

***Overview*** *Create a photo montage; use the montage as a source for a Glass Distortion effect on a cloud background; use a custom Cloning brush to bring the montage into the center of the glass image while preserving the crystal edge; increase saturation using Dye Concentration.*

PHILIP HOWE / ART DIRECTION: GREG ERICKSON © MICROSOFT CORPORATION

**1a** **1b**

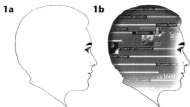

*The pencil sketch*    *Adding the time line*

**2a**

*Positioning the photo elements and their shadows*

**2b**

*The photos grouped with their shadows as they appear in the Floater List palette*

WHEN MICROSOFT COMMISSIONED PHILIP HOWE to illustrate their Encarta CD-ROM Interactive Encyclopedia packaging, he created a photo montage that included a transparent glass effect.

**1 Preparing the files.** Begin by collecting and sizing your source photos, including an image of sky with plenty of clouds. You may find it helpful to start with a sketch on paper so you can approximate sizes. Howe incorporated a 4 x 5-inch pencil drawing into the montage, scanning it at 1016 ppi. He opened it in Photoshop, made a gradient mask in an alpha channel and applied the mask to the head as a selection. Howe resized and copied a time line image provided by the client and pasted it inside the selected head atop the gradient.

In Painter, Howe sized the cloud image to match the dimensions of his pencil sketch, then retouched and added to the clouds using the Fat Stroke Airbrush variant. He used Canvas, Resize on the small source photos to size them to match the sketch.

**2 Creating the montage.** Compile your source images into a montage by copying and pasting them into a master document. To create a drop shadow behind each floating image, choose Effects, Objects, Create Drop Shadow; or create the shadows manually—as Howe did—by making a copy of the floater (Option-drag with the Floater Adjuster tool), feathering the copy (in the Controls: Adjuster palette), and filling the copy with black or gray (Effects, Fill, Current Color). Move the shadow behind the image by dragging its name lower in the Floater List, and offset it using the arrow keys. To make it easier to keep track of your floaters (or

**144** CHAPTER 6: ENHANCING PHOTOS

**2c**

*The finished montage with all elements*

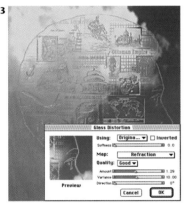

*Using Glass Distortion based on the Original Luminance of the montage to create a crystal effect*

*Using the Fat Stroke Airbrush, Soft Cloning submethod, to clone the montage into the crystallized cloud image*

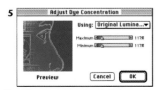

*Adjusting Dye Concentration to bring out the crystal edge of the head*

groups of floaters), double-click on their names in the Floater List palette to name them. Howe added source photos with drop shadows to the time line image and arranged them using the Floater tool. He saved the original file in RIFF format to keep the elements floating—in case the client wanted any changes—then dropped the floaters after the montage was approved.

**3 Creating a "crystal" version of the montage.** Since this step uses the luminance (or brightness information) of the montage to produce a crystal look, you'll get a more pronounced effect if your montage has good contrast. If it needs more contrast, Choose Effects, Tonal Control, Brightness/Contrast and move the Contrast (top) slider to the right. You can also use Effects, Surface Control, Dye Concentration (Howe's choice) to increase the image's saturation based on its luminance. Now create the crystal effect. Open both the cloud image and the montage, and make the montage the clone source (File, Clone Source). Choose Effects, Focus, Glass Distortion, Original Luminance and experiment with the Amount and Variance sliders. High-resolution images can accept higher slider settings and still retain definition. Click OK.

**4 Cloning the montage into the crystal.** Build a custom cloning brush and use it to bring portions of the montage into the crystal image. Choose the Fat Stroke Airbrush variant, change the method to Cloning and the submethod to Soft Cover Cloning. Begin painting in the crystal image and the montage will appear. Adjust the brush size as you work; Howe took great care to preserve the crystal effect around the edges of the image. To further define the head against the clouds, he switched to Cover method, Soft Cover submethod (the default for Fat Stroke Airbrush), chose white and carefully painted a glow around the inside edge of the back of the head.

**5 Bumping up the crystal's edge.** To further saturate the glass effect, Howe chose Effects, Surface Control, Dye Concentration, using Original Luminance (keeping the montage as the clone source). He set both Maximum and Minimum sliders to 117%.

### DIVING INTO GLASS DISTORTION

Conventional diffuser screens attach to the camera lens, breaking up or softening the image as it refracts through the screen. Painter's Glass Distortion feature works the same way but with more variety. Choose Paper Grain and experiment with refracting your image through different textures. On this photo, we used Diagonal 1 from the More Paper Textures library.

■ **Ellie Dickson** created *Wright Brothers* for an advertisement for the U. S. Postal Service. She began the image with two black-and-white photos (the plane and the two Wright brothers) supplied by the client's ad agency. She retouched both images in Photoshop, colorized them with light tints, then composited them into one image. She opened the composite in Painter and painted directly on the image using the Artist Pastel Chalk and the Just Add Water variants, building up multiple layers of colored strokes.

■ **S. Swaminathan** used Painter to combine and enhance two images, building this portrait of two friends—the dedicated Chicano Rights activist Caesar Chavez and Luis Valdez, the renowned film director of *La Bomba*, *Zoot Suit*, and *The Cisco Kid*, and director of El Teatro Campesino. (Swaminathan captured the portrait of Valdez, and Chavez was photographed by Lupe Valdez.) Swaminathan opened the Valdez image and used the curves in Tonal Control, Correct Colors to increase its brightness and contrast and to eliminate a yellow cast. He cloned the color-corrected image and used a large custom Fat Stroke Airbrush with high Color Variability settings (zoomed-out Color palette) to selectively lay down spattery, diffused brushstrokes in the clone. Using a tiny Airbush, he painted back into the blurred image to restore detail to Valdez's face, his clothing and his Aztec pendant. Swaminathan used similar techniques to enhance the image of Cesar Chavez, then copied and pasted it into the Valdez image as a floater. He used Masking brushes on the floater mask to create an irregular transparent edge on the Chavez floater. To complete the dual portrait he adjusted the opacity of the floater in the Controls:Adjuster palette for a soft effect.

■ As part of an advertising campaign, Wacom Technology Corporation commissioned **Philip Howe** to create *Portrait of Harley*. Howe started by shooting a Polaroid of his brother Harley to use as a reference. In Painter, he used the 2B Pencil variant to create a freehand sketch, then rendered the photorealistic portrait using the Fat Stroke Airbrush. Howe scanned paintbrushes, pastel sticks and pastel dust and composited the objects atop the portrait in Photoshop. Back in Painter, he painted on the image using the Oil Paint variant of the Brush, the Flemish Rub variant of the Artists brush (to break up existing strokes) and Liquid brush variants (to pull color around). Finally, he used a light touch of Glass Distortion to emphasize the brushstrokes.

■ **John Derry** used photographs he took in Japan to build *Asakusa*, part of his ongoing *City Series*. The image illustrates religion intertwined with commercial culture in the Asakusa district of Tokyo, famous for its temple and marketplace. To isolate areas of the source photos, Derry made Bézier curve selections using the Pen tool. He copied and pasted the selected areas into the composite file, where he scaled and repositioned the floaters and gave them drop shadows. To blend the masks in the center of the image with the temple prayer card beneath, Derry filled the mask in the top floater with a gradient to reveal part of the underlying image (Paint Bucket tool/Controls palette). He created an Asian-inspired pattern and used it as a background element, then added final painterly details using a modified Big Wet Oils variant and blended colors with the Just Add Water variant.

■ **Gary Clark's** current fine art work incorporates still digital photography, computer manipulation and direct painting. To begin *Dictates of Conscience* (right) he used a Canon still-video camera to capture mannequin faces in a local department store. Back in his studio, he chose one of several colored tempera studies to use as a textured background element for the piece. He scanned the study, a stalk of wheat and a piece of kiwi fruit, then enhanced the tone and color of the scans and video shots using Painter's Brightness/Contrast and Adjust Colors controls (from Effects, Tonal Control). All source images were pasted into the color study, arranged and dropped. Clark added color with the Water Color brushes, pulled forms with the Distorto variant of the Liquid brush and used Effects, Surface Control, Apply Lighting to create a sense of drama.

■ Photographer **Fred Gillaspy** shoots images with Painter in mind. For *Recuerdos de Sante Fe* (below), he used a 2¼-inch Ukrainian Kiev 88 camera (90 seconds at *f* 32) to capture the soft glow of the *luminarias*—candles in brown paper bags—set out on Christmas Eve in Santa Fe, New Mexico. He scanned and cloned the photo, then used a number of different Airbrush variants to retouch the image—eliminating autos parked in the courtyard, for example. He added brush strokes with the Just Add Water variant and retouched the foliage using textures from the Trees and Leaves library. To amplify the original photo's suggestion of heat, Gillaspy added brush strokes to suggest a lava flow along the driveway. Using a small Water brush and a tiny white Airbrush, Gillaspy burned out the center of every light source and reflection and added a light flare to each light source.

■ Photographer **S. Swaminathan** uses Painter to enhance old transparencies, some of which are over three decades old. Working as a photojournalist, he photographed the original image for *Cicero Civil Rights Riots 1966* (above) in Chicago at the event that marked the end of the nonviolent civil rights movement. Swaminathan cloned the image and used Airbrush variants to restore color and clouds to the faded transparency, then adjusted the brightness and contrast of the image. To capture the emotion of the moment rather than the details, he used Painter's Cubist Cloner Look (Brush Controls palette) to diffuse and distort the faces of the crowd.

■ The devastating Los Angeles earthquake of 1994 provided the source images for **Rhonda Campbell's** *Out of Disaster* (left). The black-and-white images of disaster and the color tree—a symbol of hope and renewal—were pasted and arranged in a single document in Painter. Campbell painted and colorized the image using the Pencils, Airbrush, Eraser and Crayons brushes. She made "progressive clones" as she painted, making it easy for her to access different stages of her work.

■ Dignity of the individual and the strength of spirit is the power behind **Dorothy Simpson Krause's** *Women of the Mills.* She used Fractal Design Color Studio to merge a black-and-white photograph of women mill workers from Lowell, Massachusetts with a photo of a New England common. She added color and texture to the image in Painter; for instance, she used a small Sharp Chalk brush to add skin tones to the women's faces.

■ **Judy Moncrieff's** most recent series of layered, montaged images, entitled *Odyssey,* uses black-and-white photographs she took while traveling through Europe. For one of the images in the series, *French Riviera,* Moncrieff began compositing a few of the photos for the background in Photoshop, then switched to Painter to add most of the other images. She colorized areas of the montage using various Airbrush variants, then blended colors with the Just Add Water variant. She increased the color saturation in the final image using Effects, Surface Control, Dye Concentration.

■ **Karin Schminke** began *Red Hawk* with a freehand sketch of a hawk using Painter's Charcoal brushes. She cloned the sketch (File, Clone) and used Painter's Tracing Paper feature (Canvas menu) to make subtle improvements to the bird's shape. She continued to clone and use Tracing Paper for five generations until she was satisfied with the form. She made another clone and added tone to the hawk using the Pencils and Charcoal brushes. Schminke opened a photograph of trees in Photoshop to adjust value, hue and contrast of the tree image. She composited the hawk and trees, then brought the montage back into Painter to add the aura with a 2B Pencil variant. Finally, she opened the image in Photoshop and added blur effects to selected areas.

■ A small original sketch and a photograph of her daughter proved to be the inspiration for photographer and fine artist **Helen Golden's** *Venus Emerging*. She scanned and sized both images, then selected the figure and copied and pasted it into the background image. She adjusted the floating figure's position until the feminine and organic forms seemed to blend naturally, then cloned the image. To integrate the color and texture of the two originals, Golden created a custom Water Color brush with a Soft Cover submethod and with the Use Clone Color option (Colors palette) checked, varying the Size and Angle settings (Brush Controls:Size) as she worked. She used the Medium Tip Felt Pens with very low Opacity and Grain settings to emphasize particular colors or forms.

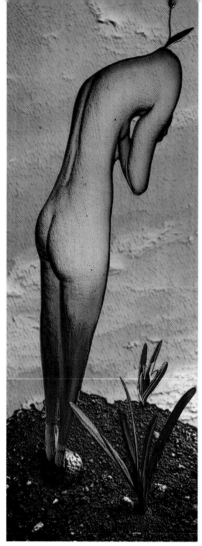

■ **Caty Bartholomew** created *Planted Nude* as a vivid symbol of personal growth. She envisioned a distorted nude that would express "growing pains" and incorporated a tulip as a symbol of hope. She began with some initial photo-compositing work in Photoshop, but wanted to avoid a slick, photographic look, so she imported the nude into Painter. Bartholomew retouched the legs and bulb with the Thin Stroke Airbrush variant, then stretched the figure disproportionately using Effects, Orientation, Scale. She cut and pasted the nude and other plants onto the dirt. To give texture and dimension to the piece, she used Effects, Surface Control, Apply Surface Texture twice: first with Original Luminance; then with Paper Grain and a Medium paper texture.

■ For this double-page illustration for IBM's *AS/400* magazine, **Jean Francois Podevin** began with conventional pencil sketches based on his own photographs. Podevin then collaborated with colleague **Larry Scher** on the computer. The team scanned Podevin's sketch and used it as a guide to position Podevin's Photo CD images. The image was composed and filter effects added in the DOS programs RIO and VIP, and then it was imported into Painter. Podevin retouched and painted on the image using the Airbrush, Water and Chalk brushes. To create the drop shadow of the final composite, the team selected the image, then floated and duplicated it. The duplicate was feathered, filled and moved behind the composite.

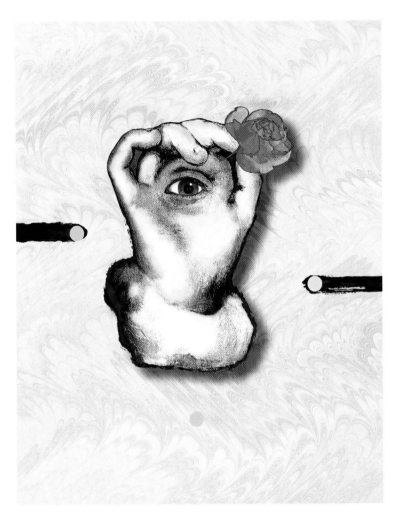

■ **Jean Francois Podevin** again collaborated with **Larry Scher** on this image for a poster announcing an Association of Media Photographers event. The team scanned a Podevin sketch which featured a tight pencil rendering of the hand. Podevin selected his own photos of a rose and an eye, and the team scanned a piece of marbled paper to use for the background. They isolated the rose using Painter's Color Mask (Edit, Mask, Color Mask), then composited the source images in the DOS programs RIO and VIP. In Painter, Podevin used various Airbrush variants to retouch the images and applied Charcoal variants to emphasize the shadows on the hand.

■ **Philip Howe** began *Trucker* with a composition sketch based on a photograph taken by associate **Ed Lowe**. Howe scanned the photo into Painter and cloned it. He painted on the clone with the Brushy variant of the Brush and several Airbrush and Chalk variants. He blended areas with the Grainy Water brush and added drama and depth with Effects, Surface Control, Apply Lighting. To further merge the photograph with his painted strokes, Howe applied Effects, Focus, Glass Distortion using Paper Grain.

■ *Swimmers 2*, one in a series of images inspired by the quiet, carefree feeling of weightlessness underwater, was created by **Cher Threinen-Pendarvis.** She made grayscale scans of three source photos—a man, a woman and a fish—and solarized the man and woman (using the technique described on page 138). She selected the male figure and copied and pasted it into the woman image. The female figure was also floated, and the glows behind the figures were created by duplicating and offsetting the two floaters. Elements were activated one at a time and tinted using Art Materials, Grad, Express in Image. She moved the image briefly to Photoshop to apply an arbitrary color map (in the Curves dialog box) to add more complexity to the color. Back in Painter, Threinen-Pendarvis painted on the water with the Oil Pastel variant, Soft Cover submethod (to preserve the smooth, photographic quality), then she used a custom Distorto variant to pull one color into another and to add more detail and movement to the water. Painterly details were added on the figures with modified Coarse Distorto and Just Add Water variants. She dropped all floating figures, then pasted in multiple copies of the fish. She emphasized the solarized edge lines around the figures with a modified Sharp Chalk variant.

■ *Rich, Mom and Ellie*, by **Ellie Dickson,** was commissioned by *Psychology Today* magazine to accompany a story on family dynamics. Dickson began by scanning a black-and-white family photo. In Photoshop, she made loose freehand selections with the Lasso and filled the selections with tints of color (using Color Mode). Dickson opened the tinted image in Painter and applied strokes with a low-opacity Artist Pastel Chalk variant, using Soft Cover submethod for a smooth look. She softened the Pastel strokes using the Just Add Water brush and intensified the image's watery look with the Distorto variant of the Liquid brush. Finally, she emphasized details in the image using a modified 2B Pencil variant.

■ "Although the program is called Painter," says renowned photographer **Pedro Meyer**, "it's important not to exclude photography from its repertoire, given that the program can also be used effectively in that medium."

*Eagles* (above) and *Fear, Anger and Hate* (left) reflect Meyer's observation of the youth of Los Angeles and how they deal with finding their identity. Although the need to belong is nothing new, what's different today is the form in which the ritual of belonging takes place. Meyer's photographic eye captures the call for unity with peers—the gang—as well the declaration of individuality and rebelliousness—for example, the upside-down flag in *Eagles* and the slogans on the wall in *Fear, Anger and Hate*.

# EXPLORING SPECIAL EFFECTS

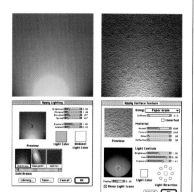

*Special effects wizard Steve Campbell relied on Painter's selections, Apply Lighting, Apply Surface Texture and Glass Distortion commands to add dimension to this piece,* The Performance.

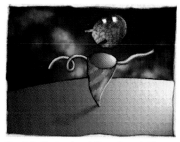

*If you use Surface Texture in tandem with Apply Lighting, you'll get more dramatic results if you choose similar lighting directions with both commands.*

PAINTER'S SPECIAL EFFECTS ARE SO NUMEROUS and intricate that an entire book could be written about them alone. Because they're so powerful, there's much less need for third-party filters than with Photoshop or other image processors. But with that power comes complexity; some of these effects have evolved into "programs within the program." This chapter introduction focuses on three of Painter's most frequently used "mini-programs"—Apply Surface Texture, Apply Lighting and Patterns—along with a handful of other exciting effects.

## ADDING EFFECTS WITH SURFACE TEXTURE

One of the most frequent "haunts" of Painter artists is the Effects, Surface Control, Apply Surface Texture dialog box. You'll find it used in a number of places throughout this book.

In Painter 4 the Surface Texture dialog box gives even greater control over the look and function of textures than in previous versions. First, the new Softness slider (located under the Using pop-up menu) allows you to create softer transitions, such as smoothing the edge of a mask or softening a texture application. Adding Softness can also increase the 3D effect produced when you apply Surface Texture Using Mask. And with the Reflection slider (bottom Material slider), you can create a reflection in your artwork based on another image.

Another very important Surface Texture control is the preview sphere, located below the image Preview. Think of the circular area displayed as your image with the lights riding above it on a dome. Although the preview sphere shows a spotlight effect, any lights you set are applied evenly across the surface of your image.

Experiment with adding more lights to the preview sphere by clicking on the sphere. Adjust an individual light by selecting it,

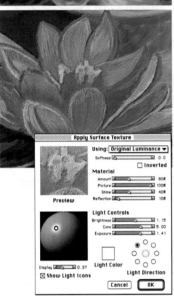

*Creating textured, dimensional brush strokes with Apply Surface Texture using Image Luminance*

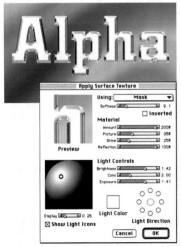

*Adding a reflection to type selections with Apply Surface Texture using Mask*

changing its color, and adjusting its Brightness and Conc (Concentration). Use the Exposure slider to control global exposure. On the other hand, you can get some interesting effects by changing your color choices for the lights. For instance, if the area to be lit contains a lot of blue, you can add more color complexity by lighting with its complement, an orange-hued light.

**Creating 3D effects.** You can use Surface Texture to enhance the surface of your image and give dimension to your brushstrokes. Image Luminance, in the Using pop-up menu, adds depth to brushstrokes by making the light areas appear to recede or "deboss" slightly. If you want to bring the light areas forward, make a clone of your painting (File, Clone), and with your original image window active, choose Effects, Tonal Control, Negative. Back in the clone, select Apply Surface Texture, using Original Luminance. The effect will be applied using the original's value information (now negative), giving you the opposite effect of Image Luminance. Experiment with the sliders to get the effect you desire. You can get a stronger 3D effect by adding a second light (a bounce or a fill light) to the preview sphere with a lower Brightness or a higher Concentration (Conc) setting.

**Applying a reflection map.** Reflections can add interest to type and to other shiny surfaces like glass or metal objects in your illustrations. The Reflection slider allows you to apply a separate image to your illustration as a reflection. Open an image and make a selection or mask for the area where you'll apply the reflection. You can use a pattern as a source for a reflection map (the current Pattern is applied automatically if you don't choose another image as clone source) or you can open an image the same size as your working file. (For inspiration, check out the Maps Pattern library in the Goodies folder on the Painter 4 CD-ROM.) If you are using a separate image as a reflection map, try bending it using Effects, Surface Control, Quick Warp to achieve a spherical or rippled look. (Quick Warp is applied to the entire image, not just to selections or floaters.) Designate it as the clone source (File, Clone Source). Then choose Effects, Surface Control, Surface Texture using Mask. Move the Reflection slider all the way to the right, and adjust the Softness slider (we used a Softness of 9.2). Experiment with the other settings.

Surface Texture works especially well when combined with other Painter tools. "Backlighting 3D Text" on page 113 uses Surface Texture, Color Overlay and Dye Concentration on several stacked floaters to create a glowing backlit effect. "Adding Diffusion and Relief" on page 162 uses Glass Distortion and Surface Texture to add brushstrokes to a photo; John Derry used a combination of Glass Distortion and Surface Texture to give the illusion of refracted water in "Creating a Tidepool" on page 166. And Steve Campbell used Surface Texture and Apply Lighting together to create gradient textural effects in "Applying Effects to Selections" on page 170.

*To get more dimension out of your lighting effects, apply lighting separately to each floating element. In the sample above, we applied the same custom lighting settings (with slightly different colors) to the background and the feathered shadow floater and text floater. To get highlights on the text floater, we applied Surface Texture using Mask. To add a greater sense of curvature, the text floater was composited with Screen Compositing Method (Controls:Adjuster palette, Floater Adjuster tool selected), which lightens while combining with the underlying image. This gives the "a" and "c" translucency on their outside edges.*

*To create a background of glowing, soft-edged circles, increase the Elevation setting and decrease the Spread of the lights in the Apply Lighting dialog box.*

## ADDING DIMENSION WITH LIGHTING

Painter's *User Guide* gives a good description of how to adjust the controls under Effects, Surface Control, Apply Lighting. Here are some tips and practical uses for the tool:

**Applying Lighting to unify an image.** Like most of the Surface Control effects, applying lighting across an entire image can help to unify the piece. (If the lighting effect is too dramatic, try using Edit, Fade immediately afterwards to reduce it.)

**Preventing hot spots**. You can avoid "burnout" of lit areas by increasing the Elevation of the light, reducing the light's Exposure or Brightness, or giving the light a pastel or gray color.

**Lighting within selections or floaters.** Add instant dimension to a selection by applying lighting within it. When lighting floaters, remember that the effect is applied to the entire floater, not just an area you may have masked. See Steve Campbell's work in this and other chapters for his use of this lighting technique.

**Creating subtle gradient effects.** To achieve colored gradient effects in an image, some artists prefer lighting with colored lights instead of filling with a gradient; they prefer the lighting command's smooth luminosity shifts over the more "mechanical" result usually achieved when using gradations.

**Painting back into lit areas.** For fine artists who want to achieve a more painterly effect, the Apply Lighting command can look a bit artificial. Artists Sharon Steuer and Chelsea Sammel (see Chapter 3) use Apply Lighting and then break up the lit area with brushstrokes, sampling color from the image as they work.

**Creating softly lit backgrounds.** On a white background, start with the Splashy Colors light effect. Increase the Brightness and Elevation on both colored lights until they form very soft-edged tinted circles on the white background. Add another light or two and change their colors. Move the lights around until the color, value and composition are working. Save and name your settings and click OK to apply the effect. Repeat this process two or three times, returning each time to your saved effect and making minor adjustments in light color, light position and other settings.

## EXPLORING PATTERNS

Under Art Materials, Patterns—new in Painter 4—there are commands that let you make seamless wrap-around pattern tiles. Once a pattern has been defined and is in the Patterns palette, it becomes the default Clone Source when no other clone source is designated. You can apply a pattern to an existing image, selection or floater with Cloning brushes, with the Paint Bucket tool (by clicking the Clone Source button in the Controls:Paint Bucket palette), with any of the special effects features that use a clone source (such as Original Luminance or 3D Brushstrokes), or by choosing to fill with a pattern or

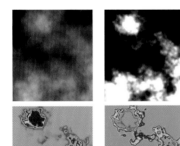

*Detail of the Carp source image for Corrine Okada's package created for The Digital Pond—notice the realistic fish scale texture (bottom). Okada scanned a photo of fish skin and used Art Materials, Pattern, Capture Pattern (top), to create a custom seamless tiling pattern. Then, to test her Pattern, she used the Check Out Pattern command (Patterns, Check Out Pattern). Okada used the wrap-around image to scroll and look for edges in her pattern. She used cloning brushes to repair any edges that weren't seamless.*

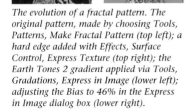

*The evolution of a fractal pattern. The original pattern, made by choosing Tools, Patterns, Make Fractal Pattern (top left); a hard edge added with Effects, Surface Control, Express Texture (top right); the Earth Tones 2 gradient applied via Tools, Gradations, Express in Image (lower left); adjusting the Bias to 46% in the Express in Image dialog box (lower right).*

clone source (Command-F). (The Fill dialog box shows a Pattern button if no clone source image is designated; if a clone source *is* available, a Clone Source button appears.) Use the pattern feature to create multimedia screen design backgrounds, textile design, wallpaper—anywhere you need repeating images.

**Defining a Pattern.** When you choose Define Pattern, Painter creates a wrap-around for the selected image. Here's a great way to see it work. Make a new document that will become your pattern tile and select Art Materials, Pattern, Define Pattern. Choose the Image Hose brush in the Brushes palette (or use any brush). Select a nozzle (choose Brushes, Nozzles to open the Nozzle palette, click on a nozzle) and begin spraying across your image and beyond its edge. Notice how the hose images "wrap around" the edges of the pattern tile you've defined (so that when an area is filled with these pattern tiles, the edges match seamlessly). Any document can be made into a pattern this way, but keep in mind that it's easier to define a blank document as a pattern and then add brushstrokes or a texture (so that the strokes wrap around) than to define an existing document as a pattern.

**Capturing a Pattern.** To make a separate pattern image, select an area of your document with the Rectangular Selection tool (or press Command-A to select the entire image) and choose Art Materials, Pattern, Capture Pattern. To offset your pattern use the Horizontal and Vertical shift options and the Bias slider to control the amount of the offset. Experiment with these settings to get non-aligned patterns—for example, to create a brick wall look, wallpaper or fabric.

**Making a Fractal Pattern.** You don't need an open document to use Make Fractal Pattern because choosing Art Materials, Pattern, Make Fractal Pattern automatically creates a pattern as a new file (with a mask) when you click OK. If you have a lot of memory allotted to Painter, you'll be able to create larger tiles; if not, the larger size options will be grayed out.

Some of the textures you can create with Make Fractal Pattern make very cool paper textures: Select the area of the fractal pattern that you want for your texture (or Select All) and choose Art Materials, Paper, Capture Texture. Or, you may want to capture the texture after you've applied effects to the pattern using Grad/Express in Image, Express Texture, Glass Distortion, Image Warp or Quick Warp.

---

**ELIMINATING "SEAMS"**

For both captured and fractal patterns, here's a way to see and repair the "seams." Select a pattern and choose Art Materials, Patterns, Check Out Pattern. This command creates a new document with a wrap-around, allowing you to paint on one side of your file and continue on the opposite side. Use Check Out Pattern to see how the edges fit together, and use brushes (Cloning brushes are especially helpful) to touch up and blend areas that don't fit seamlessly.

*After creating this topographic map, we added clouds for more atmosphere by copying the original default Fractal pattern file into our map as a floater. Utilizing the luminosity mask that Fractal Pattern builds into the file, we chose the Mask Inside button in the expanded Floater List palette (to reveal only the light areas of the floater) and adjusted the Opacity slider in the Controls:Adjuster palette to 90%.*

**Enhancing fractal patterns.** You can add any special effect to fractal (or regular) patterns and they still remain patterns. Here are two creative applications of fractal pattern.

To create a hard-edged fractal pattern with wild color, make a Fractal Pattern, setting Power to –150, Feature Size to 75 (for a relatively coarse pattern), and Softness to 0. Click OK. Select Effects, Surface Control, Express Texture using Image Luminance. Adjust the Gray Threshold and Grain sliders to 80, and set the Contrast slider at 300 for a contrasty, hard-edged effect. Click OK. Now colorize the pattern by choosing the Earth Tones 2 gradation and selecting Art Materials, Grad, Express in Image. Experiment with shifting the image's hue by dragging the Bias slider.

To make an abstract topographical map image with color and relief, create a pattern using Fractal Pattern's default settings. Give the image a "topographical" look by choosing Effects, Surface Control, Apply Surface Texture, using Mask (Amount, 200; Picture, 100%; and Shine, 0%). Tint the image with Art Materials, Grad, Express in Image and the Earth Tones 2 gradation. Now, add a little relief by applying a second pass of Apply Surface Texture, using Image Luminance (Amount, 100%; Picture, 100%; and Shine, 0%). You can use Effects, Surface Control, Image Warp or Quick Warp on the image to further increase the effect.

## MOVING LIGHTS

To access the Lighting Mover in Painter 4, so you can move lights from the Painter Settings file into a new custom library—press Command-Shift-L. To load the new library, click the Library button in the Surface Control, Apply Lighting dialog box.

## CREATING REPEATING TEXTURES WITH MAKE PAPER TEXTURE

Using Art Materials, Paper, Make Paper Texture you can generate seamless repeating textures to apply to your images. For the image below, Corrine Okada created her own repeating texture that resembled a grid of pixels to represent the digital output process. She generated the grid of beveled squares using Make Paper Texture, then applied the texture to the central portion of her image using Effects, Surface Control, Color Overlay.

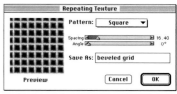

*(Left): Detail from The Digital Pond package design created by Corrine Okada. The complete illustration is featured on page 174. (Above): Okada's settings for the grid of beveled squares*

## OTHER SPECIAL EFFECTS

**Creating effects with Glass Distortion.** Try using another image as a "refractor" for your main image. (Phil Howe used this technique for the image described in "Crystallizing a Montage" on page 144.) Designate a simple, high-contrast image as a clone source (File, Clone Source), make your main image active, then choose Effects, Focus, Glass Distortion using Original Luminance. (To learn

*Using Glass Distortion, Paper Grain (Jasper Johns texture, New Textures library) to refract the edge of this Stone Serif Bold letterform. Type size, 130 points; Super Soften amount, 10 pixels.*

*Casting reflective, 3D gold type using the Gold 2 gradient and Glass Distortion, Mask. Typeface, ITC Machine. Type size, 270 points; Feather, 15 pixels.*

*Creating a vibrant chrome effect by applying the Stripes 7 gradient to black, Super-Softened Futura Heavy. Type size, 130 points; 10-pixel Super Soften.*

about displacement using Glass Distortion turn to "Diving into Distortion" on page 163, and "Draping a Weave" on page 168.)

To add a refracted paper texture to the edges of letterforms, start with a new, 500-pixel-square file with a white background. Choose a bold typeface at 130 points and set type shapes filled with black. Drop the type shapes to the background by clicking the Drop All button in the Floater List palette, then soften the edge of the letters with a 10-pixel Super Soften setting (Command-Shift-S). Select a paper texture, then choose Effects, Focus, Glass Distortion, using Paper Grain. Experiment with the sliders and different paper textures; the feathered edge of the type gives a transparent look to the texture.

To make reflective gold type with a rough-hewn bevel, create a new file 500 pixels square with a dark Paper Color. Make a large type shape (250–300 points) using a bold typeface and convert it to a selection (Shapes, Convert to Selection). Select the Gold 2 gradation and rotate it to a 45° angle, then apply it to the type by choosing Effects, Fill using Gradation. Choose the Selection Adjuster tool and in the Controls:Adjuster palette set the Feather slider to 15. Now choose Glass Distortion using Mask and drag the Amount and Variance sliders toward the middle of the slider bar.

**Expressing a gradation to make chrome.** On a light background, set a 130-point bold type shape filled with black. Drop the shape to the canvas (Drop button, expanded Floater List), then apply Super Soften (Command-Shift-S) to the whole image. Select the Stripes 7 gradation and choose Art Materials, Grad, Express in Image. The background will turn black; for a similar effect, but keeping a white background, leave the type selection active. 🐾

## TONAL CONTROL AND COLOR ENHANCEMENT

Use Effects, Tonal Control, Adjust Colors, then drag the Hue Shift slider to change the hue of your image. Use Uniform Color to shift the hue of the entire image, or use Image Luminance to change color properties only in the lighter areas.

Highpass (under Effects, Esoterica) acts like a color filter. It looks for dark areas with smooth transitions (as in a sky or shadowed background) and replaces them with abrupt edges or halo effects. It also emphasizes highlights in an image and lightens shaded areas. Keep the Radius slider to the left for a more pronounced halo effect. To further enhance Highpass, try using Effects, Tonal Control, Equalize.

*The initial, unaltered photograph*

*Adjust Colors, Uniform Color: Hue Shift, -44%; Value, 25%*

*Adjust Colors, Image Luminance: Hue Shift, 20%; Value, 25%*

*Highpass: Radius, 26.05*

# Adding Diffusion and Relief

***Overview*** *Combine Glass Distortion and Surface Texture special effects to transform a photo into a painting by creating brushstrokes and building up paint.*

CTP / PHOTO: DIGITAL STOCK

**1**

*The original Digital Stock photo*

**2**

*Applying Glass Distortion to the photo*

**3**

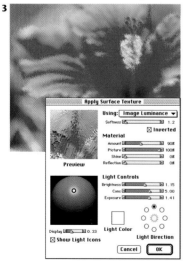

*Adding relief to the distorted image*

BY COMBINING TWO POWERFUL EFFECTS, Glass Distortion and Surface Texture, you can create a painted impressionistic look with highlights and shadows—turning a photo into a painting. This effect can be applied to an entire image, a selection or a floater, giving you much more flexibility than you would have in the darkroom working with diffuser screens and masks.

**1 Choosing an image.** Choose an image with a strong focal point and good highlights and shadows. You can achieve good results with crisp or soft-focus images.

**2 Initiating brushstrokes.** Choose a coarse paper texture—woven textures with a broad tonal range help to emulate the look of paint on canvas. We chose Fiberfill from the Weaves paper library, scaling it up to 130% (to avoid a frosty glass look in our 883 x 589-pixel image when Glass Distortion was applied). To diffuse or break up the image into strokes based on paper grain, choose Effects, Focus, Glass Distortion using Paper Grain, selecting the Refraction Map type. Use subtle settings—our settings were Amount, 0.73; Variance, 2.00; and a Softness of 1.2 to smoothe the effect—high settings can produce a faceted look. Click OK to apply your settings.

**3 Adding texture and shadows.** To add realistic relief to complete the painted effect choose Effects, Surface Control, Apply Surface Texture using Image Luminance. Use subtle to moderate settings, to avoid a harsh look and to preserve the organic quality of the original image. We used Amount, 90%; Picture, 100%; and Shine, 0%. Move the Softness slider to 1.2 to slightly increase the relief and add a soft "impasto" effect to the paint. Choose a light direction that complements the existing light in your photograph. We chose the 12 o'clock Light Direction button to complement the overhead light source in the hibiscus photo, and clicked OK.

# Diving into Distortion

**Overview** *Use Glass Distortion to displace an image using a clone source; then combine a dramatic distortion with a subtle one to create a water-stained effect.*

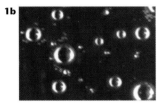
The original Digital Stock photo

The water image displacement map

Settings for the subtle distortion

The Extreme clone (left), and the Subtle clone (right)

Cloning in a dramatic water drop

PAINTER'S GLASS DISTORTION can move pixels in an image based on the luminosity of another image. We used it here to simulate water drops on a camera lens.

**1 Choosing images and making clones.** Choose an image for a displacement map that has good contrast; both crisp and soft-focus images can give good results. Because you'll be applying the displacement map image to the original image as a clone source, you'll need to size the map image to the same pixel dimensions as the image you want to distort. (Our images were 883 x 589 pixels.)

Make two clones of the image you want to distort by choosing File, Clone, twice. Save the clones, naming them Extreme and Subtle, then size and position them on your screen so that you can see both of them.

**2 Applying the distortion.** Open the displacement map image. Now, click on the Extreme clone, and designate the displacement image as the clone source (File, Clone Source). Click back on the Extreme clone and choose Effects, Focus, Glass Distortion, using Original Luminance, and chose the Refraction Map model. (Refraction works well for glass effects; it creates an effect similar to an optical lens bending light.) Our settings were Softness, 2.3 (to smoothe the distortion); Amount, 1.35; Variance, 6.00. We left Degree at 0, because it has no effect when using a Refraction map, and clicked OK. Click on the Subtle clone, and apply more subtle settings. (Our settings were Softness 15.0, Amount 0.06 and Variance, 1.00.) We wanted the diving board to curve, while preserving smoothness in the image.

**3 Restoring from the extreme clone.** We added several dramatic water drops from the Extreme clone to enhance the composition of the Subtle image. Click on the Subtle clone to make it active and chose the Extreme clone as clone source. Use the Soft Cloner brush variant of the Cloning brush to clone dramatic effects from the Extreme clone into your Subtle image. ✒

# Making a Collage with Eroded Type

**Overview** *Soften the edge of the type in source files; manipulate the type using Express Texture; apply a mask; collage the type in a composite file; add transparency effects.*

**1**

*Filling Adobe Stone Sans type with black*

**2**

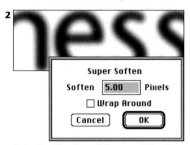

*Softening the edges of the type with a 5-pixel Super Soften setting. The gray information in the edges helps to create the eroded effect.*

**3**

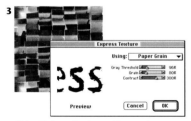

*Using Express Texture with a custom paper texture to roughen the type edges of the smaller "kindness" type*

**4**

*Pasting type floaters into the composite*

YOU CAN USE PAINTER'S EXPRESS TEXTURE command to erode the smooth edges of a typeface, resulting in an organic, textured look. For the collage above, we eroded individual words in separate source files, then combined them in a composite image and added more effects. (If you're only interested in learning to erode type, follow steps 1–3 below.) A similar process might be used to erode and collage photos.

**1 Setting the type shapes in small source files.** Use Painter's Text tool to create type in individual source files. Choose black in the Color palette to automatically fill the type shapes with black as you type. Select the Text tool and choose a font and size in the Controls:Text palette. We created a 400 x 200-pixel source file for each word, then set 110-point type using various weights of Berkeley and Stone Sans typefaces. Some of the words were scaled down later in the compositing process.

**2 Softening the type.** In preparation for softening the letters, drop the type shapes to the background by clicking the Drop All button on the expanded Floater List palette. Now build a gray edge into the letterforms that you can manipulate in the "eroding" process in step 3; one way to add a gray edge is by softening. Then type Command-Shift-S to bring up the Super Soften dialog box and experiment with different settings. We used a 5-pixel setting for the thin Stone Sans letterforms and a 10-pixel setting for Berkeley Black.

**3 Eroding the type edges.** To add an organic edge to the type's perimeter, choose Effects, Surface Control, Express Texture using Paper Grain. The Express Texture dialog box is interactive, so you can test different paper textures or switch to a new paper library without needing to close the Express Texture dialog box. Move the Gray Threshold and Grain sliders to the left to make the type thinner, and move the Contrast slider to the right to remove any gray. For the large "kindness" type, for example, we used the Puffy Turtle texture from the New Textures library and used settings of Gray Threshold, 80%; Grain, 64%; and Contrast, 300%.

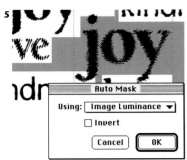

**5**

Applying a luminosity mask to the "joy" floater to mask the white area surrounding the type

**6**

The rough composite showing flat color fills and approximate sizing

**7**

Applying the Overlay Composite Method to the large lavender "peace" (left), and the Multiply Composite Method to the small maroon "kindness"

**8**

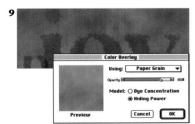

Filling the "joy" floater's mask with a gradation. Note how the type fades near the top (the darkest area of the gradation).

**9**

Using Color Overlay to add the Cloud texture and purple tint to the background

**4 Copying and pasting into the composite file.** Use the Rectangular Selection tool to select the textured type in your source file. Copy the selection, create a new file for your composite (ours was an 883 x 450-pixel file with a warm gray Paper Color) and Paste into the composite file. Use this copy-and-paste method to bring type from other source files into the composite.

**5 Making masks.** To hide the white area of the floater that surrounds the type, you need to make a luminosity mask. To do this, first select the floater in the Floater List, then choose Edit, Mask, Auto Mask (Command-Shift-M). Choose Image Luminance, leave the Invert box unchecked and click OK. Put the mask to work by clicking on the top right Mask Visibility icon in the Floater List. Repeat this process for the other type floaters in your image.

**6 Coloring, scaling and positioning.** Fill each floater with a color by selecting it in the Floater List, choosing a color and pressing Command-F, using Current Color. Use Effects, Orientation, Scale to resize selected floaters and use the Floater Adjuster tool to reposition them.

**7 Creating transparency effects.** You can achieve dramatic transparent effects using Composite Methods with layered floaters. Select a floater using the Floater Adjuster tool; in the Controls: Adjuster palette, choose a Composite Method from the pop-up menu. We used Overlay on the large "joy," "kindness" and "peace" elements, and Multiply on the smaller elements. (Turn to page 109 for a visual reference of the various Composite Methods.)

**8 Adding a gradation to a mask.** Applying a light-to-dark gradation to a floater's mask will vary the type's intensity. When used on a few type floaters, this technique can add dynamic movement to the collage. We used the gradation editor (Art Materials, Grad, Edit Gradation) to change the midpoint of a Two-Point, black-and-white gradation to 15%, making a predominantly white gradation that fades to black. (See page 18 for more about the gradation editor.) To apply a gradation to the floater's mask, select the floater and choose the Paint Bucket tool. In the Controls:Paint Bucket palette, under What to Fill, choose Mask; under Fill With, choose Gradation. Click with the Paint Bucket on the floater; the type should fade out where the mask is the darkest.

**9 Completing the collage.** We chose a purple color and applied it to the image background (click in a blank area of the Floater List to deselect all floaters) using Effects, Surface Control, Color Overlay, using Paper Grain (the Clouds texture from the Nature library) at 80% Opacity with the Hiding Power button selected. As a final touch, we selected some of the large floaters one at a time with the Floater Adjuster tool and adjusted their Opacity settings in the Controls:Adjuster palette.

# Creating a Tidepool

***Overview*** *Create a sandy background; spray plants onto the ocean floor using the Image Hose; light the scene; combine special effects to "ripple the water."*

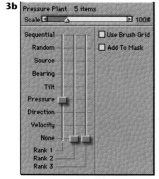

*Wheat Stalks texture applied to the blank image (left), then Super Softened*

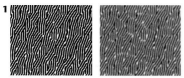

*Applying Surface Texture with Original Luminance to the sand-colored clone*

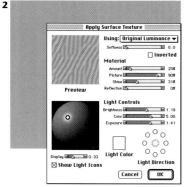

*The Pressure Plant nozzle file with images from small to large size*

*The zoomed-out Brush Controls:Nozzle palette showing Rank 1 set to Pressure*

JOHN DERRY

THE ILLUSION OF LIGHT REFRACTING through water is essential to creating a realistic underwater scene. In *Tidepool*, after using a variety of Image Hose nozzles to paint undersea plant life, John Derry engineered the look of rippling water by applying Lighting, Glass Distortion and Surface Texture to the image.

**1 Creating a soft sandy bottom.** To begin as Derry did, open a new 1200-pixel-wide image with a white background. Select black in the Color palette, choose Wheat Stalks paper texture from the New Textures library and scale it to 400% using the Size slider on the front of the Papers palette. Apply the black texture to your file with Effects, Surface Control, Color Overlay, using Paper Grain and Hiding Power at 100% Opacity. Derry liked the Wheat Stalks texture but felt it needed softening to look like rippled sand. Soften the background using Super Soften (Command-Shift-S); enter 12 when the dialog box appears. Click OK.

**2 Giving the rippled sand color and texture.** To make the background look more like sand, you can combine a sand-colored file with the gray rippled image. First, clone the gray image, (File, Clone), choose a sand color and fill the clone with the color (Command-F, Current Color, 100% Opacity). Next, combine the sand-colored clone with the gray image. Go to Effects, Surface Control, Apply Surface Texture, and choose Original Luminance. For a subtle effect use these settings: Amount, 25; Picture, 90; Shine, 30. Click the 11 o'clock Light Direction button, then move the Brightness slider up to 1.19 (to slightly increase the brightness), increase Concentration (Conc) to 5.00 (to decrease the spread of the light) and leave the Exposure at 1.41.

**3 Loading a nozzle and spraying images.** Most of the Image Hose nozzles that Derry used in this piece can be found in nozzle libraries on the Painter 4 CD, under Goodies, Nozzles. To choose an Image Hose nozzle from a Nozzle palette library, open the

**3c**

*Using short spiral strokes to Spray plants and pebbles onto the sandy ocean floor*

**4**

*Creating a soft, diffused custom light*

**5a**

*Applying Glass Distortion to initiate the ripple effect*

**5b**

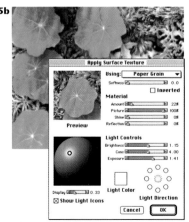

*Adding Surface Texture to complete the illusion of rippling water*

palette (Brushes, Nozzles) and click on a nozzle. To load an individual nozzle that isn't part of a library, press Command-L (or choose Brushes, Nozzles, Load Nozzle), open a folder containing nozzle files and open a nozzle. Once you've loaded a nozzle, you can choose to add it to the current library (Nozzles, Add to Library) or view it (Nozzles, Check Out Nozzle). To paint with a nozzle, select the Image Hose icon in the Brushes palette and begin painting.

To make a nozzle spray in a specific way, change the hose variant (Method, Brushes palette) or use the controls in the expanded Nozzle palette. For the undersea image, choose the Pressure Plants nozzle, select the Image Hose icon from the Brushes palette and begin painting with short, spiral strokes in your image.

Derry added strokes to the piece using a number of nozzles: Shadowed Coral and Pastel Coral (Aquatic library), Pointed Plant and Nasturtium (Nature 1 library), Pressure Plants and Pebbles (Nature 2 library). Load a library from the Painter 4 CD by clicking the Library button on the Nozzle drawer. See Chapter 11 in the Painter *User Guide* to learn how to create your own Image Hose nozzle.

**4 Applying Lighting.** To create a diffused lighting effect with soft pockets of light and dark areas, Derry modified an existing light, copied it four times, then modified the individual lights. To create a look similar to the one he achieved, choose Effects, Surface Control, Apply Lighting, Side Lighting. Reduce the Brightness, Distance and Spread settings, then click on two new locations in the Preview window to create two more lights with settings identical to the original. To reposition a light, click and drag on the large circle, and to aim the light in a new direction, click and drag on the small circle. Make further modifications to one of the three lights, then click in the Preview window two more times to create two more lights with those new settings, making a total of five lights. To create a softer effect on the whole scene, drag the Exposure slider to the left and the Ambient slider to the right. Store your custom light in the library by clicking the Save button, then click OK to apply the lighting to the image.

**5 Creating a water ripple effect.** Derry used a powerful but subtle combination of Glass Distortion and Surface Texture to create a realistic water ripple effect. To ripple your image, start with the Seismic texture from the Wild Textures library and scale it up to 400%. Now select Effects, Focus, Glass Distortion, Paper Grain and accept the default settings of Amount, 0 and Variance, 1.00.

To add a subtle bump to the transparent water ripple, choose Effects, Surface Control, Apply Surface Texture using Paper Grain: Amount, 22%; Picture, 100%; and Shine, 0%. Click the 11 o'clock Light Direction button to set a general light direction. To fine-tune your Lighting, change Brightness to 1.15 and Concentration to 4.00, and leave the Exposure at 1.41.

# Draping a Weave

***Overview*** *Paint a grayscale file that will be your source image; fill a clone of that file with a weave; use a combination of Glass Distortion and Surface Texture to wrap the weave around the source image.*

**1**

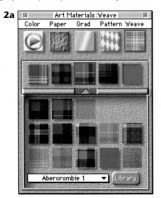

*The grayscale form file with strong values*

**2a**

*Choosing a weave in the Weaves palette*

**2b**

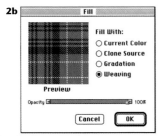

*Filling the clone with the weave*

YOU CAN USE PAINTER'S WEAVES FEATURE—located in the Art Materials palette—to fill any selection or document, using either the Fill command or the Paint Bucket tool. Weaves can be used in fashion design, and they make good backgrounds for scenes, but their flat look can be a drawback. To create the appearance of fabric—to hang behind a still life, for instance—we added dimension to a weave by "draping" it over a painted form using a powerful Glass Distortion displacement effect along with Apply Surface Texture.

**1 Making the form file.** Think of the form file as a kind of mold—or fashion designer's dress form—over which you'll drape your fabric. Create a grayscale form file that has strong value contrast and smooth dark-to-light transitions. As a reference for our 500-pixel-square form file, we draped fabric over a chair and sketched it in Painter, then cleaned up the sketch with the Fat Stroke Airbrush variant, working mostly with the Straight Lines Draw Style button checked in the Controls:Brush palette. Since any hard edges in the form file will make a noticeable break in the weave's pattern, soften your image with Super Soften (Command-Shift-S). We used a 7-pixel Super Soften setting on our file.

If you don't want to paint the form file, here's a fast, but less "organic" way to create it. Start by choosing one of the Line textures from the Simple Patterns paper library and drag the Scale slider in the Papers palette to 400%. (Alternatively, choose Art Materials, Paper, Make Paper Texture, using Line and a high spacing setting.) Choose black in the Color palette, then select Effects, Surface Control, Color Overlay, using Paper Grain and Hiding Power at 100% Opacity. Use Super Soften as you did above.

**2 Making a clone and filling it with a weave.** Choose File, Clone to make a duplicate of the form file with identical dimensions. Now choose a weave from the Weaves palette, and fill the

*Applying Glass Distortion to the weave*

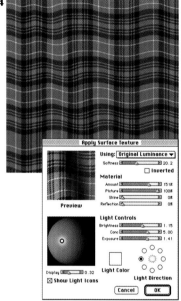

*Adding highlights and shadows to the distorted image using Surface Texture*

clone with your weave (Command-F, Weaving, 100%). We used the Abercrombie 1 weave from the Scottish Tartans library in the Colors, Weaves, Grads folder in the Painter application folder.

**3 Initiating the distortion.** Here's where the movement begins. Choose Effects, Focus, Glass Distortion, using Original Luminance. Now let Painter know the direction that you want the fabric to go when it overlies the form file. When a clone image is displaced by Glass Distortion using Original Luminance, the distance each pixel moves is based on the luminance of each pixel in the source file. We chose Vector Displacement to move pixels in a specific direction, and used the Amount slider to get a moderate "ripple" effect in the Preview (we chose 1.54), leaving Variance at 1.00. To establish the direction (and make the light areas move up and to the right, dark areas move down and to the left—based on the form file), we moved the Direction slider to 80°. We added a Softness of 15.2 to smoothe any rough edges that might be caused by the distortion of the weave. Experiment with your settings; the Softness, Amount and Direction may change based on the size of your file.

**4 Adding highlights and shadows.** Using Surface Texture adds to the illusion of folded fabric by contributing highlights and shadows based on the form file. Choose Effects, Surface Control, Apply Surface Texture, using Original Luminance. Experiment with your settings—paying special attention to how the lighting controls affect the look—and click OK. We set Softness to 20.2 (to smoothe the image and slightly increase the depth of the folds), Amount to 151%, Picture to 100% (to make the image lighter while maintaining weaving detail), and Shine to 0%, then chose the 9 o'clock Light Direction button.

---

## MOLDING A WEAVE OVER TYPOGRAPHIC FORMS

Try wrapping a weave (or other image) around type or a logo. Follow the same steps in "Draping a Weave," and remember to use the Super Soften command on the type. For the "Wow!" image we chose Angle Map type in the Glass Distortion dialog box (the angle of the distortions vary based on luminance information in the form file), and we used a high Softness setting to compensate for the extreme wrap applied to the weave. This helped to smoothe out the threads. In Surface Texture, we moved the Softness slider to 2.2, and set Amount at 171%; Picture at 100%, Shine at 40%, and chose the 9:00 Light Direction with a Brightness of 1.19.

*Type set in Adobe Reporter 2 (left), then given a Super Soften setting of 7 pixels.*

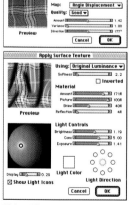

*Using Glass Distortion and Surface Texture to complete the "wrapped type" effect*

# Applying Effects to Selections

**Overview** *Create a sketch and color it; make selections; apply effects to active selections; paste items from other files into the main image.*

STEVE CAMPBELL

*Campbell's pencil sketch (left), and filling areas with the Chalk brush*

*Campbell's selections as they appear in the Path List palette*

PAINTER'S APPLY LIGHTING FEATURE is a great way to add a 3D illusion to flat art. Since that feature is one of Steve Campbell's favorites, it's no surprise he used it throughout *Post Orbit*, an illustration for a *Washington Post* story about Sony's new 3D headphones.

**1 Sketching and coloring.** Create a sketch and use Painter's brushes to color it. Campbell began with a pencil sketch that he scanned into Painter at about 3.5 inches square and 300 ppi. He chose File, Clone, then selected all and deleted the cloned image. He chose Canvas, Tracing Paper so he could use his sketch as a guide. (Campbell made a total of seven "progressive clones" throughout this job.) He used the Chalk brush to make the two background shapes and the carpet; to create activity in the color, he increased the Hue (± H) and Value (± V) Color Variability settings in the zoomed-out Color palette. He used Chalk, Airbrush and Water brushes to give color, shape and form to the figure's head, and drew the headphones with the Pen and Ink variant of the Pens brush.

**2 Making selections.** Use one or more of the selection tools to isolate areas of your image so you'll be able to add texture to them later. Name your selections as they appear in the Path List palette by double-clicking on their names. Campbell used the Lasso tool to outline the three sections of the chair, the head, the two background sections (including the pieces on each side between the headphones and

## SMOOTH TRANSITIONS

If you prefer to have selected areas blend together smoothly, select the Selection Adjuster tool, choose a selection, and increase the Feather in the Controls:Adjuster palette.

Applying a weave to the chair selection (left), then adding a gradation with an 80% Opacity setting

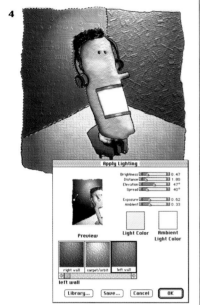

Applying a custom light to the background

Adding a shadow under one of the "orbits" using the Fat Stroke Airbrush

Campbell used Apply Lighting to darken the masked ukulele's neck.

the head) and the carpet. He grouped related selections by Shift-selecting them in the Path List and clicking on the Group button. (Read more about working with selections in Chapter 4.)

**3 Using gradations and weaves.** Activate a selection and choose a weave from the Art Materials:Weaves palette. Campbell activated the chair selection group and chose the Our Shadow Weave. Select Effects, Fill, and choose the Weaving button. Click OK. Now choose a gradation (Campbell used Night Sky) and Fill again—this time check the Gradation button. To see the weave through the gradation, drag the Opacity slider to 80%. Click OK.

**4 Applying Surface Texture and Lighting.** Add texture to active selections by choosing Effects, Surface Control, Apply Surface Texture (using Paper Grain), then give the selections more dimension with Effects, Surface Control, Apply Lighting.

Campbell applied custom paper textures to the background selections and the carpet. The left background is a video grab of a circuit board, and the one on the right is actually two textures: a line texture from the Simple Textures library, applied with no Shine setting, and a hand-drawn "hieroglyphic" texture, applied with Shine. Campbell prefers to add lighting on top of texture rather than the other way around; he feels that this method more closely imitates "real-world" lighting effects.

To light the textured selections, he created and saved three modified versions of the Splashy Color light in the Apply Lighting dialog box. He applied one of his new versions to the background, the carpet and the head, reducing its strength (if necessary) after applying with the Edit, Fade command.

**5 Creating the "orbit."** Campbell carefully drew three large, circular "orbit" shapes with the Pen tool and converted them to selections using Shapes, Convert to Selection. Then, using his custom lights, he applied lighting to each individual selection, creating a tinted, transparent look. To add to the illusion of depth, he used the Fat Stroke Airbrush variant to lighten or darken areas outside of the selections.

**6 Adding floaters.** To add other images to your work, open them as separate files. Create masks for them, then copy and paste them into your main image. The ukulele in Campbell's image, for instance, started out as a video grab that he masked in Photoshop. He opened it in Painter and used Apply Lighting to darken the fretboard, then copied and pasted the instrument into the main image where he rotated it (Effects, Orientation, Rotate) and adjusted its Opacity to 90% (Controls:Adjuster palette).

**Finishing touches.** To emphasize the headphones, Campbell added a glow with the Fat Stroke Airbrush variant. He used the same variant and the 2B Pencil to give form to the teeth.

# Building a Lively Music Poster

***Overview*** *Create type outlines in a Postscript drawing program; rasterize the EPS file in Photoshop; open it and use Painter's Image Warp to alter it; make a mask for the altered type and float it; apply gradations to the background and to the type floater; add a drop shadow to the type.*

JOHN DERRY

**1**

The rasterized Adobe Illustrator file

**2a**

Image Warp

Size ◄———————————▶ 30%

○ Linear
● Cubic          [ Cancel ]  [ OK ]
○ Sphere

*Clicking on the cap height of 1805 and pulling the first warp*

MUSIC POSTER ARTISTS OF THE LATE 1960'S were inspired by fight posters from the 1950's. John Derry drew from both of these sources when he designed *The Winter of Love* poster, created for a Jefferson Starship concert. He applied colorful gradations to simulate the effect of a split ink fountain in order to add movement to the poster, and used Image Warp to bend the typography.

**1 Preparing the type source image.** Create black-filled type outlines in a Postscript drawing program. Save the file in EPS format and rasterize it by opening it in Photoshop. (You could also set type in Painter, but if you have a lot of type, it will be easier to edit in a drawing program like Adobe Illustrator, Macromedia Free-hand or Corel Draw.) Derry set up the initial typography and graphics in Illustrator. He set the type in URW's Thunderbird Extra Condensed, a font reminiscent of '60s music posters. When Derry finished the artwork, he converted it to outlines, saved the file in EPS format and rasterized it in Photoshop as an 11 x 17-inch 300 ppi TIFF file.

**2 Warping the type file.** To distort the type, open your source file in Painter and choose Effects, Surface Control, Image Warp. To approximate Derry's effect, choose Cubic and move the Size slider

**2b**

*The finished source file with three warps*

**3**

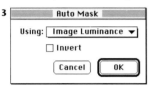

*Making a luminosity mask for the type*

**4**

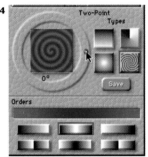

*The lower portion of the expanded Grad palette. Make a tighter spiral gradation by Command-dragging the red ball counterclockwise around the ring.*

**5**

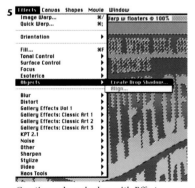

*Creating a drop shadow with Effects, Objects, Create Drop Shadow*

to 30%. Moving the slider to the left will produce a smaller-radius warp effect. To achieve the long, curved warp, Derry clicked and pulled three times: once just above the cap height of "1805," again near the baseline of "Timothy Leary," and a more subtle pull at the base of "Winter." Since Image Warp takes a while to process your adjustments, save time by making several small "warps" on your image while in the Image Warp dialog box. (If you make a mistake, click Cancel to exit the dialog box and redo your series of warps.) When you are satisfied with the preview, click OK. Derry retouched his image where the top and bottom became curved by pasting in pieces from his original file and touching up with a brush and black and white paint.

**3 Making a mask and floating.** Derry created a mask for the black lettering, then converted it to a mask representation selection so that he could float the lettering easily. Choose Edit, Mask, Auto Mask, Image Luminance to create a luminosity mask for your type. View the mask as a selection by clicking on the right-hand Visibility icon in the expanded Path List palette. When the green marquee appears, copy the item to the clipboard.

**4 Building the composite file.** Open a new file for your composite image (Derry's was 3300 x 5100 pixels). Fill it with a magenta-to-blue Two-Point spiral gradation. (In the Art Materials: Grad palette, the spiral gradation is the lower-right Types button). To make a tighter spiral, hold down the Command key and drag the red ball counterclockwise. Derry zoomed-out the palette and clicked on the top center Orders button and used the Fill command (Command-F) to fill the background with the gradation.

Paste the type floater into your composite file. Choose colors for a gradation that will contrast with the background, and then fill your floater with the gradation. Derry used a yellow-to-orange Two-Point linear gradation for the poster lettering.

**5 Adding a drop shadow.** Finally, create a soft shadow for the type: With the floater still selected, choose Effects, Objects, Create Drop Shadow. The command creates a floater group containing the original item and a duplicate (the shadow) filled with black. You can adjust the shadow's opacity in the Create Drop Shadow dialog box, although there's no preview; or, as Derry did, you can click OK with the default settings, open the group in the Floater List, select the shadow, select the Floater Adjuster tool and adjust the Opacity slider in the Controls:Adjuster palette. (Derry set the shadow's Opacity to 46%.) In the Drop Shadow dialog box, Radius and Thinness work together to control the softness of the shadow. Higher numbers in these fields will create a more diffused look. If your file is large (like Derry's), you'll also want to enter higher numbers in the X-Offset and Y-Offset boxes to make the shadow more apparent.

# Compositing Photographs Using Special Effects

***Overview*** *Use Correct Colors, Surface Texture and Painter's brushes to enhance two source images; then float elements and combine the images using Compositing methods.*

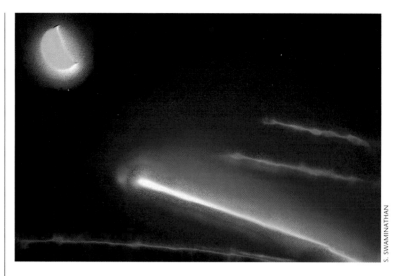

**1a**

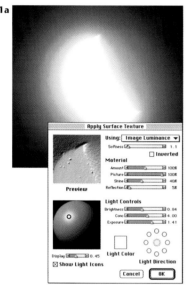

*Using Apply Surface Texture to add lighting and texture to the moon source image*

**1b**

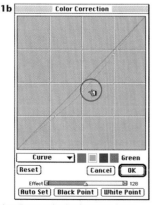

*Reducing Green color in the moon image*

TO CREATE THE EXPRESSIVE DUAL PORTRAIT *Hyakutake and the Moon,* photojournalist S. Swaminathan began by taking the original source photos using a Nikon F4 with 500 mm F.4 telephoto (with 1.4 tele-extender that increased the size of the lens to 700 mm) and Fujichrome Velvia slide film. The photo of the moon was captured at Seacliff Beach in Santa Cruz, California, using an exposure time of 1.5 seconds, and the Comet Hyakutake photo was taken in the Santa Cruz Mountains with an exposure time of 45 minutes. The long exposure time of the comet photo resulted in the stars being blurred into lovely curved lines that complement the movement of the comet through space. After scanning the two transparencies using a Polaroid Sprintscan35, Swaminathan began the process of compositing the images.

**1 Preparing the first source file.** Swaminathan opened the 1207 x 1315-pixel moon image. He selected a rectangle that included the moon using the Rectangular Selection tool, copied it, and pasted it into a new image (Edit, Paste, Into New Image). He applied dramatic highlights and shadows to the moon image using Effects, Surface Control, Apply Surface Texture.

Working with the moon image, Swaminathan performed the Correct Colors procedure to adjust the Curves, and Contrast and Brightness *after* applying Surface Texture, because he felt it gave him more control over the color and tonal ranges in the enhanced image. To correct a color cast in your image, choose Effects, Tonal Control, Correct Colors, and from the pull-down menu choose Curves. To reduce or increase an individual color component in your image, click the appropriate color icon to isolate that color, and grab the diagonal curve near the center of the grid and pull gently. You will see the color value change in your image. When you are satisfied, click OK. He reduced the Green curve to eliminate a green cast on the moon, and increased Red and Blue. He

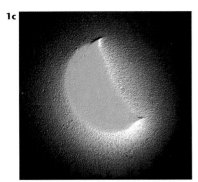

**1c**

*The dramatically enhanced and color-corrected moon source image*

**2**

*The color-corrected comet image*

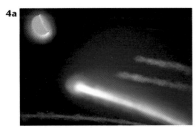

**3**

*Painting brushstrokes onto the stars*

**4a**

*The moon image, pasted and scaled*

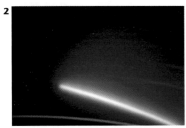

**4b**

*Detail showing particles enhanced by the Dissolve Compositing method*

also switched to the Contrast and Brightness controls and applied: Contrast +18% and Brightness –10%.

**2 Preparing the background file.** Swaminathan opened the 1135 x 1681-pixel comet image, which would become the background file. To enhance the glow of the comet, he corrected the tones and color first. He increased the Contrast and Brightness of the comet and stars using Correct Colors, Contrast and Brightness, applying these settings: Contrast, +21% and Brightness, +10%. Then, he switched to Curves, and isolated the blue component by clicking on the Blue color icon. He pulled up on the blue curve to increase blue color in the halo of the comet. Then, to add a subtle "bump" to the comet glow he used Apply Surface Texture (using Image Luminance) with these settings: Softness, 0.9; Amount, 15%; Picture, 90; Shine, 20%; Reflection, 7%; Brightness, 1.25; Conc, 5.00; Exposure, 1.41 and Light Position, 12:00.

**3 Adding expressive brush work.** To focus more attention on the comet—while enhancing the stars—Swaminathan reduced the brightness of the trailing stars in the image, then added subtle complexity to their color. First, he used the Dodge brush to reduce the intensity of the stars above and below the comet. Then, he switched to a modified Fat Stroke Airbrush and painted brushstrokes onto the stars (with the Color Variability ±H (Hue) slider set to 23%, and the Using Clone Color checkbox checked).

**4 Combining the source images.** Now it was time to move the moon into its new position, several hundred million miles across space! Swaminathan copied and pasted the moon image into the upper left corner of the comet image. With the Floater Adjuster tool selected, he chose Effects, Orientation, Scale, and dragged a corner handle to scale it to a comfortable size.

**5 Compositing the floaters.** To further emphasize the comet's tail and glow by creating a look that resembled crystalline ice particles, Swaminathan layered floaters with different compositing methods applied. He made two floaters of the comet and star image by marqueeing the comet and stars with the Rectangular Selection tool and Option-clicking twice to make two copies. After clicking the Eye icon in the Floater List to hide one floater, he selected the visible floater in the Floater List and applied Effects, Focus, Glass distortion to it (using Image Luminance and the Refraction Map type). Then using the Floater Adjuster tool, he chose the Darken Composite Method in the Floater Adjuster palette, and set the Opacity slider to 40%. He clicked the Eye icon to make the top floater visible again and applied the Dissolve Composite Method, this time with an Opacity of 80%. After dropping the floater (Drop button, Floater List), he increased the feeling of movement though space by using the Distorto variant of the Liquid brush to pull pixels in the center of the comet from the head to the end. 🖌

■ **Corrine Okada**, an innovative designer, illustrator and artist, designed *The Digital Pond* package (above), as a three-part image to illustrate services that The Digital Pond provides—communicating the transition from sketch through digital file to the final high-resolution image. After making sketches with pencil and paper, Okada began the image background and detail elements in Painter. Working in several small source files, she used brushes, her own custom paper textures and patterns, and Painter's special effects (such as Color Overlay and Surface Texture) to add color, texture and dimension to all of the elements. Finally, she opened the frog, carp, dragon fly and background files in Photoshop and completed the composition.

■ *Drummer Sam* (right), the cover illustration for the *Sacramento News & Review* Sammie Awards issue, was created by special effects genius **Steve Campbell**. His inspiration for the illustration was the original Sammie logo (shown on the monitor) designed by Steve Barberia. Campbell applied many textures and special effects within the selections. To add depth and movement to the stage floor and wall—and to make the drums look round—Campbell used Apply Lighting within individual selections, increasing the elevation and brightness of the lights to achieve soft, gradients on the surfaces.

■ **Bill Niffenegger's** illustration *AIDS* (left) for *Dentistry* magazine was honored with the APEX award for magazine covers. The piece reflects the devastating, yet sensitive, nature of the subject. The author of the book *Photoshop Filter Finesse*, Niffenegger painted the piece in Painter using a wide variety of brushes, custom paper textures, Apply Lighting and KPT Texture Explorer and Gradient Designer.

■ To accompany a *Macworld* review of Painter, **Steve Campbell** created *Paint Can* (below) with the goal of using as many of the program's special effects as possible—for instance, a custom "light bulb" Image Hose nozzle that he sprayed across the image. To achieve transparency effects, he floated nearly every item as he worked.

■ **Gary Clark** began *A Bit of Magic* (above) by using the Straight Cloner variant to bring a fractal mountain image into a blank document. (Clark generates most of his fractal images with Springer-Verlag's Beauty of Fractals Lab and Kai's Power Tools.) He incorporated a scan of a conventional watercolor abstract in the same way, then used KPT Fractal Explorer to add a fractal to the sky. To give the painting cohesiveness, he added washes of transparent color with the Simple Water variant of the Water Color brush. For the sky and water, Clark made selections with the Pen tool, then used the Straight Cloner variant to bring video grabs of cloud and water images into the selections. These areas were retouched with the Fat Stroke Airbrush variant. Clark used the Apply Lighting command to further unify the image.

■ **Dorothy Simpson Krause's** *Star in the East* (right) blends Jan Doucette's photo of a wood nymph with a scanned image of a king. She filled a clone of the composite with a gentle gold sweep using KPT Gradient Designer, then used Surface Texture to apply texture to achieve an embossed effect. In Photoshop, she opened the image and copied and pasted the original image on top of the clone using the Luminance blending mode.

■ To create *Dancers* (above), **Pamela Drury Watenmaker** began the image in Photoshop by painting flat color areas. She selected areas and saved them as channels. She then loaded each selection in turn, inverted it, deleted the rest of the image, then saved under another name in Photoshop format. She opened each file in Painter and used Glass Distortion and Apply Surface Texture—using Paper Grain for both—to the selections. Back in Photoshop, she opened the textured files one at a time and pasted them into the selections in her original file.

■ *Winter Eagles* (left) is one of a series of wildlife illustrations that **Sharon Steuer** created for a book proposal for the Smithsonian Institution. She drew the shapes in Macromedia Freehand and filled them with flat color, rasterized the EPS file in Photoshop, then brought the image into Painter, where she added volume to the flat color areas with various Airbrushes. To make the eagles and landforms more sculptural and dramatic, Steuer created custom lights and applied them to selected areas of the image, then blended the effects with the Brush, Airbrush, Dodge and Burn brushes.

■ *Information Highway* was based on an illustration **Ayse Ulay** created for *Occidental* magazine. Eight figures were placed over filled circular selections, then distorted with a KPT Glass Lens filter to achieve a spherical effect. Ulay opened a second file—a bitmapped scan of a world map—in Painter and used Color Overlay and Apply Surface Texture to tint it and add dimension. She used a KPT Glass Lens filter to turn the map into a globe. Ulay created a background in a third file with Apply Surface Texture and Paper Grain, then used Xaos Tools' Paint Alchemy to add more texture. She pasted the map and the other eight spheres into the background file and used Effects, Objects, Create Drop Shadow to make them appear to float above the canvas.

■ **Jim Benson** began *The Divorce* as a sketch with the Sharp Chalk variant. He added color to the faces with the Fat Stroke Airbrush variant and used the Brushy variant on the background. He applied Xaos Tools' Paint Alchemy filter across the entire image, then used Edit, Fade, with Undo Amount set to 75%. He also applied Effects, Surface Control, Express Texture, Paper Grain using a custom "hairs" paper texture, then fading with Undo Amount set to 95%. Benson selected the two faces and floated them, then lit each of them and the background separately using Apply Lighting with custom light settings. After more brushwork, he dropped the floaters and added the words with the Penetration Brush variant of the Brush and the Single Pixel Water variant. He opened an earlier version of the image without text and applied a Surface Texture using Paper Grain, then used the Soft Cloner variant to blend selected areas of the two images.

Page number change only on pages 178-179

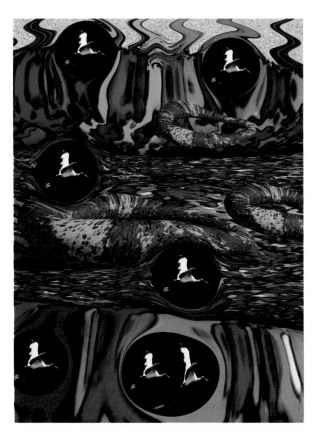

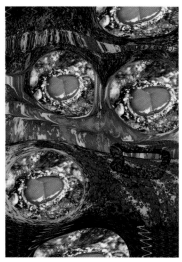

■ **Will Tait's** series of abstract images entitled *The Space Between* explores the dynamic energy that exists between varying forms of nature. Two of the images in the series (shown here) started as large, texture-mapped images in 3D Studio, which he saved as TIFF files and imported into Painter. To add blobs containing his own photos of tidepool and swamp life into the images above, he copied each photo to the clipboard, then used Effects, Esoterica, Blobs. He touched up the image with Liquid brushes.

■ Illustrator **Philip Howe** created *Meatery Couple* using a photograph taken by associate **Ed Lowe**. He used Painter's special effects on the image to create a lively surface and a warm atmosphere. Howe opened the scanned image in Painter and cloned it. He used Effects, Surface Control, Apply Lighting on the clone to get a dramatic look, then used Effects, Focus, Glass Distortion and Effects, Surface Control, Apply Surface Texture to add texture and surface activity. After painting on the image with various Chalk and Airbrush variants, he used Apply Surface Texture using Image Luminance to add a 3D brushstroke look. To add clarity to certain areas (such as the couple's faces), Howe meticulously cloned portions of the original photograph back in, using a small, low-opacity Airbrush in Soft Cloner submethod.

# MULTIMEDIA WITH PAINTER

*Film artist Dewey Reid created this pre-production comprehensive for the Nike All Conditions Gear TV commercial using scanned images and Painter's brushes, effects and Scripts; he worked back and forth between Painter and Adobe Premiere, using Premiere for timing and transitions.*

*A Current Script showing the instructions for an application of Surface Texture*

WHETHER YOU'RE AN ANIMATOR, film artist, designer, or 3D artist, Painter's multimedia capabilities offer you dozens of practical techniques. Multimedia artists appreciate the creative freedom that Painter's brushes, textures and effects offer. The ability to record painting scripts lets you make tutorials to show others how your painting was built and even lets you batch-process a series of images. If you're producing an animation or making a movie, many of the techniques and effects shown in this book can be applied to frames in a Frame Stack, Painter's native animation format, or to an imported movie clip. And Painter gives 3D artists a wide variety of choices for creating natural, organic textures to be used for texture mapping.

## WORKING WITH SCRIPTS

Painter's versatile Script feature lets you record your work, then play the process back, either in Painter or as a Quicktime, AVI or VFW movie. If you use this feature a lot, you'll soon discover its limitations: for example, its inability to record some Painter operations can change the look of the image during playback.

**How did I do that?** With Painter 4's new automatic script feature, you can reproduce what you just did using the Current Script. While you work, Painter transparently records your actions automatically—saving them as the Current Script in the Painter Script Data file, in the Painter 4 folder. You can tell Painter how long to save scripts by specifying the number of days in the Preferences, General dialog box. (The default is one day.) A word of caution: Saving several days of scripts can use a lot of hard disk space!

To work with the Current Script, open the Objects palette, click on the Script List icon, and click the Open Script button in the expanded Script List palette. Go to the Painter 4 folder and open the

To create this animated logo for Fox Television, Geoff Hull built text selections in Painter and used several Oil Paint brushes to add lively brushstrokes and saturated color to his design. Turn to page 205 to see more of Hull's work.

Use these buttons on the front of the Scripts palette to begin recording a single script (center red button) and to stop recording when you're finished (left square button).

The Wow! Effects Script library chosen in the Objects palette. Use these scripts to apply special effects to images and movies.

Current Script. The Current Script cannot be edited, but to use only a specific set of instructions from it, you *can* copy them to the clipboard and paste the instructions into a new script. Then you'll be able to use your new script to re-create a series of actions. To do this, open the Current Script, Shift-select the instructions that you want to use (you may want to work backwards from the bottom of the list, where the most recent instructions are found), and click the Copy button at the bottom of the palette. From the Script List menu, choose New Script. Type a name for your new script in the Name the Script dialog box, and click OK. The script will be saved into the current library visible in the Objects: Scripts palette. When the empty script window appears, click the Paste button at the bottom of the palette, and click the Close button. To play your new script, choose Scripts, Playback Script and select it by name.

**Recording a planned script.** To record a series of deliberate actions into a script (instead of copying and pasting from the automatically recorded script), choose Scripts, Record Script to begin recording. When you're finished working on your image choose Scripts, Stop Recording Script (or click the square Stop button on the left side of the Scripts palette). Painter prompts you to name your script. The new script will appear in the drawer of the Scripts palette, available for later playback. Choose Scripts, Playback Script, or click the forward arrow button to play the new script.

**Recording and saving a series of scripts.** If you want to record the development of a complex painting and you don't want to finish the painting in one sitting, you can record a series of work scripts to be played back, one on top of the other. Choose Objects, Scripts, Record Script, and begin your painting. When you want to take a break, stop recording (Scripts, Stop Recording Script). Include a number in the name of your script (such as "01") to help you remember the playback order. When you're ready to continue, choose Scripts, Record Script again and resume working on your image. Record and save as many scripts as you need, numbering them so you can keep track of the order. To play them back, open a new file of the same dimensions as the original, then choose Scripts, Playback Script. Choose the "01" script, and when it's done playing, choose the next script: It will play back on top of the image created by the first script. Continue playing back scripts in order until the image is completed.

**Automating a series of operations.** A recorded series of actions can save you a lot of time when you need to apply the same effect to

**PLAYING SCRIPTS ON KEY**

Painter lets you play scripts from the keyboard. End the script name with a backslash (\) plus a single letter, such as "Wow\a." To play the script using the keyboard shortcut, type Command-K followed by the letter "a." (Mac users: If you don't get a result, you may have a conflict with an extension or control panel—such as Suitcase—that uses the same key command.)

To add lighting and a paper texture to this Mediacom video clip, we played a special effects script (using Apply Lighting and Surface Texture) onto the frames.

several images or to a frame stack. Test a combination of operations (such as a series of choices from the Effects menu) until you get something you like, then choose Objects, Scripts, Record Script and repeat the series. After you've stopped recording and have saved your script, you can apply the series of operations to a selection, a floater, a still image or a frame stack by selecting your script in the Script palette and choosing Scripts, Script Options. Turn to "Automating Movie Effects" on page 191 for a detailed explanation of this technique.

**Playing a script back as a movie.** This is a great option if you want to send your script to someone who doesn't have Painter. Quicktime movies can be played on both Macintosh and PC/Windows computers with a freeware Quicktime projector such as Movie Player (included on the *Wow!* CD-ROM that accompanies this book).

Begin by choosing Scripts, Script Options. Check Record Initial State (otherwise Painter will playback the first few commands or brushstrokes of your script using whatever colors, brushes and textures are active, instead of the ones you actually used during the script). Check Save Frames on Playback, and leave the time interval Painter uses to grab frames from your script at 10, the default. (For future recordings, you may want to experiment with lower settings to get a smoother playback result.)

Next, open a new file of the same dimensions as your eventual movie file. Choose Objects, Scripts, Record Script and make your drawing. When you're finished, choose Scripts, Stop Recording Script; name and save your script. Now here's when Painter actually converts the script to a movie. First, watch your recorded script played back as Painter Frame Stack by opening a new file (same dimensions) and choosing Scripts, Playback Script. Choose your script from the list, and Painter will prompt you to create a new movie file. Name it, then specify the num-

Highly saturated colors can smear when output to video. Choose Effects, Tonal Control, Video Legal Colors to make the colors in your file compatible with NTSC or PAL video color. In the Preview, press and release the grabber to toggle between the RGB and Video Legal Colors preview, and click OK to convert the colors in your file.

> **QUICKTIME CAN'T CONVERT**
>
> Many of the prerecorded scripts that ship with Painter contain Painter commands that Quicktime cannot convert and consequently can't be turned into Quicktime movies. It's not possible to use the Record Frames on Playback function with scripts that contain commands such as File, New, or File, Clone (an Illegal Command error message will appear).

ber of layers of Onion Skin and color depth by clicking on the appropriate buttons. Click OK, and your script will unfold as a Frame Stack. When it's finished playing, save it in Quicktime/VFW movie format by choosing Save As. The Quicktime/VFW file will be smaller than a Frame Stack (if you use a compressor choice in the Compression Settings dialog box) and will play back more smoothly. (Because most compression degrades quality, compress only when you've completed the project. Film artist Dewey Reid suggests using Animation compression or None.) To read more

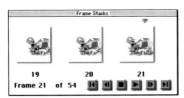

*The Frame Stack palette for Donal Jolley's animation* Turtle Rockets *showing movement in frames 19–21*

information about preserving image quality when working with movies, turn to page 187 of this chapter introduction.

**Making movies using multiple scripts.** Save a series of successive scripts, then playback the scripts as frame stacks and save them as Quicktime movies without compression to preserve quality. Open the movies in a program such as Adobe Premiere or Avid Video Shop and composite the movies together into a single movie.

## ANIMATING WITH FRAME STACKS

If you open a Quicktime or VFW movie in Painter, it will be converted to a Frame Stack, Painter's native movie format. Frame Stacks are based on the way conventional animators work: Each frame is analogous to an individual transparent acetate cel. You can navigate to any frame within a stack and paint on it or apply effects to it with any of Painter's tools (see "Animating an Illustration" on page 192).

Artists accustomed to specialized animation and video programs such as Adobe After Effects and Adobe Premiere will notice the limitations of the Frame Stack feature (there are no precise timing or compositing controls, for instance). If you use one of these programs, you will probably want to work out timing and compositing in the specialized program, then import your document into Painter to give it an effects treatment.

When you open a Quicktime or VFW video clip in Painter or start a brand-new movie, you'll specify the number of frames and color bit depth to be used in the Frame Stack. You will be asked to name and save your movie. At this point the stack is saved to your hard disk. A Frame Stack will usually take up many more megabytes on your hard disk than it did as a movie (depending on the kind of compression used), so have plenty of space available. Each time you advance a frame in the stack, Painter automatically saves any changes you have made to the movie. When you choose Save As, Painter will ask you to name the movie again. This is not a redundant Save command, but an opportunity to convert the file to another format: Save Current Frame as

When you're turning a script into a Frame Stack by checking the Record Frames on Playback box (Objects, Scripts, Script Options), a long script may result in a huge Frame Stack. There is currently no way to preview the number of frames that will be created when you enter an interval number in the dialog box, so you need to make sure you have plenty of hard disk space available.

*To record the painting process of* Mill Valley *(360 x 504 pixels, painted with Pastel and Water brushes), we made a movie using Save Frames on Playback and an interval of 10. The resulting movie was 100.6 MB with 142 frames.*

**SAVING FRAMES ON PLAYBACK**

To save a script as a movie, check Save Frames on Playback in the Script Options dialog box (Objects, Scripts, Script Options). Painter will grab a slice of your script as a frame at the interval (in 1/10th seconds) that you set. A lower setting in the interval box (such as 1 or 2) results in smoother playback than the default setting of 10, but file sizes for lower settings are larger. For instance, a short script with an interval setting of 1 resulted in a 4.2 MB Frame Stack; the same script recorded with an interval of 10 produced a 1.4 MB file.

Script Options
☒ Record Initial State
☒ Save Frames on Playback
Every [2] 1/10ths of a Second
Cancel    OK

*A storyboard frame from the MGM movie Stargate. Peter Mitchel Rubin used Painter to build digital storyboard illustrations for the movie, saving them as numbered PICT files and animating them with Adobe Premiere.*

Image, Save Movie as Quicktime or VFW format, or Save Movie as Numbered Files (to create a sequence of frames to composite in another program such as Adobe Premiere).

### Creating animated comps.

Painter provides a good way to visualize a rough animation. An animatic (a comp of an animation, consisting of keyframe illustrations with movement applied) can be comprised of images drawn in Painter; scanned elements; or numbered PICT files created in Painter, Photoshop or even object-oriented programs that can export PICT files (such as Illustrator). See "Making an Animated Comp" on page 194, featuring Dewey Reid's illustrations in a demonstration of an animatic technique. You can also alter individual frames in a movie with Painter's effects or brushes. For a demonstration of frame-by-frame painting, see "Animating an Illustration" on page 192.

**Rotoscoping movies.** There are numerous ways to rotoscope (paint or apply special effects to movie frames) in Painter. Many of the techniques in this book can be used for rotoscoping—brushwork, masking, tonal adjustment, filters, Apply Lighting, Surface Texture or Glass Distortion, for example.

**Basing an animation on a movie.** You can use Painter's Tracing Paper to trace images from a source movie to a clone to create an animation. This feature lets you shoot video and use it as a reference on which to base a path of motion.

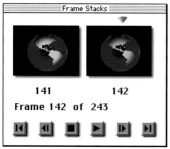

*To change the continents from brown to green in this Cascom video clip, we recorded a script while performing the Color Mask procedure and Color Overlay tinting process on one frame, then stopped recording and saved our script. After undoing the effects applied to the first frame, we chose Movie, Apply Script to Movie and took a break while Painter completed the masking and tinting process on all 243 frames. Above: The Frame Stack palette showing frame 141 with the operations applied, and frame 142 as yet untouched.*

**MANAGING LARGE MOVIE FILES**

Because an animation can involve thousands of frames, film artist Dewey Reid advises cutting a large movie into manageable sections using a compositing program such as Adobe Premiere or Adobe After Effects, then importing the sections into Painter to apply the effects. After applying the effects, use a compositing program to recompile the clips. This technique also works if you create an animation in sections in Painter and compile it in a compositing program.

**REAL-TIME COMPOSITING**

Painter has no option to set Frames Per Second (FPS) timing, so use Adobe Premiere or Adobe After Effects, where you can preview motion at 30 FPS so that it appears smooth to the eye.

**COHESIVE MOVIE LIGHTING**

Artist Dewey Reid advises using Effects, Surface Control, Apply Lighting to add cohesiveness and to smooth out transitions in a movie. For instance, using Apply Lighting with the same setting on all frames will smooth color transitions between clips and make elements from different sources blend together more successfully. Apply Lighting can also help to cover masking errors.

*Reid used Apply Lighting and Apply Surface Texture (using Paper Grain) on the character Yuri the Yak for Sesame Street (produced by Children's Television Workshop).*

*A frame from an animation based on a video clip. We began by using Painter's Water Color brushes in the Wet Layer to illustrate the frames. Because the Wet Layer sits on top of the entire Frame Stack, we chose Canvas, Dry to drop the Wet Layer's contents onto every frame in the movie when we had finished painting all of the frames. As a final touch, we applied an effects script (with Surface Texture using Paper Grain) to complete the piece.*

## USING A VIDEO CLIP REFERENCE

Painter's cloning function allows you to link two movies—a video clip and a blank movie of the same pixel dimensions—and use the video as a reference on which to base an animation. Open a video clip that you want to use as a reference, then make a blank movie (File, New) of the same pixel dimensions as your video clip. (The second movie doesn't need to have the same number of frames.) Under File, Clone Source, select the video clip. In the blank movie frame, turn on Tracing Paper (Command-T), and using the clone source as a guide, choose a brush and paint on the frame. To use the Frame Stacks palette to advance one frame in the original, click the icon circled in the palette (or press Page Up on your keyboard). Do the same to advance the clone one frame. Use Movie, Go to Frame to move to a specific frame in either clone or original. You can also apply special effects such as Surface Texture, Color Overlay or Glass Distortion (all using Original Luminance) to your new movie using the clone source.

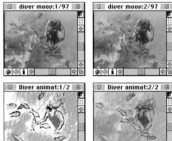

*We opened a video clip (shown here in the Frame Stack palette) and a new frame stack, both using two layers of Onion Skin. Click on the circled icon to advance one frame in the Frame Stacks palette.*

*Frames 1 and 2 of the Diver video clip (top row), and corresponding frames in the animation (bottom row), painted with the Sharp Chalk variant. Tracing paper is active on the bottom right image.*

### LIGHTS, CAMERA, ACTION!

When you recorded a *session* in previous versions of Painter only your actions were captured. But when you tell Painter 4 to record a script, your "thinking time" (the pauses between actions) is recorded. Keep this in mind if you plan to play back your script as a movie. Recorded "thinking time" can lead to series of "blank" frames. Plan to storyboard your moves so that you'll be able to execute the operations without long pauses. Here's another work-around: After you Record Frames on Playback, check out the Frame Stack, make note of any "blank" frames and choose Movie, Delete Frames. Or you can save the Frame Stack as a Quicktime/VFW movie and edit it in Adobe Premiere or Avid Video Shop.

# IMPORTING AND EXPORTING

With a little planning and understanding of file formats, still and animated files can easily be imported into Painter and exported out of Painter to other programs.

**Preserving image quality.** Because compression can degrade the quality of image files, when you obtain source files to bring into Painter, choose uncompressed animation and video clips. And because quality deteriorates each time you compress (the degree of degradation depends on the compression choice), save your working files without compression until your project is complete. If you plan to composite Painter movies in a another application such as Adobe Premiere, After Effects or Avid Video Shop, save them without compression. For an in-depth explanation of compressors for Quicktime or for Video For Windows, see Chapter 12 in the *Painter 4 User Guide*.

**Importing multimedia files into Painter.** Painter can accept Quicktime and VFW movies from any source, as well as still image PICT files and numbered PICT files exported from Postscript drawing programs, Photoshop and Premiere. To number your PICT files so

*Jon Lee of Fox Television used Painter's brushes and effects to progressively modify the logo from the comedy* Martin, *creating an animated sequence of numbered PICT files. The files were animated on a Quantel HAL.*

## CONVERTING TO GIF FORMAT

Like Photoshop's Indexed Color Mode, GIF format allows you to convert the bit depth of images (from 24-bit to 8-bit or even less) and lock in a stable palette that will be consistent between platforms. To convert your image to GIF, choose File, Save As, and select GIF in the pop-up menu. Under Number of Colors choose an option (256 colors equals 8-bit color). Under imaging method, choose Quantize to Nearest Color or Dither Colors (the latter option converts colors using a random pattern, giving a less banded result). Click the Preview button to view your choice.

that they're read in the correct order by Painter, you must use the same number of digits for all the files, and you must number them sequentially, such as "File 000," "File 001," "File 002" and so on. With all files in a single folder, use the Open dialog box to select the first numbered file in your sequence and, when prompted, select the last file. Painter will assemble the files into a Frame Stack.

**Exporting Painter images to multimedia applications.**
Since multimedia work is created to be viewed on monitors and the standard monitor resolution is 72 ppi, set up your Frame Stacks and still image files using that resolution. Most files used in multimedia have a 4 x 3 aspect ratio: 160 x 120, 240 x 180, 320 x 240 or 640 x 480 pixels. Television also has a 4 x 3 aspect ratio, but for digital television the pixels are slightly taller than they are wide. Artists and designers who create animation for broadcast usually prepare their files at "D-1 size," 720 x 486 pixels. Digital television uses a ".9" pixel (90 percent the width of standard square pixels). The narrower pixel causes circles and other objects to be stretched vertically. To create a file for D-1 maintaining the height-to-width ratio (to preserve circles), begin with a 720 x 540-pixel image. Then scale the image non-proportionally to 720 x 486. This will "crush" the image slightly as it appears on your computer screen, but when it's transfered to digital television it will be in the correct proportions.

Quicktime movie files can be exported from Painter into multimedia programs such as Premiere, After Effects and Macromedia Director. If you're using one of these programs to create an 8-bit color production, you'll save processing time if you start with an 8-bit Frame Stack in Painter: choose the 8-bit Color System Palette option in the New Frame Stack dialog box (after choosing File, New and naming your movie). If you don't set up your file as 8-bit in Painter, you should consider using Photoshop or Equilibrium Debabelizer to convert your files—they both offer excellent color conversion control.

## IMPORTING AND EXPORTING MOVIES WITH MASKS

You can create a mask in a Painter movie and use it in your Frame Stack, or export it within a Quicktime movie to another program such as Premiere or After Effects. To make a movie with a mask, choose one of the options with a mask in the New Frame Stack dialog box. (You can also make a Frame Stack from a sequence of numbered PICT files in which each file includes its own mask.) To export the movie from Painter as a Quicktime movie and include the mask, choose Save As and select the Quicktime movie option. When the Compression Settings dialog box appears, in the Compressor section, choose Animation or None from the top pop-up menu to make the mask option available, then choose Millions of Colors+ in the lower pop-up menu. Click OK.

We used a modified photo to create this repeating pattern. To generate seamless, tiled textures for 3D, use any of the commands under Art Materials, Patterns. Turn to "Exploring Patterns" on page 158 for more about working with patterns.

Many experienced multimedia artists prefer to export their Painter images as PICT files rather than as movies because they have more control over the sequence of frames. To export Painter still images to applications such as Premiere and After Effects, or to other platforms, save them as single PICT images or as a series of numbered PICT files. You can include a single mask in a Painter PICT file that can be used in compositing in Premiere or After Effects. See "Animating a Logo" on page 196 for a demonstration of exporting Painter images to another platform.

You can also import Painter-created Quicktime movies and still PICT images into Macromedia Director. Director imports these files into the Cast Window as Cast Members. A Quicktime movie comes in as single linked Cast Member, which means it will be stored outside the Director file. This keeps Director file size manageable. For more details about working with Painter and Director, see "Animating Illustrations in Director" on page 198.

## CREATING TEXTURE MAPS FOR 3D RENDERING

A *texture map*—a flat image applied to the surface of 3D object—can greatly enhance the realism of rendering in 3D programs such as Strata Studio Pro, Ray Dream Designer or Specular Infini-D. Many kinds of images can be used for texture mapping—scanned photographs, logo artwork or painted textures, for example. 3D artists especially like Painter's ability to emulate colorful, natural textures (such as painted wood grain or foliage) that can be used as color texture maps in 3D rendering. (A *color map* is an image that's used to apply colored texture to a 3D rendering of an object.) Other types of mapping use grayscale information; for instance, a *bump map* (a two-dimensional representa-

tion of an uneven surface), a *transparency map* (used to define areas of an image that are transparent, such as glass panes in a window) and a *reflectance map* (used to define matte and shiny areas on an object's surface). If you're applying more than one of these surface maps to a 3D object, you can keep them in register by using Save As or making clones of the same "master" Painter image to keep file dimensions the same. Remember to save your surface maps in PICT format so the 3D program will be able to recognize it.

These floating globes were rendered by John Odam in Studio Pro 1.5.2. He created a texture map in Painter using the Wriggle texture from the More Wild Textures library and applied the texture to the objects as follows: color map (A), bump map (B), reflectance map (C) and transparency map (D). The Studio Pro document size was 416 x 416 pixels; the texture map size was 256 x 256 pixels.

# Making a Quickshow Presentation

***Overview*** *Collect, resize and sharpen the images you want to present; save them as PICT files; drag the images and the KPT Quickshow application into a folder; customize the show.*

NANCY STAHL

USE KPT QUICKSHOW to build a self-running presentation of your artwork that will fit on a floppy disk. (Quickshow is a Mac-based freeware program; a copy is included on the *Wow!* CD-ROM.)

**1 Preparing the images.** Quickshow will resample your images if they're higher than 72 ppi, but it's better to size them yourself to avoid a "soft" look. Resize your images to 72 ppi (Canvas, Resize) and sharpen them (Effects, Focus, Sharpen). If your presentation will be playing on a variety of monitor sizes, resize your images to a maximum of 640 x 480 pixels (the size of a 13-inch monitor). Resize vertical images to a maximum of 480 pixels tall. Quickshow surrounds your images with black, so you may consider setting off dark images by adding a white border: Choose Canvas, Canvas Size and enter the same value (between 10 and 40 pixels) in each of the boxes. Save the images as PICT files.

**2 Naming the files to play sequentially.** Put the Quickshow application and all of the images into a folder: The application must be in the folder with the images for the show to work. Quickshow will play images in alphabetical or numerical order. If you have more than 9 images and you're numbering them, put a zero in front of single-digit numbers (01, 02, 03 and so on).

**3 Testing and customizing the show.** To test the show, open the folder and double-click on the Quickshow application icon. Press the Tab key to bring up the Custom Settings dialog box to program, for instance, how long each image is shown and the length of the fade between images. Press the / (slash) key to see a list of keyboard shortcuts to use to control your show (for example, pressing the spacebar to pause on an image). The show will cycle through all of the images in the folder until you press Q to quit.

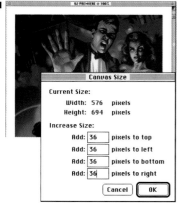

**1**

*Adding a white border using Canvas Size*

**2**

*The folder containing the numbered images and Quickshow application*

**3**

*Press the Tab key to access Custom Settings.*

## YOUR OWN TITLE SCREEN

Introduce your work with a title screen: Artist Nancy Stahl added a hand-lettered signature that she created in Painter. To make your own title screen, set type shapes and fill them with color, or use the type shapes as guides for hand lettering. Save the image as a PICT file, and name or number it so it plays first in the presentation.

# Automating Movie Effects

***Overview*** *Open a video clip; test a series of effects on a single frame; undo the effects; repeat the effects while recording; apply the session to the entire clip.*

CTP / VIDEO: MEDIACOM

**1**

*Frame 1 of the original video clip*

**2**

*The Apply Surface Texture and Apply Lighting settings chosen for the movie*

**3**

*Choosing Movie, Set Grain Position to create a "live" texture on the movie*

**4a**

**4b**

*Detail of effects on Frames 35 and 50*

WITH PAINTER'S SCRIPTS FEATURE, you can automate any series of recorded effects and apply them to each frame of an entire movie.

**1 Starting with a video clip.** Tests will be processed faster if you begin with a small video clip like the one we used—320 x 240 pixels with 67 frames. When you open a video clip, Painter converts it to a Frame Stack. (When you save the Stack, give it a new name so the original clip isn't replaced.)

**2 Testing a series of effects on a frame.** Before you test a sequence of effects on a single frame, set up multiple Undos so you can return the clip to its original state. Choose Edit, Preferences, Undo, and enter a number that matches or exceeds the number of effects you plan to use. Choose a paper texture (we chose Painted Waves from the Nature library) and apply it to Frame 1 in your movie with Effects, Surface Control, Surface Texture, using Paper Grain (we settled on Amount 22%, Picture 90% and Shine 12%). Next, we added a look of cloud-filtered sunlight by choosing Effects, Surface Control, Apply Lighting. We customized the Side Light, named it "sunlight" and saved it. (See Chapter 7 for more about lighting techniques.) When you've finished your testing, undo the sequence of effects that you applied to Frame 1. Don't worry about writing down your effects settings; Painter will remember the last settings you used in the dialog boxes.

## HI-RES MOVIE EFFECTS

If you want to apply effects to a broadcast-quality (640 x 480 pixels) video, use an editing program (such as Premiere) to create a low-resolution version on which to test a combination of effects. Because it takes a higher setting to get a result in a larger file, you may want to adjust the settings for the larger file.

**3 Moving paper grain in the movie.** To add subtle interest to your movie, you can change paper grain position on a frame-by-frame basis by choosing Movie, Set Grain Position. We chose the Grain Moves Linearly button and a 2-pixel horizontal movement.

**4 Recording and playing back the session on the movie.** Begin recording the effects by clicking the Record button in the Scripts palette, then repeat your sequence of effects. When you're finished, click the Stop button on the palette. Give your script a descriptive name, and undo your effects again. To apply your script to the movie, choose Movie, Apply Script to Movie. When the dialog box appears, find your new Script in the list, click the Playback button, and watch as Painter applies the recorded series of effects to each frame. ◐

# Animating an Illustration

**Overview** *Create an illustration; open a new movie document; paste the drawing into the movie in each frame as a floater; position and drop the floater into a new, precise position in each frame; use brushes to paint on individual frames.*

DONAL JOLLEY

**1**

*Jolley's finished Painter illustration*

**2**

*Beginning a new Frame Stack, 3 x 3 inches, 72 ppi, with 35 frames*

**3**

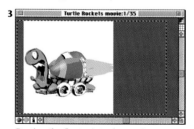

*Pasting the floater into the movie*

**4**

*Entering coordinates for the second floater*

CREATING AN ANIMATION—whether you use Painter or draw on traditional acetate cels—is labor-intensive because of the sheer number of frames required to get smooth motion. But working digitally does have advantages. You can save a lot of time by copying and pasting a single illustration onto multiple frames; corrections to digital art are easier to make than with conventional methods; and, thanks to the Frame Stacks player, you can see results immediately, instead of needing to film each individual cel in stop-motion.

To begin *Turtle Rockets*, a cartoon "teaser" used between segments of a youth outreach video, Donal Jolley painted a not-so-pokey turtle with Painter's brushes, then typed in floater coordinates to precisely indicate motion. Once the basic animation was in place, Jolley painted speed blurs, flame, smoke, and even a wad of gum picked up by one of the skateboard's wheels.

**1 Planning the animation and illustrating.** It's a good idea to do a quick storyboard sketch on paper to visualize the path of motion for your animation. To keep the process simple, choose a subject that won't need to be redrawn in every frame—no bird with flapping wings, for instance. Jolley sketched a turtle on a skateboard moving from right to left across a 3 x 3-inch frame.

Create an illustration in Painter, choosing a file size no more than a few inches square at 72 ppi. Use Painter's brushes to paint just the essential image; you'll be adding the details to each individual frame later. When you've finished your illustration, choose Edit, Select All, then copy it to the clipboard. It's now ready to be pasted into a movie. To fill his movie more completely with his image, Jolley created an illustration file two inches wider than the movie file would be (5 x 3 inches at 72 ppi). He rendered a line sketch of the turtle, rockets and flame using the Fine Tip Felt Pens variant. Jolley added color using the Oil Paint variant of the Brush, modeled forms with the Fat Stroke Airbrush, added linework and shadows using the Felt Marker variant and blended color with the Just Add Water variant.

**2 Starting a new Frame Stack.** To open a new movie file, choose File, New. Choose a small size so Painter will play the movie quickly, then click the Movie Picture Type, and enter enough frames to give you a smooth animation. Jolley created a 3 x 3-inch movie at 72 ppi with 35 frames to start, and added more

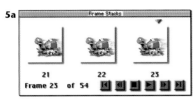

The red marker shows that Frame 23 is active.

Detail of Frame 25, showing motion blur

Frame 28 with Tracing Paper/Onion Skin (three layers) turned on

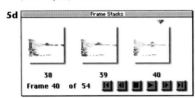

The Frame Stack palette, showing the movement in Frames 38–40

Shaping the flame and adding smoke on Frame 40

frames as he needed them using Movie, Add Frames. His finished animation was 54 frames. Click OK, name and save your movie, and in the New Frame Stack dialog box, choose Jolley's options: three layers of Onion Skin and 24-bit color with 8-bit mask.

**3 Positioning the first floater.** Paste your illustration into the movie file—it will come in as a floater. Use the Floater Adjuster tool to move it into its starting position, then double-click on its name in the Floater List palette. Jot down the numbers that appear in the Top and Left boxes (Jolley's numbers were Top, 4 and Left, 200) and click OK. Click the Drop button in the Floater List palette to drop the floater onto Frame 1.

**4 Offsetting floaters to create movement.** To put a floater into the next frame, go to Frame 2 by clicking on Page Up on your keyboard. Paste the illustration again, double-click on its name in the Floater List, and in the Top and Left boxes, add or subtract the number of pixels you want the character to move in the frame. Since Jolley wanted his turtle to move from right to left with no vertical variation, he entered 190 in the Left box for Frame 2, leaving the 4 in the

**MOVIE AUTO-SAVE**

Painter saves your movie every time you advance a frame.

Top box unchanged. When you've positioned the floater, drop it and advance to the next frame, continuing this paste-and-move process until you have filled all of your frames. To avoid a staccato effect, add or subtract the same number of pixels each time. (Remember to drop the floaters each time, too.) Jolley used a consistent, 10-pixel difference between frames, resulting in a smooth-moving image.

**5 Adding variety to the animation.** When the illustration has been positioned and dropped in all of your frames, add to the feeling of motion by painting on individual frames. Look at the Frame Stacks palette to check your progress. You can also view previous frames "ghosted" in your main image—much like an animator's light box—by choosing Canvas, Tracing Paper (Command-T). The number of previous frames displayed is determined by the number of Onion Skin layers you chose when you opened the movie. To change the number of layers, close the file, reopen it, and choose a new number of layers. Use Command-T to turn the Onion Skin layers on and off as you work.

Jolley painted on individual frames to give more life to the animation. He used the Gritty Charcoal variant to paint the dirt—altering it slightly in each frame—and the Oil Paint variant to paint the gum picked up by the first skateboard wheel. He shaped the flame by adding white, then used the Just Add Water variant to smear the pigment. Jolley also created speed blurs by smudging the turtle's back using the Just Add Water variant.

# Making an Animated Comp

***Overview*** *Set up a layered illustration file with floaters; record the movement of a floater using scripts; play the script back into a movie.*

DEWEY REID

*Reid's original street scene illustration*

*Painting the mask on the background*

*The topmost floater showing the dropped-out area that will reveal the background scene underneath*

*The Dino character showing the painted mask (left), and with the background dropped out*

TO VISUALIZE MOTION in the early stages of creating an animation, Dewey Reid often makes an animated comp (a conceptual illustration with a moving element). Adding motion is a great way to help a client visualize a concept, and it's more exciting than viewing a series of still images. Reid's storyboard, above, shows frames from a movie created by recording a script of a moving floater.

Using scripts and the Record Frames on Playback feature, you can record a floater's movement. When you play the script back, Painter will generate a Frame Stack with the appropriate number of frames, saving you the tedious work of pasting in and moving the character in each frame. After you've made your Frame Stack, convert it into a Quicktime (or AVI/VFW on the PC) movie for easier and faster playback, using a freeware utility like Movie Player.

**1 Beginning with an illustration.** Begin with an image at the size you want your final movie to be. Reid started with a 300 x 173-pixel street scene illustration from his archives.

**2 Setting up a layered file with floaters.** Like conventional animation where characters are drawn on layers of acetate, this animation technique works best when all elements in the image are floated on separate layers. You may want to create masks for the various elements in separate documents, then copy and paste them into your main image. (For more about floaters and masking, turn to Chapter 5.) An easy way to try this technique is to drag items from Painter's default Floaters palette into your image—like the hat, the piggy and the monkey, for example.

Reid envisioned three floating "layers" for this comp: a background image (the street scene), a copy of the street scene with a painted mask, and a dinosaur positioned between the two street scenes that would move from left to right across the "opening" created by the painted mask in the topmost street scene floater. Reid used the Masking Pen variant of the Masking brush to paint a mask on the original street scene image, then he converted the mask to a mask representation selection by clicking on the far right Visibility button in the Path List palette. He floated two copies of the image by Option-clicking twice with the Floater Adjuster tool.

**2d**

*The Dino floater, selected in the Floater List and in starting position (with the selection marquee turned off), ready to be moved by the arrow keys*

**3a**

*Setting up Scripts, Script Options to Save Frames on Playback*

**3b**

*Saving and naming the script*

**4**

*The Dino script selected in the Scripts palette*

**5**

*Choosing the Quicktime button in the Save Movie dialog box*

In a separate document, Reid painted a mask to isolate Dino the dinosaur from the background, and turned the mask into a selection by clicking on the far right Visibility button in the Path List palette. He copied

**HIDE THE MARQUEE**

Turn the marquee off (Command-Shift-H) before you record a script or the marquee will be recorded and will be visible when you play back your script.

Dino to the clipboard and pasted him into the street scene RIFF file. In the zoomed-out Floater List palette, Reid dragged Dino between the two street scene floaters and unchecked the Show Selection Marquee box. (Hiding the marquee makes it easier to see while you're positioning your character.) Using the Floater Adjuster tool and the arrow keys, Reid positioned the dinosaur so that only the red nose was visible behind the left front building, establishing Dino's starting position in the animation.

**3 Recording the script.** Choose Scripts, Script Options; uncheck Initial State, check Record Frames on Playback and enter a number for Every 1/10ths of a Second (Reid chose 5). Select the floater that will be moving by clicking on its name in the Floater List and turn its marquee off (Command-Shift-H). Choose Scripts, Record Script and hold down an arrow key to move the floater smoothly in the RIFF file. When you have completed the path of motion, choose Scripts, Stop Recording Script and name the script. Return the character to its starting position using the Floater Adjuster tool or arrow keys.

**4 Playing back the script into the movie.** Choose Scripts, Playback Script and choose your script from the list. When prompted, name your movie a different name than the RIFF file. Click the Save button, and Painter will convert your RIFF image to a movie (leaving the original RIFF intact) and will add the movie frames needed.

As the movie is generated, you will see the frames accumulating in the Frame Stack palette, and corresponding movement in the movie window. When Painter finishes generating the Frame Stack, remove the floaters that are floating above the movie by selecting them in the Floater List and deleting them. (If you don't, you won't be able to see your movie.) Finally, press the Play button on the Frame Stacks palette to play your movie!

**5 Converting the Frame Stack to Quicktime or VFW.** To be able to play the movie without having Painter loaded, convert the Frame Stack to Quicktime or VFW format: Choose File, Save As, and when the dialog box appears, choose Save Movie as Quicktime/VFW. Give your movie a new name (such as "Dino movie.qtime"), and when the Compression Settings dialog box appears, select a choice from the top pop-up menu (Reid recommends Animation or None). 🖌

# Animating a Logo

**Overview** *Make a clone of existing artwork and modify it with Painter's brushes and effects; save it, make another clone, and alter the new clone; continue to progressively make and alter clones, restoring the image when needed by pasting a copy of the original logo from the clipboard.*

JON LEE / FOX TELEVISION

Starting with the existing Martin logo

**2a**

Lee began manipulating the logo by selecting and scaling a portion of the cloned image (left). Then he selected and inverted a portion of the next clone in the sequence (right).

"IMPROVISATIONAL, FRESH, SPONTANEOUS, and very flexible!" says Jon Lee, Director of Art and Design for Fox Television, when describing his artistic experience with Painter. For the Fox TV program *Martin*, Lee built an animated title sequence like a painting, saving frames at different stages of development. He created a wild, hand-done, organic look to express the comedic street sensibility of the TV show.

Lee created a series of 35 keyframes in Painter (keyframes are the frames that establish essential positions in an animated sequence), eight of which are shown above. When he finished, he moved them from his Macintosh to a lightning-fast Quantel HAL system, where he added dissolves to blend one frame into the next. (Dissolves can also be achieved on the Macintosh desktop in Adobe After Effects or Adobe Premiere.)

**1 Beginning with existing art.** Lee began by opening the existing Martin logo in Painter. He copied and pasted it into a new file measuring 720 x 486 pixels (the aspect ratio of the Quantel HAL) with a black background, then dropped the floater by clicking the Drop button in the Floater List palette.

**2b**

*Adding colored boxes to Frame 05 with the Rectangular Selection tool and the Fill command*

**2c**

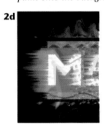

*Using a variety of Liquid brushes to pull paint onto the background in Frame 07*

**2d**

*A motion blur effect applied in 14 (left), and then cloned and filtered in 15*

**3a**

*Adding hand lettering and colored brush strokes to a clone of Frame 15 in Frame 16*

**3b**

*Restoring readability with a floater in 17*

Choose an image that you want to manipulate in your animated sequence and open it in Painter. Name your file "01" and save it in PICT format. In order for a numbered sequence of files to automatically play in numerical order, the files must be named using the same number of digits, such as 01, 02, 03 and so on.

**EASIER ANIMATION EDITING**

For keyframe editing flexibility, creative director Jon Lee advises using a sequence of numbered files. You can remove frames that don't work without interrupting the flow of the animation, since the remaining files stay in numerical order.

**2 Manipulating progressive clones.** After planning how many keyframes you'll need and how the artwork will progress through the frames, begin your manipulation. Clone the first document (File, Clone) and use Painter's tools and special effects on your clone. If you don't like the result of a brushstroke or applied effect, undo it and try something else. When you're satisfied with the result, name the file "02," and make another clone from it. The new clone will become the next canvas for your experimentation. Working quickly and intuitively, Lee treated the logo with a wide variety of brushes, filters and Surface Control effects, saving progressive versions in a numbered sequence.

**3 Restoring the logo.** After a few progressively altered clones, your image may become unrecognizable. To restore the original to some degree, go to your original file, select all and copy, then paste it into your current clone. Adjust the Opacity (Controls: Adjuster palette, Floater tool selected) and drop the floater. Lee used this technique to periodically restore the readability of the logo, working it back into the progressive image.

**Outputting the Painter files.** When Lee was finished with the series of PICT frames, he used Electric Image Projector (a subprogram within Electric Image) to automatically shuttle the files over to the Quantel HAL platform for compositing and output to Beta videotape for broadcast. The workstation is set up with the Quantel HAL and Mac systems side-by-side; they're connected with an Intelligent Resources card that helps convert the digital imagery from one platform to another. Part of the translation process involved converting RGB color to the NTSC video color system for television.

On the HAL, Lee "stretched" the 35 original frames to 90 frames; the HAL added the appropriate number of dissolves between each pair of keyframes to make the animation even and smooth. To create a 10-second title sequence at 30 frames per second, Lee needed 300 frames total. He made a loop of the 90-frame sequence and let it cycle until it filled the necessary frame count.

# Animating Illustrations in Director

*Overview Make a storyboard; create pencil and watercolor illustrations in Painter; import the images into Director and animate them.*

**1**

*Rabinowitz's conventional pencil sketches*

**2a**

*The 2B pencil sketch of the fourth background file*

**2b**

*The fourth background colorized with a with Water Color brush*

**2c**

*The colorized car and motorcycle drawings. The motorcycle zooms past the car when they're both on the bridge.*

IN THE WHIMSICAL ANIMATION *Big Move*, illustrated in Painter and animated in Macromedia Director by Abbie Rabinowitz and Eric Rosene, the viewer watches through a small window as two artists and their cat travel from Oakland to San Francisco. Rabinowitz designed *Big Move* as a promotional piece and moving announcement for the partners. She originated the concept and created the art in Painter, then turned to Rosene who used his expertise in Director to enliven Painter images with movement and sound. They planned the animation so the background scene would move while the car remained centered in the frame.

**1 Planning the movie.** Rabinowitz wanted the promotional piece (including a sound track) to be small enough to fit on a floppy disk and to be compatible with a variety of computers. To keep your animation file size small, choose a small Director Stage Size (Rabinowitz chose 304 x 200 pixels) and use 8-bit color. Make storyboard sketches (Rabinowitz used paper and pencil) to work out the concept and to determine what drawings will be needed in the animation. Design your storyboard sketches to fit the proportions of your Stage Size.

**2 Creating the drawings.** Using your storyboard sketches as a reference, create drawings in Painter. Use a resolution of 72 ppi, and make your images the size of your Director Stage, or wider if you want to pan horizontally. Using her sketches as a reference, Rabinowitz created a friendly, old-fashioned scene with the 2B Pencil variant of the Pencils brush. She added transparent washes of color with the Simple Water variant of the Water Color brush. Rabinowitz built a total of seven background files, each 640 pixels wide by 200 pixels tall, across which she could pan to create the illusion of a car traveling between the two cities. To make the transition between background images, she copied the right side of one background image and pasted it into left side of the next one. In addition to the seven background pieces, she drew a car, its wheels and a motorcyclist.

**3**

*Two of the cloned and rotated drawings*

**4**

*Setting up a Stage Size in the Director Preferences dialog box*

**5**

*The Director Transform Bitmap dialog box showing settings 8-bit Mac System palette*

**6**

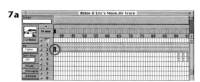

*The Director Cast Window with the imported Painter PICT images and various other Cast Members in the production*

**7a**

*The Director Score, showing Frames 37–95; Channel 2 shows 12, the first car Sprite selected.*

## QUICK TRANSFORM ACCESS

To access Director's Transform Bitmap dialog box without using the pull-down menu, double-click the Cast Member in the Cast Palette to access the Paint Window, then double-click on the Bit Depth button in the Tools palette.

**3 Cloning and rotating the car illustration.** Rabinowitz cloned the drawing of the car (choose File, Clone) five times to make six copies, then she rotated each car image to a different angle to match the background images and simulate uphill and downhill travel. She rotated the cars in Painter because she had more visual control than in Director. (Rotating is accomplished in Director by specifying numbers in the Transform Bitmap dialog box.) To rotate an image in Painter, select it with the Rectangular Selection tool, then choose Effects, Orientation, Rotate, grab a corner handle, drag it to the angle you need, and click OK. This command creates a floater, but don't worry about dropping it: just save your image as a PICT file to import into Director and the file conversion will drop the floater to the background.

**4 Setting up a small Director file.** To set up a Stage Size in Director that matches the one used by Rabinowitz, choose File, Preferences. In the Stage Size section of the dialog box, choose Custom, and set up a 304-pixel-wide by 200-pixel-tall production by typing the numbers in the appropriate fields.

**5 Changing the color depth.** To give the animation a cohesive look, imported images should have a consistent color palette and bit depth. To display similar colors on a variety of computers, Rabinowitz converted her RGB images to an 8-bit Mac System palette. There are three ways to accomplish this. One way is to set your monitor's bit depth by choosing Control Panels, Monitors, 256 Colors. Since color in Director is dependent on your monitor's bit depth, it will adjust the files as they are imported as Cast Members.

The second way to convert to an 8-bit palette uses Director. To change a Cast Member's color palette, select the Cast Member you want to edit in the Cast Window by clicking, Shift-clicking multiple members or choosing Select All. Then choose Cast, Transform Bitmap, and in the dialog box, choose 8-Bits for Color Depth and the System–Mac Palette.

The third conversion method involves using another program such as Debabelizer or Photoshop. To accomplish a conversion in Photoshop, open the image and convert it from RGB to Indexed Color; when the dialog box appears, choose the appropriate options for resolution, color palette and dither (which mixes the pixels of available colors to simulate the missing colors). Refer to Photoshop's *User Guide* for more information.

**6 Importing illustrations into the Director Cast.** To import your Painter images into Director, select File, Import and choose a PICT file (or files) that you want to bring into your production. The PICT files will appear in the Director Cast Window (Window, Cast).

**7b**

The corresponding stage frame, with the car (Sprite 12 in Frame 37) selected

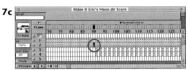

**7c**

The Score showing car cast member 12 in Channel 2, Frame 90 selected.

**7d**

The Stage, car position in Frame 90

**7e**

The Stage, car position in Frame 103

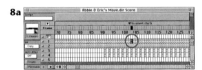

**8a**

The Score showing the background cast member in Channel 1, Frame 103 selected

**8b**

The Stage, showing the background moved from its original position in Frame 115

**7 Understanding layering in the Director Score.** You'll need to add your Cast Members to the Score to make them a part of the action. The *Score* allows layered Cast Members to move independently of each other on the Stage. The Score is comprised of tiny *Cells*—each Cell contains information about a single Cast Member. A horizontal row of cells is called a *Channel* (which shows movement over time), and a vertical column is a *Frame* (showing all Cast Members in a single moment in time). A *Sprite* is the image of a Cast Member that performs on the Director Stage. It contains information about the Cast Member's location on Stage and any changes you make to it while on Stage (such as scaling or applying ink effects) without changing the original Cast Member. Rabinowitz placed the background Cast Members into Cells in Channel 1, the back-most channel. The car was placed into Cells in Channel 2, in front of the background images in the layering order.

**8 Animating the background.** To re-create Rabinowitz's panning background effect, select a Cell in the Score in Channel 1. In the Cast Window, select the background Cast Member you created in step 2 and drag it onto the Stage and into the selected position in the Score. Rabinowitz worked out the background animation first. She started with a stationary background in Frames 1–102, then created movement over time in Frames 103–747.

Use *In-betweening* (Score, In-between Linear) to calculate motion and create intermediate Frames between key Frames. To move a background element from left to right, first select Channel 1, Frame 1 in the Score, drag the background Cast Member onto the Stage, and align the Cast Member in Channel 1, Frame 1 with the right side of the Stage. Select a new Cell in the same Channel (try Frame 200), and drag the Cast Member again from the Cast palette to a new horizontal location, aligned with the left side of the Stage. Select both Frames and use Score, In-between Linear (Command-B) to create the intermediate frames. To arrive at a speed you like, begin with one background image and experiment with how many frames it will take to move your background steadily across the entire stage. In the Director's Control Panel palette, set the Frames per Second to 30 (as Rabinowitz did) and preview your animation. She felt that slower movement complemented the low tech, old-fashioned look of the images.

**9 Animating the car.** To animate a character in front of your background, select a Cell in the Score in front of your background layer (such as Channel 2 or 3), and in the Cast Window, choose a Cast Member to drag onto the Stage and into the selected position in the Score. (Remember that in Director, channels with lower numbers are behind those with higher numbers.) With the Sprite still selected on Stage, press the Score Ink Type pop-up menu and choose Matte Ink to "mask out" or hide the car's

**9**

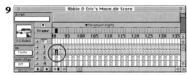

*The car in the Score in Channel 2, Frame 91, with Matte Ink selected; the wheels are shown in Channels 3 and 4.*

**10a**

*The Director Paint Window with the background image (top) and the newly created cast member (bottom)*

**10b**

*The family in the Cast Window (top); layered in front of the car in the Score, in Channel 9, Frame 519 (middle); and on the Stage (bottom)*

bounding box and reveal the scene behind the Cast Member in the Score.

To simulate driving on a bumpy road, Rabinowitz selected the appropriate Sprite Cell for the car in the Score, then used the arrow keys to move the individual sprite up or down one or two pixels on a frame-by-frame basis. She nudged the car up or down a few pixels in Frames 35–90 (while it was "idling"), then moved it horizontally in Frames 90–115. She positioned the car on the Stage in Frame 90, and then she selected Frame 115 and dragged the car onto the Stage in a new position—then selected both Frames 90 and 115, (the starting and ending frames), and used the In-between Linear command to calculate motion between the frames. After this sequence the car stays centered in the frame, jostling along on the "bumpy" road. (The jostling was accomplished by copying the car Sprite and pasting it into a later frame, in-betweening, and then selecting individual Sprites on the Stage and moving them up or down with the arrow keys a pixel or two.) To enhance the bumpy road effect and to simulate turning wheels, Rabinowitz overlapped the car tires (Cast Member 20) in Channels 3 and 4 with slightly different positions in every other frame.

**10 Isolating items from the background and bringing them forward.** Rabinowitz wanted to bring three items in front of the car in her animation: the bridge railing, a building, and an image of a family. It was easier for her to do small touch-ups like this in the Director Paint window than to go back to Painter. The items needed to be isolated from the background image and layered in a channel in front of the car in the Score. To do this, she created copies of the background files that contained those elements and opened them individually in the Director Paint Window. (To edit a Cast Member while preserving the original, select the Cast Member in the Cast palette and make a copy by choosing Cast, Duplicate Cast Member or pressing Command-D. The duplicate will appear in the Cast Window.) Rabinowitz used the Eraser and Pencil from the Paint Tools palette to isolate the elements that she needed. (The Pencil works just like Painter's Single Pixel Scribbler Pencils variant.) When you close the Paint Window, the edited Cast Member appears in the Cast Window. To bring the Cast Member forward on the Stage, first select the appropriate numbers in the Score (in a higher-numbered Channel), then select the edited Cast Member in the Cast Window and drag it into position on the Stage.

**Exporting the animation.** The production was exported as a Projector movie (File, Create Projector) that contained the resources needed to replay the movie without the Director application. To compress the Projector movie into a self-extracting archive, the team used the compression utility Disk Doubler. 🐿

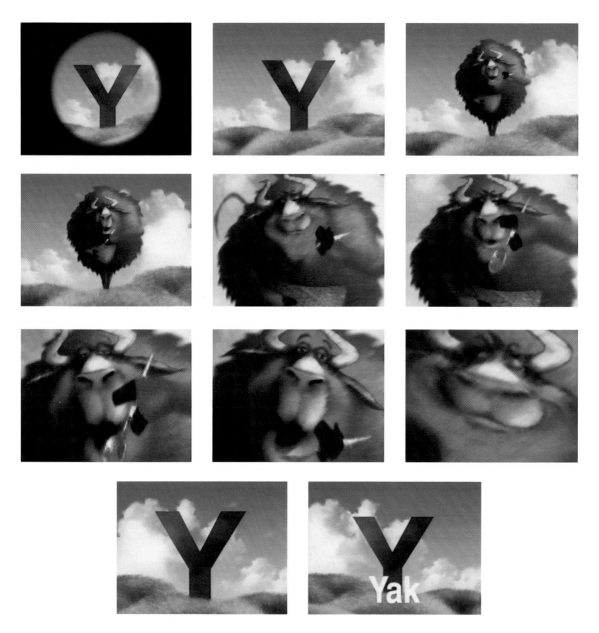

■ **Dewey Reid**, of Reid Creative, illustrated the 30-second animation *Yuri the Yak* for Sesame Street, a production of Children's Television Workshop. In the story segment, Yuri the Yak travels the countryside eating yellow yams and yogurt, and teaching the letter "Y."

Reid stresses the importance of preproduction planning in animation. He created the Yuri the Yak animation with an astounding total of only 35 drawings (it could have taken hundreds). His background in conventional animation helped him determine which drawings to make, saving time and a lot of work.

Reid used Painter to create individual parts of the Yak, such as the head, body and arms. He opened the illustrations in Photoshop and created a mask for each image, then saved the illustrations as PICT files in a numbered sequence. (He prefers using PICT files rather than Quicktime movies, since PICT files allow higher quality. Also, a sequence of PICT files allows for more flexibility—it's easier to remove a frame or two, if necessary.)

He imported the masked files into Adobe After Effects, created animation cycles for each of the Yak parts, then joined animation cycles together.

A virtuoso with atmospheric effects, Reid completed his artistic vision by adding subtle lighting and texture. He opened the animation in Painter as a Frame Stack. After recording a script of Apply Lighting and Surface Texture effects, he chose Movie, Apply Script to Movie to add the effects to every frame.

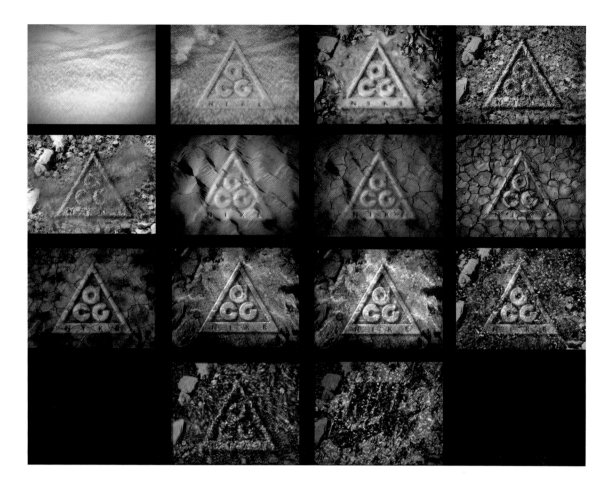

■ Creative director and film artist **Dewey Reid** engineered the preproduction for the *Nike All Conditions Gear* TV commercial while working with Colossal Pictures.

To begin the preproduction visualization, Reid scanned a variety of images, then used Painter to create keyframes to establish the essential positions in the animated sequence. He imported the Nike logo (by copying it from Illustrator and pasting it into the Painter file as shapes while both applications were running); converted the logo shapes to selections (Shapes, Convert to Selection) and applied a feather to the selections. He built an emboss with Effects, Surface Control, Apply Surface Texture (using Mask), creating the illusion that the logo pushes up through the scanned images. Reid saved the keyframes as numbered PICT files, then used Adobe Premiere to create transitions (such as Cross Dissolves) between the keyframes. He manipulated a few of the masks in Adobe After Effects.

Back in Painter, Reid painted clouds of dust with the Fat Stroke Airbrush variant and used Effects, Surface Control, Image Warp to subtly change the shape of the clouds. He imported the dust image into Premiere and moved the dust across one segment of frames.

After working out the timing in Premiere, Reid used Painter to add a series of special effects to the entire movie to increase the 3D look. A whiz with scripts, he opened the movie as a Frame Stack and treated it with an effects script that included third-party filters, Apply Lighting, and Surface Texture (using Image Luminance).

**Peter Mitchell Rubin,** a gifted and innovative storyboard artist, used a variety of Painter's brushes and compositing controls to create the storyboards for the MGM movie *Stargate.* The Giza, Egypt sequence is shown here. Rubin outputs his illustrations from Painter as numbered PICT files, then animates them in Adobe Premiere.

Rubin's love of drawing shows in his storyboards. He works very quickly, in gray, at 72 ppi. His document size depends on the amount of detail needed, but is usually under 600 pixels wide. The aspect ratio depends upon how the film is shot. Rubin organizes the thousands of drawings that he creates for a film in folders according to scene. He sets up Quickeys macros to automate actions wherever possible.

When Rubin adds other elements to an image, he pastes the element, drops it, then paints into it to merge it seamlessly into the composition. He also uses Painter's Cloners brushes. For example, he created the texture in Frame 15 (left column, third frame down from top) by photographing the actual set sculpture used in the movie, scanning it and cloning it into his drawing.

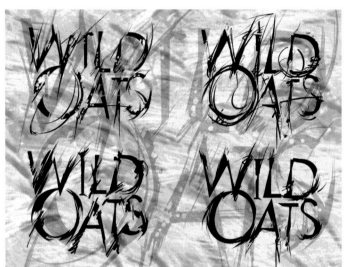

■ As both a broadcast designer for Fox Television and a freelance graphic designer, **Geoff Hull** employs a spontaneous, progressive approach when designing with type.

Hull began *Fox Logo Pattern* with a black background. He imported a solid and an outline version of the Fox logo (using File, Acquire, Adobe Illustrator file—which creates a new file). He copied the shapes from the new file and pasted them into the larger background file; then converted the two logo shape groups into two floaters. Working quickly and intuitively, he painted on the logo floaters with various Oil Paint brushes and saturated color. To build a layered look, Hull made additional copies of the floaters and added more brushstrokes. In busier areas, he erased portions of floaters by removing the floater's mask layer with a Masking brush.

To create the animated title sequence for the TV show *Wild Oats*, Hull envisioned a hand-done calligraphic look. He began the image with a white background and set type in Painter using the font Earthquake, a typeface from the T26 foundry. After setting type shapes filled with black, he made a clone (File, Clone) and erased its contents. He chose Canvas, Tracing Paper and expressively traced the letterforms. Hull made a series of progressive clones, switching clone sources (File, Clone Source) among the original and several later versions of the title sequence.

Hull created *The Crossing Guard* storyboard for a Miramax Films movie title and trailer. He began with a black background and set individual letterform shapes in Painter using Mason from the Emigre font library. After converting the shapes to floaters, he filled them with color and erased portions of the letters with a Masking brush. He also used Effects, Orientation, Scale on the floaters to vary the size of the elements.

# PRINTING
# AND
# ARCHIVAL
# CONCERNS

*Sybil's Fear, by Dorothy Simpson Krause, was created for a Media West Editions Pixel Pushers exhibition. Krause printed the image at 30 x 22 inches on an Iris 3047 printer. She plans an edition of 75 prints.*

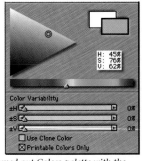

*The zoomed-out Colors palette with the Printable Colors Only box checked*

HOW WILL YOU PRESENT YOUR PAINTER ARTWORK to the world? As a limited-edition digital painting, printed with archival media by a specialized printer or service bureau, matted, framed, and hung on a gallery wall? As an illustration in a magazine, a part of a page layout that's output to negative film by an imagesetting service bureau, turned into a printing plate and printed on an offset press? As a desktop color print? As part of a slide show? For each of these and other output options, there are things you can do to prepare your Painter file so the output process runs more smoothly. Check with your printer or service bureau for specific output requirements.

## COLOR FOR PRINTING

Most types of printing involve the use of four-color process, or CMYK (cyan, magenta, yellow, black) inks and dyes. Painter's native color mode is RGB (red, green, blue), which has a larger color *gamut* (range of color) than the CMYK color model. (An illustration that compares RGB and CMYK color gamuts is on page 3 in Chapter 1.) Although Painter doesn't let you specify CMYK color mixes like Adobe Photoshop and some other programs do, it does allow you to paint in and see Printable Colors—those colors within the RGB gamut that are realizable in CMYK. You can also output CMYK EPS files for offset printing directly from Painter.

**Using Printable Colors.** It's a good idea to use Painter's Printable Colors functions when you'll be turning a file over to an imagesetting service bureau for output in a form that will be used for CMYK printing. To paint with Printable Colors, check the Printable Colors Only box in the zoomed-out Colors palette. To preview an existing RGB image in Printable Colors, choose Effects, Tonal Control, Printable Colors. Click, drag and release the grabber

*Pressing and dragging with the grabber hand in the Printable Colors dialog box to toggle between RGB and Printable Colors*

hand to toggle between the broader-gamut image and a Printable Colors preview. To convert your image to Printable Colors, click OK.

**Making CMYK conversions in another program.** Some Painter artists prefer to work in the broader RGB color gamut and convert their images to CMYK in another imaging program such as Photoshop or Equilibrium Debabelizer, because these programs allow more control of how the conversion is made. There are several good resources that give detailed explanations of color conversion using Photoshop, including the *Adobe Photoshop User Guide, The Photoshop 3 Wow! Book*, and *Photoshop in 4 Colors* (Peachpit Press). Some service bureaus—for example, Cone Editions—prefer to receive RGB files from artists and make the conversion themselves using custom color tables they create in Photoshop especially for that image. (See "Making a Fine Art Master Print" on page 218 for an explanation of Cone Editions' process.) Check with your printer or service bureau to work out a conversion method.

**Writing EPS-DCS files from Painter.** Many illustrators prefer to have control over the prepress process by ordering their own four-color film for illustrations. Rather than an electronic file, they send the film separations and a laminated proof (a Matchprint, for example) to the client. Whether you or someone else will be ordering the film, check with the service bureau operator who will be doing the output. They should be able to tell you the correct setup for the equipment that will output your job. Many service bureaus prefer to place your art in a page layout program and set the line screen there before sending it to the imagesetter. If this is the case, you'll need to prepare your EPS-DCS files without line screens by checking the Suppress Screen Angles box in the EPS Options dialog box that appears when you save a file in EPS format.

## FINE ART PRINTING

If you plan to present your image as fine art, choose a service bureau or master printer who specializes in output for fine art printmaking. The expertise needed differs greatly from that of a commercial service bureau accustomed to making film and proofs for offset printing. Choose a printer who has experience working with artists and who understands archival and editioning issues. (See Appendix C for a list of service bureaus that specialize in working with fine artists.)

*Pulling a print on the Vutek system (top), and a close-up view of the nozzle heads on the Vutek machine (bottom)*

**Digital watercolors with the Iris.** Iris printers (Iris is a division of Scitex) are special inkjet machines capable of producing images with luminous color and no visible dot, making the output desirable for fine art printmaking. The Iris sprays water-soluble vegetable-based CMYK dyes (similar to watercolors) through four extremely narrow nozzles. The paper or other substrate is taped to a rotating drum in the machine and sprayed with millions of droplets per second. Many fine art printers retrofit the Iris 3047 (the largest of the Iris printer line) so it can handle thicker substrates. Cone Editions, The Digital Pond and Nash Editions were among the first printers to pioneer this technique; they moved back the printing heads, allowing 400-lb. watercolor paper, canvas and metal to be taped onto the drum.

**Outputting to large canvas.** Richard Noble is a traditionally trained artist and commercial illustrator who has worked with the computer for several years. He researched large output options and discovered Vutek, a large-format, low-resolution technology originally devised to print billboards. Noble established a partnership with Vutek and adapted the technology to print large-format fine art. The machine sprays acrylic-based pigments through four nozzles simultaneously, producing soft-edged images very much like an airbrush painting on canvas. Once they dry, the acrylic-based pigments are not water-soluble and offer permanency similar to that of acrylic paint. Images can be printed up to 4 feet wide and as long as you like, with enough canvas remaining around the perimeter of the image for stretching around a frame. Although the prints look good right off the Vutek, you can add even more dimension by working back into them with conventional brushes and acrylic paint. Since the Vutek prints at 18 ppi, files can be fairly small. For example, to produce a 4 x 6-foot painting, you'll need to set up a 864 x 1296-pixel file (only about 5 MB).

**Digital watercolors with desktop printers.** Desktop inkjet printers can deliver beautiful color prints if they are set up properly. The affordable HP Desk Writer (or Desk Jet) 560C and 660C and the Epson Stylus are great little printers not only for pulling proofs before sending images to an Iris, but also for experimental fine art prints. Inkjet inks are water-soluble; try painting into a print with a wet brush. Although most desktop printers work best with slick paper, archival-quality cotton papers produce excellent results on

*Detail of* Old World, *by Bonny Lhotka. She hand-worked and treated Rives BFK paper, then printed the image on a Hewlett-Packard XL 300.*

**TRY COLORSYNC WITH RGB**

You can get good results when printing from Painter using a desktop inkjet (such as the HP 550C or 560C) without first converting your image to CMYK. In the Print dialog box, choose Best Quality, and in the Options dialog box, choose Colorsync from the pop-up menu.

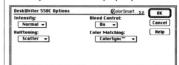

*To check color and detail before printing on an Iris inkjet, Cher Threinen-Pendarvis proofed* Sunrise *as an 8 x 10-inch Fujix Pictrography print. The print was sent along with the digital file to the service bureau (The Digital Pond), where the image was printed at 12.5 x 20 inches on bright white Somerset paper.*

some machines. For example, the HP 550C/560C series prints on thicker acid-free papers if you feed the paper manually. (Two suggested papers are 80–120 lb. Arches cold-pressed watercolor paper and Rives BFK printmaking paper.)

## TURN OFF POSTSCRIPT

If possible when printing Painter artwork files with Postscript inkjet printers (such as the Hewlett-Packard XL300 and 1200c), turn off the Postscript option. If you leave it on, the Postscript software prevents the printer from producing the scatter spray that is desirable in a fine art print, giving you instead a halftone dot pattern. A scatter spray overlaps colors on the surface of the print where they mix, giving a result similar to fine dithering.

## PHOTOGRAPHIC IMAGING OPTIONS

Many new technologies are available for Painter output at graphic art service bureaus and photo labs that use digital equipment.

**Imaging to transparencies using a film recorder.** Small- and large-format film recorders are used to image digital files such as Painter artwork to transparencies ranging from 35mm to 16 x 20 inches. For output via a film recorder, images should be in landscape orientation (horizontal) to take full advantage of the width of the film.

To avoid *pixelation* (a jaggy, stair-step look caused by lack of sufficient resolution) on transparencies generated by a service bureau's film recorder, here are some guidelines from Chrome Digital (San Diego) and The Digital Pond (San Francisco) for creating or sizing your files. Most professional-quality 35mm film recorders (such as the Solitaire 16 series) use a minimum resolution of 4000 lines; for this resolution, your image should be 4096 x 2732 pixels. The minimum resolution for 4 x 5-inch transparencies is 8000 lines, requiring an 8192 x 5464-pixel file. For even more crispness, devices such as the Solitaire 16XPF will image at a resolution of 16,000 lines (a 16,384 x 10,928-pixel file). Two new, powerful film recorders used to create 4 x 5-inch, 8 x 10-inch and larger-format transparencies are the LVT (from Light Valve Technology, a subsidiary of Kodak) and the Lightjet (from Cymbolic Sciences, Inc.). Plan to create huge images (up to 800 MB) to take full advantage of the resolution capabilities of these machines.

**Output to a digital positive.** Prints made from the Fujix Pictrography 3000 offer better registration, permanency and more natural color than a dye-sublimation print such as the Kodak XL7700 or 3M Rainbow. The Fujix uses a laser to image the digital

*Dorothy Krause and Bonny Lhotka print Krause's image,* Procession *on the Alpha Merics Spectrum printer. The large-format printer is outstanding for printing on thick material. The Spectrum's variable "Z" axis can be adjusted to the thickness of the substrate, allowing it to print on materials up to 3/4" thick (such as the wood shown in the photo above).*

file onto a "donor" sheet, which is then printed onto photographic paper using a single-pass, silver-halide printing process. The appearance and permanency (about 20 years) of the Fujix are similar to those of a photographic Cibachrome (C-print). Prints can be laminated with a coating that includes an ultraviolet inhibitor, extending the life of the print.

**Printing your images as Fujichrome.** For fine art images, Fujichrome prints made from transparencies offer excellent detail and saturated color, and can be ordered with a high gloss. Prints can be made from 35mm slides or 4 x 5-inch transparencies. To print to the maximum size of 20 x 24 inches, a 4 x 5 transparency is recommended. The permanency of the Fuji print is 40–50 years, and this can be extended by adding a lamination with an ultraviolet inhibitor. Diane Fenster, a noted fine artist and photographer produces much of her digital work as large-format Fujichrome prints.

## NON-SILVER PRINTING PROCESSES FOR PHOTOGRAPHERS

Sometimes getting the kind of print you want involves doing research. Three innovative artists who use photography in their work—Helen Golden, Judy Moncrief and Karin Schminke, researched non-silver printing processes for photographers at a workshop at Golden's studio in Palo Alto, California. They created hand-painted substrates and sub-images which would later have digital images printed on them. In preparation for the workshop, the artists printed digital files to the HP Design Jet 750 and the CalComp Tech Jet 1751—imaging onto acetate negatives. At the workshop they tested and prepared Kwik-print surfaces—painting the solution onto Stonehenge—an archival paper that they had "sized" to accept the Kwik-print solution. For instance, Schminke made surfaces that consisted of large patterned imagery and some smaller textures. She'll use the colored prints created with the Kwik-print process as a base layer/substrate; other images will be printed on top using a large-format inkjet printer such as the CalComp Tech Jet 1751.

*Taping an inkjet printed acetate negative to a piece of paper that has Kwik-print coating applied to it*

*Hand-painting back into a Kwik-print image*

*Developing the exposed Kwik-print image with running water and rubbing the excess paint with a sponge*

*With Kwik-print image hanging behind, an image is prepared for overprinting.*

*The overprint is first printed on acetate to check scale, color and placement.*

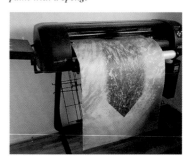

*Printing the first overprint on a CalComp Techjet 175i*

Prairie Reflection, *by Karin Schminke. Elements for the image were created with the non-silver Kwik-print process described on page 210.*

*Detail of* The Game *by Carol Benioff, an Iris print overprinted with a copperplate etching*

*Detail of* Day Job *by Bonny Lhotka*

## EXPERIMENTAL PRINTMAKING

In today's world of experimental printmaking, anything goes if it works with your vision of the image you're printing. For instance, many different substrates can be used successfully with inkjet printers; among the favorites are archival-quality papers with a high cotton content. Browse your local art store for Saunders handmade watercolor paper, Arches hot-press and cold-press watercolor paper, Rives BFK printmaking papers, and Canson drawing and charcoal papers. You can hand-feed these papers into a studio desktop printer, or request that a fine art service bureau create an Iris print with paper that you supply. Fine art service bureaus often keep special fine art papers in stock—Cone Editions, for instance, has about 80 different papers on hand. Some service bureaus also print on canvas, film and metal.

**Mixing media.** Prints from an Iris and other inkjet printers can be modified with traditional tools and fine art printing processes, such as embossing, intaglio and silkscreen. (Turn to page 214 to read about Carol Benioff's technique of overprinting a copperplate etching on top of an Iris print.)

If you plan to hand-work an inkjet print with media such as pastels, pencils or oil paint—make the print on rag paper with enough body to hold together when you apply the traditional media to the print. Arches 140-pound watercolor paper and Rives heavyweight printmaking paper are good choices.

**Making translite transfers.** This technique was pioneered by Jon Cone. First, he printed a digital image onto Translite film using an Iris printer. He soaked archival quality paper (such as Rives BFK), and when it was partially dry, he transferred the image from the Translite "plate" onto the dampened printmaking paper using an embossing press—producing a monoprint with softly graduated color.

**Overprinting a digital file onto a monotype.** To create a surface that she would later use in the printing of *Day Job*, Bonny Lhotka used acrylic paint to create a one-of-a-kind monotype "plate," by painting acrylic onto prepared acetate. She laid a piece of rag paper onto the "plate" in preparation for transferring the painted image onto the paper. (To transfer the image onto the back of the paper she used a custom-made 40-lb roller.) After transferring, she lifted the paper off the "plate," then allowed it to dry. In preparation for printing, she applied two coats of Communicolor ProofPlus Precoat Inkjet Receiver to the transferred image. Finally, she used a large-format Novajet inkjet printer to overprint the digital file on top of the transferred monoprint. She believes that the overprinting process produces a broader range of color than possible with a standard inkjet print, resulting in a print with more depth.

*Bonny Lhotka creates one-of-a-kind "monotype" substrates to use as unique surfaces in the printing of her digital images.*

Fine artist and printmaker Bonny Lhotka shares some of her experiences while experimenting with various surfaces and printers:

"Artists can purchase primed or raw canvas and add their own surface. One-of-a kind substrates are much cheaper than commercially available canvases and can yield a more interesting print. I have printed on muslin, cheesecloth, silk, linen, buckram and drapery fabrics. First, stretch the material on a frame and coat it with white gesso. Let the gesso dry overnight before applying an inkjet receiver (from Communicolor in Seattle). Cut the fabric from the stretcher being careful not to make any creases. Store these sheets rolled face out with a sheet of smooth butcher paper laid over the surface. Roll each sheet onto a 4" tube until you are ready to use it.

"Aluminum or copper, with a thickness of .003 to .005-inch and 36 inches wide, is a particularly interesting surface to print on. The metal must first be cleaned with a strong washing vinegar and roughed with steel wool or sandpaper. This is followed with a coating of artist's gesso. I generally run the metal through an etching press to flatten it out. Once the digital file is printed and sealed, the aluminum can be embossed using a cardboard plate by pressing the two in the etching press or using a hydraulic press. Both sides of the sheet can be printed on, allowing for the plate to be folded to create a dimensional image. The advantage is that the metal is more durable than paper and can be displayed without glazing.

"Par glass is a stiff fiberglas material less than 1/8-inch thick. It can be coated with rabbit skin glue and an inkjet receiver. After printing and coating with UV protection, the sheets look like stained glass. It's possible to burn the edges of this material to give the art a fragmented look.

"Twinrocker Handmade Papers creates custom papers for art editions. They can be made with a watermark to identify an authentic edition of digital prints (as an additional safe guard against unauthorized prints being made from a digital file). While big deckles are a desired aesthetic element and the mark of a hand made sheet, they can create problems when used with inkjet printers. The Alpha Merics is the only printer I've tried that prints on the sheets with the biggest deckle. When printing a hand-made sheet with a large deckle on an Iris 3047, tape the deckle down."

*White Buffalo, by Gary Clark, was printed by Cone Editions on Somerset paper at 12 x 28 inches. Clark plans an edition of 20.*

## PERMANENCY CONCERNS

Inks used by inkjet printers—including the Iris—are fugitive, which means they can fade when exposed to ultraviolet light. A few fine art printers (notably, Cone Editions and Nash Editions) have developed their own silkscreen coatings to protect Iris prints from fading. The coating merges with the ink on the substrate and doesn't change the appearance of the print. (Both Iris and desktop inkjet prints are water soluble. Keep them dry unless you purposely want to spot or mix the color with water.)

**Treating inkjet prints in a studio setting.** If you are printing your images to a desktop inkjet printer such as the HP 560 and 660C or the Epson Stylus, you can treat prints yourself so they'll last much longer. Artist Bonny Lhotka suggests buying a can of Golden MSA Varnish with UVLS (soluble with mineral spirits) from your local art supply store. Use a protective respirator

*Willow Pond, by Dennis Orlando was printed with an Iris 3047 by Cone Editions on Somerset, a bright white paper. The print was approximately 30 x 20 inches; Orlando plans an edition of 150.*

*Point Lobos Calm Light, by Cher Threinen-Pendarvis, was printed on Rives BFK printmaking paper on an Iris 3047 by Harvest Productions. The 22 x 17-inch fine art print was hand-worked with pastel pencils; Pendarvis plans an edition of 50.*

CERTIFICATE OF AUTHEN

Title **Swimmers 2**

Image Size **12 x 18"**　　　　Edition # **2/50**

Edition Size **50**　　　　Artist Proofs **5**

Date Created **July 1, 1995**　　Date Purchased **July 14,**

Art Media **Iris print on Rives BFK**

Uniqueness of this Print **This print is hand-worked with pe**

Artist *Cher Threinen-Pendarvis*

The above information contains all the information pertaining to this Edition. As or watercolor, do not display this artwork in direct sunlight. Frame it under UF3 pl

*Detail of a sample certificate of authenticity*

*Dorothy Krause printed* Centaur *on canvas using an Iris 3047 at 46 x 31 inches in an edition of 20. The print was hand-worked after printing: Krause rubbed metallic pigment into the female figure and wrapped gold leaf around the outer edges and sides of the stretched canvas.*

and gloves for the process because the fumes from this coating are *very* toxic. To further minimize contact with dangerous airborne particles, dilute the varnish and apply it to your artwork with a brush.

**Caring for prints.** After a UV-protective coating has been applied to your print, treat it as you would a watercolor and avoid displaying it in direct sunlight. Frame it using UV-resistant glazing (glass or Plexiglas) and preserve air space between the surface of the print and the glazing.

## FINE ART EDITIONS FROM DIGITAL FILES

Some artists scan finished, traditionally created artwork and then print it on an Iris. This process is actually *replicating* an original piece of work and is not original digital art. When artwork *originates* as a digital file—using a program such as Painter—and is then printed to an Iris, that print becomes an original. (Think of your Painter image as a kind of "digital printing plate" stored in your computer.)

**Advantages of digital editions.** Printing a digital edition has advantages over traditional, limited-run printing methods. Any number of multiple originals can be made from a digital file without loss of quality: the "digital plate" won't deteriorate. Also, the setup charge for the digital process is usually much less than when an edition is printed conventionally. And while an edition printed with traditional methods needs to be printed all at once, with digital editions, an artist may request prints from the fine art service bureau as needed.

**Planning an edition.** An edition should be carefully tracked and controlled, just as it would be if printed with traditional methods. It's wise to make a contract between the master printer and artist, stating the type of edition, the number of prints in the edition and that no more prints will be made. When an original is sold, the artist should give the buyer a certificate of authenticity that contains the name of the artist and the print, the date sold, the edition size, the print number, the number of artist proofs, the substrate, and any details of hand-working done on the print. Once the edition is complete, the artist should destroy the digital file, just as the screen would be destroyed after a silkscreen edition. (See "Making A Fine Art Master Print" on page 218.)

# Combining Digital and Intaglio Printmaking

**Overview** *Make a print using a traditional printmaking method; scan the print; use the scan as a guide to create a colored image in Painter; output the digital file to an Iris printer; overprint the traditional print on top the Iris print in register.*

CAROL BENIOFF

1a

Photograph of the copperplate etching. The composition is created in reverse.

1b

Grayscale scan of the black-and-white intaglio print

CAROL BENIOFF'S INNOVATIVE PRINTMAKING method combines classic intaglio techniques with digital printing. An award-winning fine artist and illustrator, she has illustrated for magazines such as *Atlantic Monthly* and *Parenting*—and her work appears in the 1995 *CA Illustration Annual*. Currently she works with The Graphics Arts Workshop in San Francisco: one of the oldest artists' cooperatives in the United States, it has been in existence since the 1930s. To create *The Game*, a self-promotional piece, Benioff overprinted a copperplate etching on top of an Iris print made on Daniel Smith archival printmaking paper.

**1 Making an intaglio print.** Benioff planned the 6 x 7-inch copperplate knowing that she would be adding a dimension of colored imagery created in Painter. Using primarily a hard ground etching technique, she etched fine lines into the acid-resistant coating on the copperplate with a fine-point diamond stylus. When making a classic hard ground etching, an artist scribes lines into an acid-resistant coating, exposing the metal underneath. Then the plate is soaked in a acid bath to etch the drawing deeper into the plate. The acid-etched lines hold the ink, yielding warm, velvety black lines when printed.

Benioff rolled black ink onto the plate, working it into the lines with a cardboard dauber, then rubbed off excess ink with tarlatan

**2**

*The two images: A painted landscape (left), and a watercolor tint image to match the etching (right)*

**3**

*Photograph of the Iris print composite*

**4a**

*Inking the plate (left) and making registration marks on a clear acetate sheet to help align the copperplate to the Iris print (right)*

**4b**

*After lifting the press felts on the intaglio press, Benioff carefully pulled the finished print off the copperplate.*

(starched open-weave muslin). Next, she chose a piece of archival printmaking paper and soaked it, so it would absorb the ink better. After letting the paper partially dry, she made a print using an etching press.

When the print was dry, she scanned it and saved the scan to use as a guide to help develop two color images (described in step 2). Benioff's grayscale scan was 2400 x 2800 pixels.

**2 Creating color images and compositing.** Open your scan, make a clone (File, Clone), and delete the contents of the clone (Select All, and press the Delete key). Now, turn on Tracing Paper (Command-T). Using the scan as a guide, paint a colorful image that will complement your traditional print.

Benioff created two images: a painted landscape and a loose watercolor version of the etched composition. The landscape was designed to add dynamic tension to the composition. To begin the landscape, she sketched larger shapes with the Large Simple Water Watercolor brush, then added details with the Artists Pastel Chalk and the Brushy Brush. When the image was complete, she saved it for use later in the process.

To paint a second image, which would add colored tints to elements in the etching, she made a second clone of the scan, again deleting the contents. Using the scan as a guide, she painted a loose color composition with the Simple Water brush variants.

Benioff composited the images in Photoshop by merging the second image with the first using the Image, Apply Image and the Multiply blending mode. To merge two color images in Painter, open both images and make the second image active. Select All, Copy, and Paste it into the first image. Choose a Compositing Method in the Controls:Adjuster palette that complements your image.

**3 Choosing paper for the print.** To achieve a good ink impression of the copperplate, paper should be softened by dampening so that it will mold to the detail etched into the plate. This poses a problem when printing over an Iris print, because Iris prints bleed when wet. To resolve this problem, Benioff extensively experimented with different papers. She found that some very soft papers will soak through—even when you spritz the back of the paper to dampen it slightly—destroying the water-based Iris image. The paper she chose is fibrous enough to soften and swell when slightly moistened but thick enough that the dampness did not soak through to the inks on the front. To print *The Game*, Benioff settled on Daniel Smith archival printmaking paper.

**4 Overprinting the etching.** After preparing the copperplate with ink, Benioff made an acetate template to register the image on the paper and plate. The elements in the Iris print needed to align perfectly with the copperplate, so she carefully traced the position of the figures and table onto the acetate. She aligned the template, the plate and the paper (Iris print) on the press bed and pulled the print.

# Building an Experimental Desktop Print

***Overview*** *Create colorful, textured elements for a collage; roughen and coat the paper prior to printing; print the final image on a desktop inkjet printer.*

BONNY LHOTKA

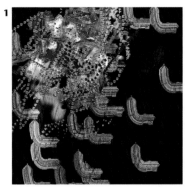
*Lhotka's color sketch, created in Painter*

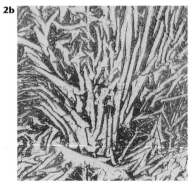
*Painting on the scanner bed*

*The original scanned "paint skin"*

"MOST OF MY ORIGINAL WORK has a strong tactile quality," says Bonny Lhotka of her printmaking experimentation. She often uses traditional printmaking equipment to prepare rich, complex surfaces for her digital collage work. To create *Old World*, Lhotka used three digital source files and composited them into a collage, then wrinkled and coated the paper before feeding it through her desktop inkjet printer. You may want to loosely follow Lhotka's image-making process and also experiment with your own effects.

**1 Sketching with color.** Open a new file and make a colorful, abstract sketch. Lhotka opened an 8-inch-wide, 100-ppi file with a black background. She created an abstract, color sketch using a variety of brushes in Painter, in much the same way she would paint an image with traditional tools. She saved the image for use later in the process.

**2 Making a "paint skin."** To create source images that she calls "paint skins," Lhotka applies paint directly on the glass surface of her scanner (or to a sheet of acetate) and scans it. To create your own paint skin in a process similar to Lhotka's, paint a textured design on a piece of clear acetate with acrylic paint. If you like, make marks in the paint with a palette knife or flat brush. When the paint dries, place the acetate on the scanner bed and scan it.

**3 Compositing in Photoshop.** Lhotka began the composite in Photoshop though she could have done the work in Painter. Without a preconceived idea, she opened the Painter file (from Step 1) in Photoshop where she flipped, inverted and distorted the image. She copied and pasted the paint skin image (from Step 2) into the developing, 11 x 11-inch, 300-ppi Photoshop composite as a layer (in Painter, it would have been a floater). She turned the skin nega-

The image showing the emerging map-like design

The boat scan, ready to paste into the composite

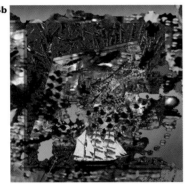

The image as sent to the desktop printer

Ironing the dampened, crumpled paper

Painting a dark acrylic wash onto the paper to enhance the wrinkled effect

Positioning the paper on the etching press to flatten it before printing

tive (Image, Map, Invert) to change the color spectrum to blue tones. As the image evolved, a map-like configuration emerged. She selected some of the dark areas in the skin layer with the Magic Wand and deleted them to make those areas transparent.

To give her image more depth, Lhotka created a new background image for the composite by copying a portion of her original sketch and resizing and softening it. She pasted the working composite into the new background image, combined the two layers using the blending modes, then flattened the image.

**4 Refining the image in Painter.** To make the evolving image appear more like a map, Lhotka opened the image in Painter and used the program's brushes and effects. She used the Magic Wand (Edit, Magic Wand) to select shapes in the top and right side of her image and filled the selections with blue (Command-F, Current Color) to create a sky and bodies of water. Then she painted an island chain in the lower right using a variety of brushes. She gave the sky and water more depth by reselecting all of the solid blue areas with the Magic Wand and filling the selections with a blue-to-white Two-Point gradation (Effects, Fill, Gradation). Lhotka created drop shadows beneath the "land masses" in her map and added linear elements and arrows to suggest an abstract compass. She chose a scan of a model boat from her archives and pasted it into the composite image. As a final step to finish the image, she used Effects, Tonal Control, Adjust Colors and experimented with the Hue Shift, Saturation and Value sliders.

**5 Preparing the paper and printing.** Many desktop inkjet printers will accept thicker papers that have been pretreated for more uniform printing. If your printer can do this, try using an archival-quality paper with a high rag content such as Rives printmaking or Arches watercolor paper. Lhotka used a cream-colored, heavyweight Rives paper. To give the paper an antique look that enhanced the Old World feel, she dampened and crumpled the paper, then flattened it with a steam iron. To add to the wrinkled look, she applied a wash of acrylic that soaked into the creases. She dried the paper and ran it through an etching press to flatten it.

As a final step before printing, she precoated the paper with an inkjet precoat (from Communicolor in Seattle) to enhance the uniform application of the inks and maintain color fidelity. She printed the 11 x 11-inch image on a Hewlett-Packard XL300 inkjet printer. She set the XL300 to print without Postscript software, which allowed the device to print the inks in a scatter pattern similar to that of an Iris, but coarser. The inkjet inks soaked into the paper and helped integrate the image with the character of the prepared paper itself. To protect the print from fading, Lhotka brushed a solvent-based UV varnish (from Golden Varnishes) onto the finished print. 🖌

# Making a Fine Art Master Print

***Overview*** *Make a custom color conversion of a Painter image; choose a textured, handmade paper that will enhance the image; after a first, light printing, paint an iridescent polymer onto some areas of the print; print the image a second time; apply a UV-protective coating to the print; document the edition.*

**1a**

*Cone at the Power Mac 9150 that's connected to the Iris system*

**1b**

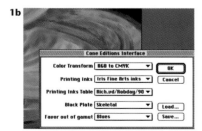

Cone Editions Interface

| | | |
|---|---|---|
| Color Transform | RGB to CMYK | OK |
| Printing Inks | Iris Fine Arts inks | Cancel |
| Printing Inks Table | Rich.vd/Robdog/90 | |
| Black Plate | Skeletal | Load... |
| Favor out of gamut | Blues | Save... |

*One of Cone's custom ink settings*

JON CONE OF CONE EDITIONS PRESS has been making prints and editions for artists since 1980. In 1985, Cone Editions began using computers in printmaking, pioneering techniques such as digital gravure, digital silkscreen and various digital monotype techniques. The firm has made Iris prints since 1992 and has become a leader in Iris printing technology, sharing methods, materials and techniques with other fine art service bureaus.

When he makes a fine art Iris master print, Cone interprets the artist's image in a collaborative manner. Often the selection of a paper, a special color transformation or perhaps even an experimental printing method can enhance an image. Cone used all three of these to realize the Painter image above.

**1 Resizing and converting the color mode.** An image may need to be resized to take advantage of the Iris printer's resolution (300 dpi) and replication capabilities. The Iris achieves the look of a much higher resolution because of the way the ink sprays onto the paper. Although the optimal resolution for files that will be printed on the Iris is 300 ppi, the printer can interpolate resolutions of 150 ppi or 100 ppi to produce high-quality prints.

Because Painter does not yet have a monitor-to-output calibration loop, Cone uses Adobe Photoshop. He has written a proprietary color transformation engine for Photoshop that he uses to convert images from RGB to CMYK. This interface also helps him calibrate the Iris, allowing the monitor to show a close approximation of the printed image. After converting this image, Cone used Photoshop's

## IRIS FACTS

The Iris printer's drum spins at 110 inches per second; up to 1 million droplets of ink per second are sprayed at 90 mph through each of its four nozzles. Using only cyan, magenta, yellow and black inks, it can simulate millions of colors.

**2**

*Positioning the paper on the Iris drum*

**3a**

*Carefully painting the iridescent polymer coating on the print*

**3b**

*Drying the iridescent solution*

**4**

*Stopping the printer to show how the cyan, magenta, yellow and black inks are printed in sequence on the substrate*

**5**

*Using a silkscreen process to add a protective archival coating*

Image, Adjust, Curves dialog box to compensate for out-of-gamut blues that had been lost. (Since RGB has a broader color gamut than CMYK, out-of-gamut colors are dulled when an image is converted to CMYK.) The black plate was adjusted separately to bring out detail in the darkest areas of the image. Finally, a proprietary plug-in Iris format RIP (raster image processor) was used to save the image in a form that the Iris can use for printing.

**2 Choosing a paper and setting up the Iris.** Cone selected a sheet of heavy, handmade paper with a very soft, large surface grain and an exaggerated deckled edge that would complement the vivid color and lively brushstrokes in the image. He taped the paper to the drum of the Iris.

**3 Printing, painting and drying.** Cone used the Iris to print this particular image twice. For the first pass, he adjusted the ink tables in the Iris's RIP to print a faint version of the image. With the print still taped to the drum, Cone brushed an experimental iridescent solution (composed of titanium dioxide-coated mica and hydroscopic polymer) onto the lily only. Then he dried the hand-painted coating with a hair dryer.

**4 Printing the image a second time.** Cone loaded a new set of rich-printing color ink tables into the Iris's RIP and made a second printing pass. The transparent Iris inks adhered to the polymer coating on the lily as easily as they did to the uncoated paper; the iridescent polymer provided a subtle reflection, adding luminance to the lily.

**5 Applying a protective coating to the print.** Michael Pelletier, Systems and Production Manager for Cone Editions, applied a silkscreen coating of hindered amine light stabilizers (HALS) and UV absorbers (UVA) to the finished print. This solvent-based coating developed by Cone carries the protective additives deep into the printed image where they fully encapsulate the dyes, helping to produce what Cone Editions says is "the longest-lasting archival Iris print available today."

**Documenting the edition.** The artist now signs the finished print to make it the "right-to-print proof" against which future prints in the edition will be compared. After the artist has signed approval, an edition can be printed on demand while the image file is stored safely on CD-ROM at Cone Editions. A documentation sheet signed by both master printer and artist details the size of the edition, number of proofs printed, methods used and dimensions. Most importantly, it specifies that no other proofs or prints can or will be made. (After completing an edition, Cone destroys all copies of the image file.) Each print will bear a unique print identification number and will be signed and numbered in pencil by the artist.

■ **Carol Benioff**, an award-winning illustrator and fine art printmaker, created the narrative series *Air, Earth, Water and Fire* for a direct-mail self-promotion. She developed the four images simultaneously, beginning with pencil sketches. Because she would print the images to a direct-to-plate printer instead of as a fine art print (as shown on pages 214–215), Benioff planned to composite the etching digitally with color imagery developed in Painter. She etched the four copperplates using classic hard-ground etching and aquatint methods—adding a touch of dry point to darken the shadows. After printing the plates she scanned each etching, cloned the scan, turned on Tracing

Paper and painted each color illustration with the varients of Simple Water watercolor brush. After drying the Wet layer, she added detail using modified Colored Pencils and Artist Pastel Chalk, then blended color using the Just Add Water brush. She opened both images in Photoshop and composited them with Image, Apply Image using the Multiply Blending mode, then flattened the image and made a CMYK conversion. Benioff placed the illustrations into a page layout program and prepared the files for prepress. The self-promotion card series was printed on a five-color direct-to-plate GTO DI Heidelberg printer.

■ **Helen Golden** created *Reflections And Breezes* by beginning with two source images, a photo she took of a window at an Italian country inn and a scan of a pen-and-ink drawing. After painting on the source images with Painter's brushes, she used both Painter and Photoshop to composite the pieces into one picture. Then she painted on the composite image using the Wet layer and Watercolor brushes in Painter.

Golden plans to print three different versions of the digital file, on different surfaces and using different printers. She printed the first version on prepared canvas at 48 x 30 inches, coating the print with Golden UV Filtering Varnish to protect it and to add a sheen that would enhance the feeling of transparency in the windows. She plans to print the second version on Tuxedo Parchment paper at a slightly smaller size. Tuxedo Parchment has a translucent look reminiscent of the soft light emanating from the window. The third version will be 48 x 30 inches, and will be built using two layers: a heavy coated paper topped with Hewlett-Packard Clear Acetate Film. The printed film is placed over the print on the paper, producing an image with both transparency and greater color depth. All three of these prints will be printed on the Hewlett-Packard DesignJet 755CM. Golden plans an edition of 30 works.

To begin *Metaphor* (left), one work in her series *Variations on a Theme*, **Judi Moncrieff** shot many photos of flowers at an orchid ranch in Livermore, California. Inspired by the beauty of the rare flowers, she chose one photograph from the shoot as a basis for the digital image and worked with it in Painter and Photoshop—adding textures, color and brushstrokes in Painter. Moncrieff prepared canvas by painting it with gold and bronze acrylics and interference colors. Then she treated the canvas with an inkjet precoat and printed it on a large-format Encad NovaJet 3 Printer with an Onyx RIP. After drying the print, she worked back into it with gold leaf, pencils, inks and pastel. The size of the final print is 34 x 46 inches.

■ **Bonny Lhotka**, known for her experimental mixed-media printmaking, created the digital file (above) for *Day Job* in Painter, by painting with brushes and using floaters to composite several source files. Before printing the digital image, Lhotka prepared a one-of-a-kind surface using gold and ochre-colored acrylics. She painted an abstract design on a nonporous surface, to create a monotype that she could transfer to a piece of rag paper using a large roller. After drying and coating the surface of the monoprint with inkjet receiver to help it absorb the ink, she printed the image on top of it using an Encad NovaJet 3. The final print is shown at right.

■ In creating the series *Women of the World*, fine artist **Dorothy Krause** spent as much time preparing surfaces and working the printed image as she did making the original images on the computer. She created the digital work for *Lady of the Flowers* (the digital file above and the printed work, left) and *Marketplace* (the digital image shown below, left) in Painter and Photoshop. Both images were printed on the Alpha Merics Spectrum printer, which prints on 4 x 8-foot materials up to 3/4-inch thick.

For *Lady of the Flowers*, Krause coated loosely woven linen with spackling compound and modeling paste, then rolled it to make it crack and chip. *Marketplace* was printed directly onto a plywood surface, then textured heavily with modeling paste. She glazed the border with washes of oil color.

To help unify the series, Krause rubbed metallic pigment onto the printed surfaces of the works until they looked like a blend of old stucco and burnished metal. Next, she added a 2-inch deep structure with cross supports to the back of each piece and textured and colored the surfaces. Then she brought some of the same texture and color into the images. As a last step, she drew onto the works with graphite, scratched their surfaces with a scribe and added bits of gold leaf.

Krause plans an edition of 20 works based on each of these digital images. She may decide to print each of the works on a different printer, on a different surface and at a different size.

# 10

# MAKING MOSAICS AND WEB GRAPHICS

Matthew Angorn illustrated Ruben, a regular character featured in the late-night Insomniacs Asylum™ suite created by the Warner Bros. Online team. To see more work from the Insomniacs Asylum™, turn to page 234.

Multicamel, *a tongue-in-cheek mosaic created by Steve Campbell*

WHAT DOES PAINTER OFFER AN ARTIST designing graphics for the World Wide Web? In addition to its powerful natural media painting and compositing tools, image hose brushes, mosaics and floaters with masks, Painter can help you with image prep for Web screens: For example, use shapes to set type for titles or draw polygons, convert the shapes to a floater and define the area as a clickable region for use on your screen. Or open source video in Painter as a frame stack and grab stills to use as graphics or as references for your screen illustrations.

In addition to tips and techniques for artists who create graphics for online subscriber services (such as America Online) and the World Wide Web, this chapter includes examples of Painter 4's new "mini-program" Mosaics. (If you need help with the painting techniques or selection methods referred to in this chapter you can find more information in Chapters 3, 4 and 5.)

## WORKING WITH MOSAICS

Tile mosaics became a popular medium at about 200–300 BC in the Roman Empire and Greece; floors and walls of many building were decorated with mosaics made of small pieces of glass, stones and shells. They were most often built to celebrate a historic event or for religious purposes. And early Christians built mosaics from bits of sparkling glass, illuminating the walls and ceilings of their churches with biblical scenes designed to inspire the viewer.

**Inspiration for mosaics.** You can build mosaics using Painter 4's new Mosaic brush and dialog box—by drawing them from scratch, by basing them on a line drawing that you've scanned, or by creating a clone-based mosaic using an existing piece of art or a photo. Keep in mind that because of the nature of the Mosaic

*Using a colored pen-and-ink sketch of the king of beasts as reference for a mosaic. Top: The cloned sketch (with tracing paper turned on) shows the mosaic in progress with recently applied tiles. Bottom: The same stage with tracing paper turned off. Click tracing paper on and off without closing the Make Mosaic dialog box by using the checkbox.*

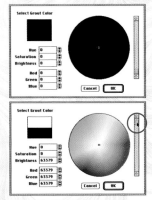

*Using the Make Mosaic dialog box to design a small narrow tile for the lion mosaic (above)*

*The default grout color is black, shown here (top) in the Select Grout Color dialog box, which uses the Apple color wheel. Dragging the value slider up lightens the color of the grout (bottom).*

tool, your decorative design or photo reference should have a strong compositional focal point. If you want to use a photo that has a busy background, consider simplifying it first by desaturating or blurring the background. (For tips on neutralizing busy backgrounds, see the beginning of Chapter 6.)

**Laying down tiles.** Here's a way to try out Painter's Mosaics. Open a new blank file, or a reference on which to base your mosaic. Visualize the forms in your design before you begin laying down the tiles, and rotate your page (by clicking on your image and dragging with the Rotate Page tool) to accommodate your drawing style so you'll be able to make smooth, controlled strokes to describe the forms.

Choose Canvas, Make Mosaic (or press Command-Option-M), to open the Mosaic dialog box. Opening the dialog box will turn the background of the currently active image black, the default grout color. If you have the Art Materials, Color palette open, you can use it to change grout color. For example, to change the grout to a color in the Color palette (instead of using the Apple color wheel in the Select Grout Color dialog box), click in the field, press Option and click on a new color in the Color palette. Then choose a contrasting color in the Color palette to paint some tiles. Switch colors again and continue to make tiles. Once you have tiles in place, you can sample color from an existing tile by pressing the Command key as you click on it. You can undo an action without closing the Make Mosaic dialog box by pressing Command-Z. To erase a tile, press the Control key and stroke with the Mosaic brush over the tile. While working on a mosaic, save it in RIFF format to preserve the resolution-independent nature of the mosaic. (Because mosaic tiles are mathematically described, a mosaic can be resized without loss of quality.)

To read more about working with Selections and Shapes, turn to Chapters 4 and 5 of this book. For an in-depth explanation of Painter's mosaic-building tools check out Chapter 13 of the *Painter 4 User Guide*. And to read more about using a photo-reference for a mosaic, turn to "Building a Clone-Based Mosaic" on page 228.

## CREATING GRAPHICS FOR THE WEB

Painter has tools that make it easy to adapt graphics for the World Wide Web: For instance, you can save in GIF and JPEG (the two most popular image formats used on the Web). And you can tell Painter to do some of the coding to help you set up image maps or linked graphics. Here are some tips for creating Web graphics in Painter.

First, there are two basic uses for images on a Web screen. One is an in-line graphic or "static" image embedded in the page without a link to another location—for example, an embedded background graphic. The second use for graphics is as a "hot spot," or "button." A hot spot is a clickable region on your artwork that will allow the user to hyperlink (or travel) to another location on the

*A row of interactive buttons on the* Lenny Kravitz *Web site* Music *screen designed by Hugo Hidalgo with BoxTop Interactive for client Virgin Records. The center button features a colored animation, inviting the viewer to click there first.*

**Save As GIF Options**

Number of Colors:
- ○ 4 Colors
- ○ 8 Colors
- ○ 16 Colors
- ○ 32 Colors
- ● 64 Colors
- ○ 128 Colors
- ○ 256 Colors

Imaging Method:
- ● Quantize to Nearest Color
- ○ Dither Colors

Transparency:
- ☐ Output Transparency
- ● Background is WWW Gray
- ○ Background is BG Color

Misc Options:                Threshold ▓▓▓░░░░  25%
☐ Interlace GIF File

Map Options:
☒ NCSA MAP file          ☐ CERN Map File

[ Preview Data ]  [ Cancel ]  [ OK ]

*Saving an image in GIF format, reducing the number of colors from millions (24-bit) to 64 colors (6-bit). Use the checkbox to choose a server type if you want Painter to create a Map Definition file for the image so that the hot spots on the image are defined.*

## ON-SCREEN TYPE AND COLOR

Type on-screen can be difficult to read in small sizes, so it's important that it be as clear as possible. For both type and drawings, flat color with crisp edges often works best. Anti-aliasing and gradations don't compress well—they can become blotchy.

Web, either within the same Web site or at another site. There are two general types of hot spots. The simpler one is a button that links to one location (URL, or Uniform Resource Locator). The second is an image map—an image that has been divided into regions, each of which lets you link to a different URL.

**Making an image map.** You can choose any kind of graphic as an "image map": title type or a particular word in a sentence, a photograph or an illustration you've painted. Define an image map by selecting all or part of an image (by dragging around it with a selection tool and floating it). Double-click on the floater name in the Floater List to access the Floater Attributes dialog box. Use the checkbox to make it a WWW map clickable region.

**Using Web-friendly file formats.** The JPEG and transparent GIF formats that Painter supports are the most popular file formats used in web page design. Transparent GIF files make use of the mask you've saved with the file, allowing a graphic to be placed on the page with an irregular edge or with holes cut into it to reveal the background underneath. Make a transparent GIF by choosing File, Save As, GIF. In the Save As GIF Options dialog box, use the Preserve Transparency checkbox. Click the Preview button to make sure your mask is working.

We suggest using GIF format to save simple line art and flat-color graphics without gradations and soft edges. Save photos and painted artwork in 24-bit JPEG format. When you Save As GIF or JPEG, choose the server type (CERN or NCSA) that your service provider recommends. Painter will create the map definition file for you, writing a text file that defines the hot spots.

**Building small files that load fast.** Many Web-savvy designers recommend making graphics files small, between 20 and 30K, because most folks surfing the Net will not wait for images that take a long time to load. The average modem speed is 14,400 baud and graphics of 20–30K will load within about 30 seconds. To make GIF images small, use Painter's Save As GIF Options dialog box to compress the number of colors from millions to 256 (8-bit) or fewer. Save as GIF in the exact pixel dimensions needed for the page design. When you use JPEG format to preserve the 24-bit color of an image, experiment with the JPEG Encoding Quality settings to determine how much compression an image can withstand. JPEG is a lossy compression (it removes information, which can't be restored when the image is compressed), so make sure to use File, Save As to create the new JPEG file with a different name, preserving your master file.

**Creating a subdued background.** Painter has tools for creating exciting patterned backgrounds, but a busy, contrasty pattern can take attention away from the subject of the screen and overwhelm your audience. Here are two suggestions that will help you make a

*Detail from the* Sequoyah Online *hub screen, designed by Lynda Weinman, shows the use of a subtle background.*

*Hugo Hidalgo created buttons, patterns, type and glows in Painter for the Lenny Kravitz site. Click the glowing button (above), and Netscape boots Simple Player. Click the forward arrow to play the Quicktime movie. See more work from the Kravitz site on page 236.*

See more work from the Kravitz site on page 236.

## SHRINKING A COPY

If you're doing detailed painting to be displayed on the Web at 72ppi, you may want to create your art at a higher resolution so you can zoom in and paint the details. Then use Canvas, Resize to shrink a copy of your image down to 72ppi. Sharpen areas that become soft (Effects, Focus, Sharpen).

## A MASTER TIME-SAVER

To make Web page updates easier, always save a master RIFF or Photoshop 3.0-format file with live floaters for each screen design. When you want to replace an image on a screen, clear the old one and paste in the new (double-click the floater's name in the Floater List and enter the specifications in the Floater Attributes dialog box). Save As in GIF format using a new name.

background pattern more subtle: Turn down the contrast using Effects, Tonal Control, Brightness/Contrast, or Effects, Tonal Control, Correct Colors, Brightness and Contrast. Or desaturate the background (using Tonal Controls, Adjust Colors) to call attention to brighter-colored content. To desaturate, move the Saturation slider to the left. Click OK when you see the look you want in the Preview window.

**Adding movie stills and video to your page.** You can open a movie in Painter and capture frames for static images or hotspots. And you can save a Quicktime or AVI/VFW movie using very small compression such as Adobe Premiere's Cinepak, so it can be played within the Netscape 2.0 browser. Clicking on a button that's linked to a movie causes Netscape to boot Simple Player, and you can click the forward arrow to play the movie with sound.

## IMAGE MAPS OR SINGLE LINKS?

Image maps are made by dividing a single image into several hot spots, or clickable areas, that link to different places. There are two types of image maps: client-side and server-side. Server-side maps require the additional use of CGI (Common Gateway Interface) scripts, and must be posted to a working Web server for viewing and testing. Client-side maps are preferred by most designers, because they can be programmed exclusively in HTML, without the need for CGI, and can be tested from a hard drive without being posted to a server. (One drawback with client-side maps is they currently they are supported only by Netscape version 2.0 and higher. Most HTML pages that use client-side image maps also include a server-side image map for this reason.)

An advantage to using image maps, rather than single-linked images, is that one image will download much faster than a series of smaller images. Using an image map also presents the opportunity to make freeform graphics that are not confined within the rectangular bounding boxes of their own documents, but Web designer Lynda Weinman recommends using image maps only when you need to: They are harder to program than single-linked images and can be taxing on servers and hard to troubleshoot. An alternative would be to break apart a single image into multiple images that could be programmed to link independently, using standard HTML codes. For example in:

    <a href=""><img src=""></a>

you would put the destination of the link, into the quotes within the <a href=""> tag; the destination could be either another HTML page or an image at the same site. You would put the image that would be linked (the hot spot) within the quotes of the <img src="">tag, and close everything with the </a> tag.

# Building a Clone-Based Mosaic

**Overview** *Choose a photo reference and retouch it if needed; make a clone of the retouched photo; use the Make Mosaic dialog box to design and lay down colored tiles in the clone.*

S. SWAMINATHAN

**1**

*The original photograph*

*Increasing the contrast in the source image*

**2b**

*Detail of the retouched source image*

MOSAICS HAVE BEEN USED AS A NARRATIVE and decorative art form since Hellenistic and Roman times. Because of its graphic nature the mosaic is a medium that can be used to express strong emotion. S. Swaminathan created the digital mosaic *Soul of Homelessness*, based on his photograph of a homeless man. His vision was to create an abstracted mosaic portrait of the man that would portray the dignity he projected.

**1 Selecting a source image.** Because the mosaic look is very powerful, choose a photo with a strong focal point and meaningful content, so the technique does not overpower the image. The photo should also have a broad tonal range and good color detail to help build value and color complexity into the tiles. Swaminathan began with a 675 x 920-pixel photo.

**2 Retouching and cloning.** To separate the subject from the background, Swaminathan used a modified Fat Stroke Airbrush to simplify the background of the photo, adding soft blue and white strokes. He also increased the contrast in the image using Effects, Tonal Control, Brightness/Contrast. When he was satisfied with the retouching, he cloned the image. Choose File, Clone to make a clone of your source image. In preparation for laying down colored tiles

---

**MOSAIC QUICK KEY**

To quickly access the Make Mosaic dialog box without visiting the Canvas menu, press Command-Option-M.

**3a**

*Designing a horizontal tile to use on the face*

**3b**

*Using Tracing Paper to view the clone source while positioning tiles on the clone*

**4a**

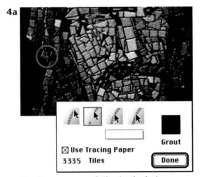

*Erasing a course of tiles in the hair*

**4b**

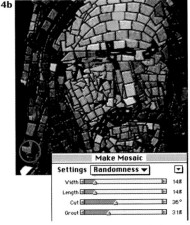

*Adding new irregular tiles in the hair*

in the clone based on the color of the clone source image, check the Use Clone Color checkbox in the Color palette.

**3 Laying tiles.** With the clone active, open the Make Mosaic dialog box (Canvas, Make Mosaic), and check the Use Tracing Paper checkbox so you can see the source image while laying down the tiles. To design a custom tile, begin by setting Dimensions for the tile; choose a Width, Length and Grout size. Make a stroke on your image to test the settings. Press Command-Z to Undo a test stroke without closing the Make Mosaic dialog box. Experiment with the settings until you get just the look you want.

Swaminathan began with the face, which would become the focal point of the mosaic portrait. As he worked, he varied the size of the tiles, using larger tiles for the broader areas of the face (the forehead and cheeks), and smaller tiles to render detailed areas (the shadowed right side of the man's nose, eyes and eyebrows).

Generally, he worked from the center out, beginning with the face and hair and then rendering the shirt, shoes and background. To depict the long hair (and to contrast with the more uniform shapes of tiles on the subject's jacket) he designed narrow, irregularly shaped tiles. To customize the Randomness Settings of tile shapes and grout (as Swaminathan did), press the Settings pop-up menu to access the Randomness sliders. Begin by moving the Cut slider to the right to increase Randomness in the shape of the tile ends. To vary the spacing between tiles, move the Grout slider to the right. Experiment with each of the sliders individually until you arrive at the look you want.

**4 Completing the image.** To refine the tile design, Swaminathan sampled color from existing tiles (by pressing the Command key and clicking on a tile), and applied the color to other tiles. To erase tiles, click the Remove Tiles icon and drag the cursor over the tiles that you want to remove. Click back on the Apply Tiles icon and drag with the Mosaic brush to add new tiles.

**Adding highlights and shadows.** Finally, Swaminathan used a subtle application of Apply Surface Texture to add the realistic highlights and shadows you would see on the slightly uneven surface of handmade tiles. Choose Effects, Surface Control, Apply Surface Texture using Image Luminance. Try these settings: Softness, 0; Amount, 20; Picture 100; Shine, 25; and Reflection, 0. Click OK.

**SAMPLE WITH A CLICK**

To sample color from an existing tile in your mosaic, press the Command key and click on a tile. You won't see the Mosaic brush's crosshair cursor change to the Dropper tool when you're working with the open Make Mosaic dialog box, but you *will* be able to sample the color.

**CORRECTION SHORTCUT**

To remove tiles without clicking the Remove Tiles icon, press the Control key and drag the Mosaic brush over the tiles that you want to remove.

# Creating a Web Page with an Image Map

***Overview*** *Scan elements; build a patterned background using the scanned elements; create floaters and designate an image map in Painter; finish the HTML.*

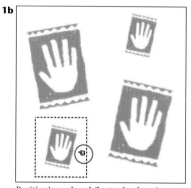

1a

The grayscale scan of a hand graphic

1b

Positioning a hand floater by dragging with the Floater Adjuster tool.

LYNDA WEINMAN, AUTHOR OF THE BOOK *Designing Web Graphics,* creates graphics and animation for movies, TV commercials, music videos and World Wide Web sites. To build the Web site *Sequoyah Online* for an alternative elementary and junior high school in Pasadena, Weinman used Painter to create a background pattern, a logotype, graphics, and image map buttons. She designed the site to be viewed with any browser and used her own site, http://www.lynda@lynda.com. to develope the prototype.

**1 Laying out the pattern tile.** As the basis for the background, Weinman planned a tile that would be easy to make into a seamlessly repeating pattern: None of the graphic elements would touch the tile edges, and the texture behind the graphics would be randomized and not too coarse. (For information on creating a more complicated pattern in which elements touch the edges and the "seams" have to be edited, see "Exploring Patterns," in Chapter 7 on pages 158–160.)

Choose a design element that you want to use in your pattern. To capture an element to use in her pattern design, Weinman scanned a hand graphic and opened the scan file in Painter. You may want to follow Weinman's process of scaling, rotating and duplicating to create your own design.

Select your design element with a selection marquee or the Lasso tool and copy it to the clipboard. Then open a new image to use for developing your pattern tile (Weinman's was 200 x 200-

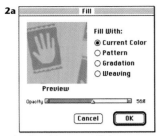

Filling the tile with an overall tint

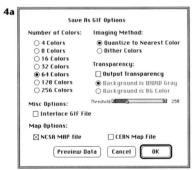

Adding relief with Apply Surface Texture

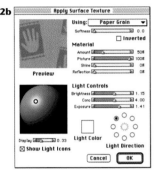

Moving the pattern in the Capture Pattern window to look for seams

Saving the file as a GIF with 64 colors.

Detail of the background file with pattern

pixels), and paste the copied graphic into it. Before dropping the pasted graphic, Weinman used Effects, Orientation, Scale to reduce its size. She reduced its Opacity to about 50% using the Controls: Adjuster palette. Then she chose Effects, Orientation, Rotate and turned the graphic by dragging on a corner handle. She made a copy by Option-clicking on the graphic with the Floater Adjuster tool, dragged the copy to a new position, and rotated the copy to the right. She Option-clicked, scaled and rotated to produce more elements to balance the design within the pattern tile.

When you have all of the elements of your tile in position, click the Drop All button on the expanded Floater List to drop the floaters (they must be merged with the canvas to use the Capture Pattern command in step 3).

**2 Coloring and texturing the tile.** Next, Weinman added a subtle brown color and texture to the tile. To color your tile, give it a transparent overall tint by filling it (Effects, Fill at about 50% Opacity.) Now make a mask so you'll be able to color the darker areas (the hand graphics in this case) without affecting the background (Edit, Mask, Auto Mask using Image Luminance, clicking the Invert Mask checkbox.) Give the graphic a darker tint with Color Overlay (Effects, Surface Control, Color Overlay, using Mask, clicking the Dye Concentration button).

Next, to add a colored texture to the entire tile, choose an interesting Paper texture; you may want to scale your texture down using the Scale slider on the front of the Art Materials, Paper drawer. Then apply Color Overlay using Paper Grain, clicking the Hiding Power button. Finally, add highlights and shadows that will enhance the texture using Effects, Surface Control, Apply Surface Texture using Paper Grain. (Use the same Paper texture, at the same size you used to apply the Color Overlay.)

**3 Capturing the Pattern.** When you have colored and textured your tile, it's ready to make into a pattern. To capture your pattern, choose Art Materials, Pattern, Capture Pattern. Click and drag in the Preview window to check your pattern for any seams. If you need to eliminate seams, refer to "Exploring Patterns," in Chapter 7. Weinman also captured her tile as a paper texture (Art Materials, Paper, Capture Texture) so she could apply it to her files as a repeating texture.

**4 Setting up a page.** This step sets up the Web page design itself. There are no absolute size restrictions on Web pages. They can be any length, because the viewer can scroll. But it's best to make the page no wider than 640 pixels (the width of the average monitor screen display). Weinman created her new page file at 500 x 600 pixels, to fit within the default page size of Netscape 2.0, a popular and versatile browser.

For your prototype Web page design, create a new file and fill it with your pattern (Effects, Fill, Pattern). When you've filled the

*The masked logo (top) and hand graphic with type (bottom) shown using Canvas, View Mask*

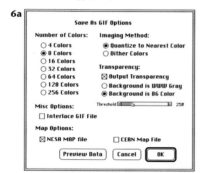

*The finished hand GIF with type; relief added with Apply Surface Texture*

**6a**

**Save As GIF Options**

**Number of Colors:**
- ○ 4 Colors
- ● 8 Colors
- ○ 16 Colors
- ○ 32 Colors
- ○ 64 Colors
- ○ 128 Colors
- ○ 256 Colors

**Imaging Method:**
- ● Quantize to Nearest Color
- ○ Dither Colors

**Transparency:**
- ☒ Output Transparency
- ○ Background is WWW Gray
- ● Background is BG Color

**Misc Options:**
- ☐ Interlace GIF File

Threshold ▣▬▬▬▬ 25%

**Map Options:**
- ☒ NCSA MAP file
- ☐ CERN Map File

[ Preview Data ]  [ Cancel ]  [ **OK** ]

*The GIF Options dialog box with settings for Transparency and colors*

**6b**

GIF Output Preview

[ OK ]

*The GIF Options preview window shows the logo background "dropped-out," so the user can test the mask and preview transparency.*

file with your pattern, choose File, Save As, GIF. Choose the number of colors and click the Quantize to Nearest Color radio button. (For advice on reducing Web page color palettes, see page 226.)

**5 Setting type and filling it with a pattern.** It's often easier to build source graphics in separate files and paste them into the final screen image when all of the elements are done. Start a new file the same width as the page and as high as the graphic you want to add. Using the Text tool with black as the current color, set large bold letters for a logotype. Weinman made a 500 x 100-pixel file and typed "Sequoyah" using Hot Coffee, a font by Ethan Durham at Fonthead Design (http://www.mediabridge.com/fonthead/main.html).

Since you'll be treating all the letters as a unit, group the selected type shapes (Command-G) and collapse them to make one floater (Collapse button, in the expanded Floater List). (A mask is saved when you convert a shape to a floater. Click the top right [Masked Outside] button in the expanded Floater List.) To fill the logotype floater with a gray version of her pattern, Weinman used Effects, Fill, Pattern and then stripped the color out by using Effects, Tonal Control, Adjust Colors, and dragging the Saturation slider to the left. She added texture to "Sequoyah" (Effects, Surface Control, Surface Texture using Paper Texture) using the Paper she had saved in step 3, so it lined up perfectly with the pattern fill. Then she added the subhead type to the logotype file with the Type tool, in a gray color she sampled from the logotype using the Dropper.

Next she created another new file (416 x 283 pixels) and copied and pasted her original hand scan into it. She masked the hand floater (Edit, Mask Auto Mask using the Current Color, black), and clicked the masked outside button in the Floater List. Then, as she had done for the logotype, she filled it with the pattern, grayed it out, and added text.

**6 Embossing.** For the logotype and the graphic, Weinman built a crisp-edged embossed effect that would display well on the screen using limited bit depth. To do this you'll need to make two copies of your graphic. Select the Floater by clicking on it with the Floater Adjuster tool. Now, Option-click twice to make two more copies, one for the highlight (the middle one in the Floater List) and one for the shadow (the bottom one in the list). Select the shadow floater in the Floater List and use the arrow keys to offset it a few pixels to the left and up to create a hard-edged shadow (you'll be simulating lighting from below, right). Then darken it by choosing Effects, Tonal Control, Adjust Colors and dragging the Value slider to the left. Now select the highlight floater in the Floater List, move it a few pixels down and to the right, and lighten it (this time the Value slider goes right).

After collapsing the floaters (select all three floaters in the Floater List, press the Group button, and then press the Collapse button), drop the floater to the canvas with its mask, by clicking the Drop with Mask checkbox and then the Drop button.

**6c**

*Selected rectangular floaters that will define bounding boxes of the buttons*

**7a**

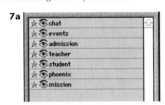

*The Floater List with the named floaters*

**7b**

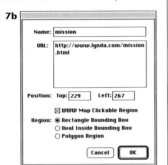

*Entering the URL into the information field*

**8a**

*The image map's HTML code as it appears in Simple Text*

Now, save the image as a transparent GIF with a reduced color palette (Weinman saved the gray logotype and the graphic with 8 colors). Choose File, Save As, and select GIF format. In the Save As GIF Options dialog box, click the Preserve Transparency radio button, and choose the number of colors. Preview the transparency (by clicking the Preview button) to make sure it works; for example, the background needed to show through the counters of the "e," "q," "o" and "a" in "Sequoyah" and through the hand in the graphic.

**7 Completing the layout and making the image map.** Open the background file (from step 4; this was Weinman's 500 x 600-pixel pattern-filled file). Then copy and paste your logotype and graphics images into it (from steps 5 and 6; for example, the "Sequoyah" and hand graphic files). Position the elements and drop the floaters by clicking the Drop button in the expanded Floater List.

Painter allows you to define an image file as an image map (a document that's divided into nonoverlapping regions, each of which lets you link to a different URL or location on the Web). Open the finished layout and drag with the Rectangular Selection tool to create a marquee around one of the button elements that will become a clickable region. Click to float the item. Repeat this process for as many clickable regions as you need.

Now tell Painter what to include in the map definition file: Double-click on each floater name in the Floater List to open the Floater Attributes dialog box. Enter a new name for the floater in the Name field, if you like. Use the checkbox to select WWW clickable map (the Region button will default to Rectangle), and type the URL into the URL field. Choose File, Save As, GIF, and when the Save As GIF Options dialog box appears, use the NCSA map or CERN map checkbox, depending on which type your Web server requires.

**8 Finishing the HTML.** Ask your service provider where the CGI script for image maps is stored and how to use it (CGI is an acronym for Common Gateway Interface). Or convert the image map information to a client-side image map for use within the HTML document. You can find more information about image maps (including client-side) on page 227. And check out these URLs on the World Wide Web to learn how to set up programming for client-side and server-side image maps: http://www.utexas.edu/learn/pub/maps/ and http://www.hway.com/ihip/.

**8b**

*The anatomy of one of the clickable regions in the map defintion file that Painter automatically generates.*

Painter will make the map definition file for you—which lists each region, defines each region using $x$ and $y$ coordinates and lists the URL it links to. You'll also need additional HTML programming to make the links work.

# Building an Online Suite

***Overview*** *Scan pencil sketches into Photoshop; paint flat color onto layers; take the image into Painter to render details with brushes and textures; convert the color palette; compress the files.*

©1996 WARNER BROS.

© 1996 WARNER BROS.

*The original pencil sketch*

*The in-progress layered file in Photoshop with flat color*

*Flat type shapes with a drop shadow applied*

© 1996 WARNER BROS.

*Angorn created an irregular edge for the rock by making a freehand selection, and floating it, in the final logo button before it was distorted to fit the right wall. He gave the type a three-dimensional look with Effects, Apply Surface Texture using Mask.*

IF YOU'RE ONLINE LATE AT NIGHT, check out the work of the Warner Bros. Online creative team on America Online (use Keyword: Insomniacs). Some might say that Matthew Angorn's cartoon style is reminiscent of 1960s psychedelic art. Angorn coordinated with other members of the Warner Bros. Online team—art director Suzanne Abramson, director of production Rikk Galvan, producer Kelly Goto and assistant producer Julie Noiman—to create the artwork for the "rooms" in the *Insomniacs Asylum*™ suite. He worked with many separate elements (layers in Adobe Photoshop and floaters in Painter) so it would be easy to make the changes required by the production team.

**1 Making sketches and scanning.** Angorn began each room in the suite by scanning a pencil-and-paper sketch using Adobe Photoshop's File, Acquire command. He saved the scan for the Lounge (the site hub, shown above), as a 1389 x 806-pixel file. Although the final art used online would be smaller, he preferred to work at a larger size so he could zoom in and paint details.

**2 Adding flat color to the sketch.** Using the sketch as an underlay (it was on the Background layer in Photoshop), Angorn blocked in large areas of color, creating new layers as he needed them. He saved the files in Photoshop 3 format so he could open them in Painter, automatically preserving the layers as floaters.

**3 Creating elements using shapes.** All of the furniture was drawn with the Painter's Pen tool using Bézier curves. He converted the shapes to floaters (Shapes, Convert to Floater), then distorted them into the perspective of the room using Effects, Orientation, Distort. Type was set with the Text tool and converted to floaters in the same way.

**4 Adding brushstrokes and texture.** Enjoying the natural feel of Painter's brushes and its ability to apply textures, Angorn began rendering the characters who inhabit the room, each on its own floater. Using the Feather Tip Airbrush, he blocked in general values. To add detail to the people, he used both the Fat Stroke Air-

*Angorn drew the* Insomniacs Asylum™ *logo type with the Pen tool; then floated elements and applied color fills, brushstrokes and Apply Surface Texture*

**5**

*Close-up detail showing a few of the regular Insomniacs*

**6**

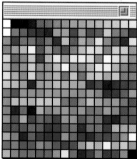

*Noiman used DeBabelizer to convert the 24-bit file to an 8-bit BMP file (top) with these colors.*

brush and the Large Chalk variant (at about 70% opacity). On the furniture and type elements, he used Effects, Color Overlay and Effects, Apply Surface Texture using Mask, then touched up the highlights and shadows with the Feather Tip Airbrush.

**5 Adding painted details.** Using a small modified Feather Tip Airbrush, Angorn added highlights and shadows to the lounge regulars and the furniture, and added final touches to the logo buttons. When the details were complete, he saved the files in Photoshop 3.0 format, to make it easy for assistant producer Julie Noiman to prepare the files to be sent to America Online.

**6 Converting and compressing.** Noiman opened the files in Photoshop and saved a new version of each one, reducing the file size from 1389 x 806 pixels to 500 x 290 pixels at 72ppi, the resolution used for screen display. After reducing the number of layers by combining some of the smaller elements with the Merge Layers command, she saved each layer into its own file. Then she opened the new files in Equilibrium DeBabelizer and converted each 24-bit working file with millions of colors into an 8-bit nondithered BMP file with 256 colors. (America Online accepts both 4-bit [16 color] and 8-bit [256 color] files.)

To prepare the files to be sent to the America Online producers, Noiman moved the illustration file, (now in BMP format) to a PC running Windows 95. She saved individual files in ART format with Johnson-Grace ARTpress, a compression format used by AOL. Originally created for working with photos, ARTpress works well with any continuous-tone images.

At AOL, producers programmed the art into their system and database and sent files back to the Warner Bros. Online team. Goto and Noiman wrote code for links to screens and developed script content for the site, adding stories and photos with a language similar to HTML. 👁

*Cafe.com, reached by clicking the Cafe.Com button on the Lounge back wall, was created using the same layering and brush techniques as the Lounge (Salon hub screen shown on page 232).*

■ **Hugo Hidalgo**, a gifted artist and innovative web designer working with Boxtop Interactive, built the graphics for the *Lenny Kravitz* web site for client Virgin Records. The site features many exciting screens that work together in a unified design. Hidalgo used tiled patterns built from images he had captured from video. He opened each video clip in Painter as a frame stack, and saved single frames by choosing File, Save As, Save Current Frame As Image. He also used the video grabs and photos supplied by the client to build button graphics in Painter.

To make it more inviting to enter the site, Hidalgo created an animated color button for the *Main Hub* (top). He put together a simple low-memory color animation for the button, by making different color versions, saving the series as numbered files, and animating them in GIF Builder, a nifty freeware program that animates GIF 89a files, written by Yves Piquet (yvespiquet@ia.epfl.ch). First, Hidalgo applied a red color to the button with Effects, Color Overlay, using Image Luminance and Dye Concentration and saved the file as "01." He cloned the file and used Effects, Tonal Control, Adjust Color to change the Hue from red to purple. He saved the second file as a numbered file ("02"), and repeated the process to save the other files, moving around the color wheel.

For the *Videos* screen (bottom), Hidalgo drew a vertical, irregular shape with the Pen tool in a separate source file that included a pattern made from a montage he had built from video grabs. He converted the shape path to a selection and used the selection to capture a section of the montage that he could paste into the final *Videos* screen image. The vertical pattern also appears on several other screens within the site.

He designed the *Videos* screen to take advantage of Netscape 2.0's ability to play movies with sound by clicking a button on a web page. Hidalgo programmed the buttons to link to small video clips stored in a folder. He used Adobe Premiere to compress the clips using Cinepak compression to about 1 MB in size. When the user clicks on a button linked to a video clip, Netscape boots Simple Player and saves a movie to the user's hard disk. To play the movie, the user clicks the Simple Player forward arrow button. You can visit the Kravitz site at http://www.underground.net/lenny kravitz.

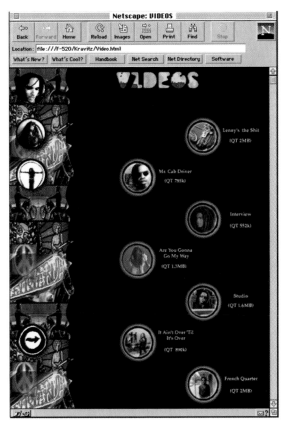

■ To build the images for the *UPN* web site, **Hugo Hidalgo** used Painter's brushes, special effects and image map features.

He began the *Main* opening screen (top) by scanning a black-and-white photograph of an Art Deco building. He cut the top off the building to make room for the glowing logo that was to come. He cloned the photo (File, Clone) and after deleting the contents from the clone, he used Tracing Paper to make a drawing with the Pencil brushes. Then, he cloned portions of the photo into the drawing. He applied tints to his image using the Wet layer and the Simple Water Watercolor brushes. Then he used various Airbrushes to add atmosphere. Hidalgo built the logos for the *Main* screen in separate source files.

He set type shapes and drew Bézier shape paths to build the Telescape and Info logo outlines, and added realism to both logos with various Airbrushes, Effects, Apply Surface Texture, and Apply Lighting. When the logos were complete, he copied each one and pasted it into the final *Main* screen image.

Taking advantage of Painter's ability to make an image map definition file, Hidalgo created two links for the *Main* screen image, making the *Telescape* and *Site Info* logo floaters into hot spots (clickable regions). Using the Rectangular Shape tool, he dragged a shape around each logo to define the bounding box of the button, and entered the appropriate information into the Floater Attributes dialog box for each region.

The *Telescape Lobby* (bottom), can be reached by clicking on the *Telescape* button on the *Main* screen. Hidalgo used the same techniques he used to build the *Main* screen to create the *Telescape Lobby* image and other rooms in the site. Check out the *UPN* site at http://www.upn.com.

# Appendix A
# Images on the *Wow!* CD-ROM

*These vendors provided photos or video clips from their collections for the* Wow! CD-ROM *in the back of this book.*

**Artbeats**
*Three volumes (3 CDs each) of backgrounds and textures, including Wood and Paper; sizes to 16.5 MB*

**Cascom International**
*Select Effects: A three-volume set of digitized clip video, including high-tech animation, titling effects and moving backgrounds; sizes to 320 x 240 pixels*

**Color Bytes**
*3 Sampler volumes (nature and urban photos); 2 Designer volumes (background and texture photos); sizes to 25 MB*

**Digital Stock**
*42 standard photo volumes (e.g., Active Lifestyles, AntiStock™, Skylines of North America, Medicine & Health Care, Urban Textures, Transportation, Undersea Life); sizes to 24 MB*

**Digital Wisdom**
*Body shots: One volume of photographs shot with twelve models in various business situations against a white background; sizes to 4 MB*

**Form and Function**
*Wrapture Reels: One volume of animated textures including time-lapse clouds, rushing water, and hand-drawn animations; sizes to 640 x 480 pixels*

**MetaTools**
*KPT Power Photos: 10 volumes of object and background photos, many with masks; sizes to 18 MB*

**Mediacom**
*Adclips: One volume (2 CDs) of video clips including Recreation, Corporate, Historical, Lifestyles, Wildlife; sizes to 320 x 240 pixels*

**PhotoDisc**
*34 standard photo volumes; 12 Signature Series (from a single photographer) discs; 12 Object Series (with clipping paths) discs; 4 Fine Art disks; sizes to 28.5 MB*

**Visual Concept Entertainment**
*Pyromania 1 and 2: 2 volumes of digitized video of explosions, fireworks, smoke, and other incendiary displays; sizes to 640 x 480 pixels*

**Xaos Tools**
*Fresco: One volume of painterly computer-generated textures; sizes to 30 MB*

**Image Farm**
*Five volumes; Arizona Desert, Berlin Walls, Cottage and Country, Real Rock and Streets of London; high quality photographic textures and backgrounds; sizes to 18 MB.*

# Appendix B Vendor Information

## IMAGE COLLECTIONS

**Artbeats, Inc.**
2611 S. Myrtle Road
Myrtle Creek, OR 97457
541-863-4429  541-863-4547 fax

**Cascom International**
806 4th Ave South
Nashville, TN 37210
615-242-8900  615-256-7890 fax

**Color Bytes, Inc.**
2525 S. Wadsworth, Suite 308
Lakewood, CO 80227
800-825-2656  303-202-9200
303-202-5946 fax

**Digital Stock Corp.**
400 South Sierra Avenue, Suite 100
Solana Beach, CA 92075
800-545-4514  619-794-4040
619-794-4041 fax

**Digital Wisdom, Inc.**
300 Jeanette Drive, Box 2070
Tappahannock, VA 22560
800-800-8560  804-443-9000
804-443-3632 fax

**Form and Function**
1595 17th Avenue
San Francisco, CA 94122
415-664-4010  415-664-4030 fax

**Image Farm**
110 Spadina Ave., Suite 309
Toronto, Ontario
Canada M5V 2K4
416-504-4161  416-504-4163 fax

**Mediacom**
12701 Cottage Mill Terrace
Midlothian, VA 23113
804-794-0700  804-794-0799 fax

**MetaTools, Inc.**
6303 Carpinteria Avenue
Carpinteria, CA 93013
805-566-6200  805-566-6385 fax

**PhotoDisc, Inc.**
2013 4th Avenue, 4th Floor
Seattle, WA 98121
800-528-3472  206-441-9355
206-441-9379 fax

**Visual Concept Entertainment**
P.O. Box 921226
Sylmar, CA 91392
818-367-9187  818-362-3490 fax
http://www.vce.com

**Xaos Tools, Inc.**
600 Townsend Street, Suite 270 East
San Francisco, CA 94103
415-487-7000  415-558-9886 fax

## HARDWARE

**Apple Computer, Inc.**
800-767-2775

**Epson America** / *Desktop color printers*
P.O. Box 2854
Torrance, CA 90509
800-289-3776  800-873-7766

**Hewlett-Packard** / *Desktop color printers*
16399 West Bernardo Drive
San Diego, CA 92127
619-592-8308

**Iomega** / *Removable drives*
1821 West Iomega Way
Roy, Utah 84067-9977
800-456-5522  801-778-3000

**IRIS Graphics** / *Specialized inkjet printers*
Six Crosby Drive
Bedford, MA 01730
617-275-8777

**Pinnacle Micro** / *Optical drives*
19 Technology
Irvine, CA 92718
714-727-3300  714-727-1913 fax

**Wacom** / *Drawing tablets*
115 Century Road
Paramus, NJ 07652
800-922-6613

## SOFTWARE

**Adobe Systems** / *After Effects, Dimensions, Gallery Effects, Illustrator, Pagemaker, Photoshop, Premiere*
1585 Charlston Road
P.O. Box 7900
Mountain View, CA 94039-7900
800-833-6687

**Aladdin Systems** / *Sitcomm*
165 Westridge Drive
Watsonville, CA 95076-4159
408-761-6200

**Baseline Publishing, Inc.** / *Screenshot*
1770 Moriah Woods Boulevard, Suite 14
Memphis, TN 38117-7118
901-682-9676

**Fractal Design Corp.** / *Color Studio, Dabbler, Painter, Poser, Sketcher*
335 Spreckles Drive, Suite F
Aptos, CA 95003
408-688-8800

**Insignia Solutions, Inc.** / *Soft PC*
1300 Charlston Road
Mountain View, CA 94043
415-694-7600  415-694-3705 fax

**Letraset** / *Envelopes*
40 Eisenhower Drive
Paramus, NJ 07653
800-343-8973 x 7210
800-634-3463

**Macromedia** / *Director, Freehand*
600 Townsend Street, Suite 310-W
San Francisco, CA 94103
800-989-3762
415-252-2000

**MetaTools, Inc.** / *Kai's Power Tools, KPT Vector Effects, KPT Convolver, KPT Quickshow*
6303 Carpinteria Avenue
Carpinteria, CA 93013
805-566-6200  805-566-6385 fax

**Netscape Communications Corp.**
Netscape, Netscape Navigator
501 East Middlefield Road
Mountain View, CA 94043
415-528-2555

**Strata, Inc.** / *Studio Pro*
2 West St. George Boulevard, Suite 2100
St. George, UT 84770
800-787-2823
801-628-9756

**Xaos Tools, Inc.** / *Paint Alchemy*
600 Townsend Street, Suite 270 East
San Francisco, CA 94103
415-487-7000  415-558-9886 fax

# Appendix C Fine Art Service Bureaus

*These North American service bureaus specialize in fine art printing with Iris equipment.*

**David Adamson Editions**
Glen Echo, MD
301-320-9386

**Adgravers**
Detroit, MI
313-259-3780

**Altron Color Imaging**
Moncton, NB, Canada
506-852-3510

**Cannonball Graphics**
San Jose, CA
408-453-1470

**The Color Space**
Peter X (+C) Design
New York, NY
212-366-6600

**Colibri Digital Imaging**
Old San Juan, PR
809-721-4069

**Cone Editions**
East Topsham, VT
802-439-5751

**Cone-Laumont Editions, Ltd.**
333 West 52nd Street
New York, NY 10019
212-245-2113

**Digicolor**
Seattle, WA
206-284-2198

**Digicolorado**
610 South Lipan Street
Denver, CO 80223
303-777-6720

**Digital Graphics, Inc.**
Burlington, MA
617-270-3670

**Digital Image Plus**
Chicago, IL
312-464-0416

**The Digital Pond**
San Francisco, CA
415-495-7663

**Duggal Color Projects**
New York, NY
212-242-7000

**Finer Image Editions**
Van Nuys, CA
818-373-1100

**Harvest Productions**
Placentia, CA
714-961-1212

**Hunter Fine Art**
Kennebunkport, ME
207-967-2802

**Imagestation**
Kihei, HI
808-536-1718

**Mesa Digital Communications**
New York, NY
212-691-9888

**Nash Editions**
Manhattan Beach, CA
310-545-4352

**New American Platinotype**
Medford, MA
617-391-3006

**Paris Photo Lab**
Los Angeles, CA
310-204-0500

**Today's Graphics**
Philadelphia, PA
215-567-0332

**Tulip Graphics**
Berkeley, CA
510-843-8171

**Tulip Graphics**
San Francisco, CA
415-544-0900

**Urban Digital Color**
San Francisco, CA
415-626-8403

# Appendix D
# Contributing
# Artists

**Matthew Angorn**
4100 W Alameda Avenue, # 207
Burbank, CA 91505
818-977-0868

**Richard Biever**
601 W. Water Street
Newburgh, IN 47630-1151
812-426-7761
812-853-7411

**Jeff Brice**
2416 NW 60th Street
Seattle, WA 98107
206-706-0406

**Ben Barbante**
1245 Chula Vista Drive
Belmont, CA 94002
415-508-9814

**Caty Bartholomew**
198 Seventh Avenue #4R
Brooklyn, NY 11215
718-965-0790

**Carol Benioff**
3311 Jennings Street
San Francisco, CA 94124
415-467-5014

**Rhonda Campbell**
2256 Rimrock Dr.
Bishop, CA 93514
619-397-2571

**Steve Campbell**
1880 Fulton #5
San Francisco, CA 94117
415-668-5826

**Gary Clark**
823 Lightstreet Road
Bloomsburg, PA 17815
717-387-1689
717-389-4352

**James D'Avanzo**
1446 Jennings Road
Fairfield, CT 06430
203-255-6822

**Ellie Dickson**
185 West End Ave. #3L
New York, NY 10023
212-724-3598

**Pamela Drury Wattenmaker**
17 South Palomar Drive
Redwood City, CA 94061
415-368-7878

**Linda Davick**
4805 Hilldale Drive
Knoxville, TN 37914
615-546-1020

**John Derry**
Fractal Design Corporation
335 Spreckles Drive, Suite F
Aptos, CA 95003
408-688-5300

**John Dismukes**
2820 Westshire Drive
Los Angeles, CA 90068
213-464-2787

**Mary Envall**
1536 Promontory Ridge Way
Vista, CA 92083
619-727-8995

**Grace Ferguson**
2226–11th Avenue
Oakland, CA 94606

**John Fretz**
500 Aurora Avenue N, #406
Seattle, WA 98109
206-623-1931

**Kerry Gavin**
154 East Canaan Road
East Canaan, CT 06024
203-824-4839

**Fred Gillaspy**
465 Sugarloaf Road
Scotts Valley, CA 95066
408-354-2809

**Helen Golden**
460 El Capitan Place
Palo Alto, CA 94306
415-494-3461

**Rhoda Grossman**
216 Fourth Street
Sausalito, CA 94965
415-331-0328

**Francois Guerin**
33 Rue Alexandre Dumas
75011 Paris, France
0-11-331-43-73-36-62

**Andrew Hathaway**
805 Page Street
San Francisco, CA 94117
415-621-0671

**Hugo Hidalgo**
9014 Reichling Lane
Pico Rivera, CA 90660
310-942-7526

**Philip Howe**
540 First Avenue South
Seattle, WA 98104
206-682-3453

**Geoff Hull**
4054 Cartwright Avenue
Studio City, CA 91604
818-761-6019

**Donal Jolley**
2607 Murray Ridge Road
San Diego, CA 92123
619-277-7120

**Rick Kirkman**
2432 W. Peoria, Suite 1191
Phoenix, AZ 85029
602-997-6004

**Dorothy Simpson Krause**
32 Nathaniel Way
P.O. Box 421
Marshfield Hills, MA
617-837-1682

**John Lee**
2293 El Contento Drive
Los Angeles, CA 90068
213-467-9317

**Bonny Lhotka**
5658 Cascade Place
Boulder, CO 80303
303-494-3472

**Susan LeVan**
30 Ipswich Street, Studio 211
Boston, MA 02215
617-536-6828

**Craig MacClain**
9587 Tropico Drive
La Mesa, CA 91941
619-469-9599

**Pedro Meyer**
1333 Beverly Glen #1004
Los Angeles, CA 90024
310-475-3631
Pedromeyer@aol.com

**Judi Moncrieff**
4543 SW Water Avenue
Portland, OR 97201
503-294-9947

**Bill Niffenegger**
1007 Grand Boulevard
Cloudcroft, NM 88317
505-682-2776

**Richard Noble**
899 Forest Lane
Alamo, CA 94507
510-838-5524

**John Odam**
2163 Cordero Road
Del Mar, CA 92014
619-259-8230

**Corinne Okada**
657 Evert Avenue, Apt.1
Palo Alto, CA 94301
415-325-3549

**Dennis Orlando**
79 Brookline Road
Ivyland, PA 18974
215-345-4525

**Chet Phillips**
6527 Del Norte
Dallas, TX 75225
214-987-4344

**Jean Francois Podevin**
5812 Newlin Avenue
Whittier, CA 90601
310-945-9613

**Abbie Rabinowitz**
24 Clarendon Street
San Francisco, CA 94114
415-566-5706

**Dewey Reid**
c/o Microsoft Corporation
1 Microsoft Way, 13/1052
Redmond, WA 98052-6399
206-703-1412

**Peter Mitchell Rubin**
c/o Production Arts Limited
310-915-5610

**Chelsea Sammel**
482 South Street
Holister, CA 95023
408-636-7443

**Larry Scher**
11821 North Circle Drive
Whittier, CA 90601
310-699-8797

**Karin Schminke**
5803 NE 181st Street
Seattle WA 98155
206-483-3011

**Beth Shipper**
13738 Fairgate Drive
Poway, CA 92064
619-486-4429

**Nancy Stahl**
470 West End Avenue
New York, NY 10024
212-362-8779

**Anna Stump**
c/o Penner
1883 Cabernet Drive
Chula Vista, CA 91913
Stump@Bilkent.edu.tr

**S. Swaminathan**
Golden Light Imagery
P.O. Box 1547
Capitola, CA
408-722-3301

**Jeremy Sutton**
245 Everett Avenue
Palo Alto, CA 94301
415-325-3493

**Sharon Steuer**
205 Valley Road
Bethany, CT 06524
203-393-3981

**Will Tait**
1357 93rd Avenue
Oakland, CA 94603
415-329-3684

**Ayse Ulay**
146 South Michigan Avenue, #101
Pasadena, CA 91106
818-796-4615

**Trici Venola**
911 Marco Place
Venice, CA 90291
310-823-7308

**Lynda Weinman**
2096 Lilac Lane
Glendale, CA 91206
http://www.lynda.com

# Appendix E Art & Photo Credits

*The following are credits for images and photos in the Basics sections of each chapter.*

### Chapter 1
Facing page 1: *Pouring it on with Painter*, Steve Guttman

Page 2: *Cat's Eye*, Cher Threinen-Pendarvis

Page 4: *BICtopus*, Rick Kirkman; *Mosaic Effect*, Jim Benson (photo: Digital Stock)

Page 5: *Mosaic Effect*, Jim Benson (photo: Digital Stock); *Parthenon* (photo: Photo Disc)

Page 10: *Life*, Cher Threinen-Pendarvis

### Chapter 2
Page 13: *Firey Deer*, and *Along Tomales Bay*, Cher Threinen-Pendarvis

Page 14: *Value Study* inspired by Michelango, Cher Threinen-Pendarvis; detail from *Bend in the Epte*, Dennis Orlando; *Color Study* based on Hans Hofmann's *Twilight*, Jim Benson

Page 15: *Zinnias*, and *A Landscape with Figures*, based on Gauguin's *Mahana no atua*, Cher Threinen-Pendarvis

Page 16: *Before and After*, photo: Cher Threinen-Pendarvis

Page 17: *Island Tie-Dye*, Cher Threinen-Pendarvis

### Chapter 3
Page 29: *Aloha*, Cher Threinen-Pendarvis

Page 30: *Still Life with Apples*, *Coastal Meadow*, and *Michelangelo-inspired Charcoal Study*, Cher Threinen-Pendarvis

Page 31: *A Peaceful Coexistence* (Elephant and Deer), *San Simeon Watercolor*, and *Portrait of Sabina Garros*, Cher Threinen-Pendarvis

Page 32: *King of Beasts*, Cher Threinen-Pendarvis; Detail from *Ktema*, John Dismukes; *Extraordinary Cruise*, Jim Benson (photo: Digital Stock)

Page 33: Detail from *Tennis Woman*, Nancy Stahl; Detail from *Harley*, Richard Noble; Detail from *Point Lobos Calm Light*, Cher Threinen-Pendarvis

### Chapter 4
Page 75: *Diving Deeper*, Cher Threinen-Pendarvis (photo: Digital Stock); *Love*, Cher Threinen-Pendarvis; *Dry*, Jim Benson (photo: Photo Disc)

Page 78: *Fish*, Cher Threinen-Pendarvis

Page 81: *Sibyl:* Cher Threinen-Pendarvis (inspired by Michaelangelo)

Page 82: Anderson Valley Apples, Cher Threinen-Pendarvis

### Chapter 5
Page 102: Editorial illustration for *Professional Speaker* magazine, Rick Kirkman

Page 103: *Wow! Factor* poster, Cher Threinen-Pendarvis; *Hangliding*, (photo: Digital Stock)

Page 104: *Cowboys*, (photo: Photo Disc)

Page 107: *Outrigger Restaurant* logo, Cher Threinen-Pendarvis

### Chapter 6
Page 126: *Balinese Girls*, (photo: Digital Stock); *San Francisco* (photo: Photo Disc)

Page 127: *Borrego Desert* (photo: Cher Threinen-Pendarvis); *Flower*, Cher Threinen-Pendarvis (photo: Digital Stock); *Classic Solarization*, Cher Threinen-Pendarvis (photo: Photo Disc)

Page 128: *Glass distortion, line conversion, and embossing effects*, Cher Threinen-Pendarvis (photos: Photo Disc); *Looking Sharp* (photo: Photo Disc)

Page 129: *Snowboarder Posterization*, Cher Threinen-Pendarvis (photo: Craig MacClain; *Vignette*, Jim Benson (photo: Digital Stock)

### Chapter 7
Page 156: *The Performance*, Steve Campbell

Page 157: Detail from *Water Lilies*, Cher Threinen-Pendarvis; *Chrome Type*, Cher Threinen-Pendarvis

Page 158: *ABC*, Cher Threinen-Pendarvis; *Soft Custom Lights*, Cher Threinen-Pendarvis

Page 159: *Carp*, Corrine Okada; *Organic Fractal Patterns*, Cher Threinen-Pendarvis

Page 160: *Topographic image with Clouds*, Cher Threinen-Pendarvis; *Detail from The Digital Pond package*, Corrine Okada

Page 116: *Glass-Distorted Type* and *Chrome Type*, Cher Threinen-Pendarvis; *3D Gold Type*, Jim Benson; *Point Lobos* photo, Cher Threinen-Pendarvis

### Chapter 8
Page 180: *Nike All Conditions Gear* TV advertisement frame, Dewey Reid

Page 181: *Fox Television* animated logo frame, Geoff Hull

Page 182: *Mediacom* video frame; *Pastel Lemon*, Cher Threinen-Pendarvis

Page 183: *Turtle Rockets* Frame Stack palette, Donal Jolley; *Mill Valley*, Cher Threinen-Pendarvis

Page 184: Frame from *MGM Stargate* movie storyboard, Peter Mitchel Rubin; Frame Stack palette showing operations applied to *Mediacom* video clip; *Yuri The Yak*, Dewey Reid (for Sesame Street, produced by Children's Television Workshop)

Page 185: *Trolley animation*, (video clip: Mediacom); *Diver animation*, (video clip: Gazelle Technologies Digital Video Library), Cher Threinen-Pendarvis

Page 186: *Martin TV title*, Jon Lee, Fox Television; ; *Gondolas* (photo: Photo Disc)

Page 187: *3D Globes*, John Odam

### Chapter 9
Page: 206: *Sybil's Fear*, Dorothy Krause

Page 207: *Golden Gate* (photo: Photo Disc)

Page 208: *Vutek photos*, courtsey of Richard Noble; detail of *Old World*, Bonny Lhotka

Page 209: *Sunrise*, Cher Threinen-Pendarvis

Page 210: *Alpha Merics Spectrum prniter* photo, courtesy of Dorothy Krause; *Kwik-print photos*, courtesy of Helen Golden, Judi Moncrieff and Karin Schminke

Page 211: *Prairie Reflection*, Karin Schminke; Detail of *The Game*, Carol Benioff; Detail of *Day Job*, Bonny Lhotka

Page 212: *Monotype substrate*, courtesy of Bonny Lhotka; *White Buffalo*, Gary Clark; *Willow Pond*, Dennis Orlando

Page 213: *Point Lobos Calm Light*, Cher Threinen-Pendarvis; *Centaur*, Dorothy Krause

### Chapter 10
Page 224: *Ruben, Insomniacs Asylum™*, ©Warner Bros.; *Multicamel*, Steve Campbell

Page 225: *King of Beasts*, Cher Threinen-Pendarvis

Page 226: *Music* screen, from the *Lenny Kravitz* Web site, Hugo Hidalgo, BoxTop Interactive

Page 227: Sequoyah Web page, Lynda Weinman; Elements from the *Lenny Kravitz* Web site, Hugo Hidalgo, BoxTop Interactive

# Appendix F Reference Materials

*Here's a sampling of recommended references for both traditional and digital art forms.*

## ART BOOKS

### Art Through the Ages
Fifth Edition
*Revised by Horst de la Croix and Richard G. Tansey*
Harcourt, Brace and World, Inc.
New York, Chicago, San Francisco, and Atlanta

### The Art of Color
*Johannes Itten*
Van Nostrand Reinhold
New York

### Drawing Lessons from the Great Masters
*Robert Beverly Hale*
Watson-Guptill Publications
New York

### Mainstreams of Modern Art
*John Canaday*
Holt, Reinhart and Winston
New York

### Printmaking
*Gabor Peterdi*
The Macmillan Company
New York
Collier-Macmillan Ltd.
London

### The Natural Way to Draw
*Kimon Nicolaïdes*
Houghton Mifflin Company
Boston

### The Photographer's Handbook
*John Hedgecoe*
Alfred A. Knopf
New York

### TypeWise
*Kit Hinrichs with Delphine Hirasura*
North Light Books
Cincinnati, Ohio

## COMPUTER IMAGERY BOOKS

### Adobe Photoshop Handbook
(Photoshop 3 Edition)
*Mark Siprut*
Random House Inc.
New York, NY

### Photoshop in 4 Colors
*Mattias Nyman*
Peachpit Press
Berkeley, CA

### Designing Web Graphics
How to Prepare Images and Media for the Web
*Lynda Weinman*
New Riders Publishing
Indianapolis, Indiana

### The Illustrator Wow! Book
*Sharon Steuer*
Peachpit Press
Berkeley, CA

### The Photoshop 3 Wow! Book
*Linnea Dayton and Jack Davis*
Peachpit Press
Berkeley, CA

## PUBLICATIONS

### Communication Arts
Coyne & Blanchard, Inc.
410 Sherman Avenue
Palo Alto, CA 94306

### Computer Artist
Ten Tara Boulevard, Fifth Floor
Nashua, NH 03062

### Design Graphics
Design Editorial Pty. Ltd.
11 School Road
Ferny Creek
Victoria 3786 Australia

### Graphis
Graphis US, Inc.
141 Lexington Avenue
New York, NY 10016

### How
Ideas and Techniques for Graphic Design
104 Fifth Avenue
New York, NY 10011

### Print
RC Publications
104 Fifth Avenue
New York, NY 10011

### Step-by-Step Graphics and Step-by-Step Electronic Design
Step-by-Step Publishing
6000 Forest Park Drive
Peoria, Illinois 61614

# Index